SHARING CARE

Sociology of Children and Families series

Series editors: **Esther Dermott** and
Debbie Watson, University of Bristol, UK

The Sociology of Children and Families monograph series brings together the latest international research on children, childhood and families and pushes forward theory in the sociology of childhood and family life. Books in the series cover major global issues affecting children and families.

Forthcoming in the series:

Black Mothers and Attachment Parenting
A Black Feminist Analysis of Intensive Mothering in Britain and Canada
Patricia Hamilton, December 2020

Out now in the series:

Social Research Matters:
A Life in Family Social Science
Julia Brannen, December 2019

Designing Parental Leave Policy:
The Norway Model and the Changing Face of Fatherhood
Elin Kvande and **Berit Brandth**, July 2020

A Child's Day:
A Comprehensive Analysis of Change in Children's Time Use in the UK
Killian Mullan, July 2020

Find out more at

bristoluniversitypress.co.uk

SHARING CARE

Equal and Primary Carer Fathers and
Early Years Parenting

Rachel Brooks and Paul Hodkinson

BRISTOL
UNIVERSITY
PRESS

First published in Great Britain in 2021 by

Bristol University Press
University of Bristol
1-9 Old Park Hill
Bristol
BS2 8BB
UK
t: +44 (0)117 954 5940
e: bup-info@bristol.ac.uk

Details of international sales and distribution partners are available at bristoluniversitypress.co.uk

© Bristol University Press 2021

British Library Cataloguing in Publication Data
A catalogue record for this book is available from the British Library

ISBN 978-1-5292-0597-8 paperback
ISBN 978-1-5292-0596-1 hardcover
ISBN 978-1-5292-0601-2 ePub
ISBN 978-1-5292-0599-2 ePdf

Cover design: blu inc, Bristol
Front cover image: VeaVea, stocksy.com

Bristol University Press uses environmentally responsible print partners.

Printed in Great Britain by CMP, Poole

We would like to dedicate this book
to our children: Hannah, Martha and
Daniel, and Laurie and Asher.

Contents

Acknowledgements

We would like to thank all the fathers who generously gave up their time to talk to us, and tell us in such detail about their experiences of sharing care. We are also very grateful to the Faculty of Arts and Social Science at the University of Surrey for funding the research upon which this book is based, and colleagues in the Department of Sociology at Surrey for providing such a supportive environment in which to write the book – particularly Ranjana Das, who gave us invaluable feedback on the material in a number of the chapters. We are also indebted to Anna Tarrant for her insightful suggestions on the whole manuscript, and Esther Dermott and Debbie Watson for their support of this project as editors of the excellent Sociology of Children and Families series. In addition, Rachel would like to thank her children, Hannah, Martha and Daniel, for their interest in the book and, in general, having made 'caring' such a pleasure. Paul would also like to thank his children, Laurie and Asher, for ensuring that cuddles are never in short supply and that life is never, ever dull, and especially his partner, Holly, for her ongoing and unwavering support.

We have made some of the arguments in this book in two journal articles, which draw on the same research. Some of the material from Chapter 5 was originally published in P. Hodkinson and R. Brooks (2018) 'Interchangeable parents? The roles and identities of primary and equal carer fathers of young children', *Current Sociology* (advance online access) and is included courtesy of Sage. Material from Chapter 6 was originally published in R. Brooks and P. Hodkinson (2019) 'Out-of-place: The lack of engagement with parent networks of caregiving fathers of young children', *Families, Relationships and Societies* (advance online access); and is republished with permission of Policy Press (an imprint of Bristol University Press UK).

1

Sharing Care: An Introduction

Beyond 'being there'

His relationship always had been '50/50', Scott says, and his unusual level of involvement in the care of his one-year-old child – which contrasts with the more traditional arrangements taken up by most of his friends – feels like an extension of that, though it was also enabled by other factors, including parity of earnings between him and his partner. Following a year of parental leave that was split between them, they both now work flexibly in order to enable each to have weekday time alone with their one-year-old and limit their use of day care. They also share childcare tasks as evenly as they can in the evenings and on weekends and, although he works longer hours than her overall, he is also the one more likely to take time off if their son is sick because his work offers greater holiday entitlements. He is proud and happy about the arrangement, and his boss – a mother herself – has been supportive, even if colleagues occasionally quip about his 'days off' or 'babysitting'.

Sharing care has not been all plain sailing. Scott's partner struggled emotionally on her initial return to work after seven months and found it difficult to hand over a significant portion of daytime care duties, which also led to feelings of guilt for Scott himself. Meanwhile, although she had established valuable relationships with other mothers, he has often felt isolated when caring on weekdays, with ventures out into daytime public spaces punctuated by insecurities about how he might be judged by others and envy of the apparent camaraderie of groups of mums he encounters. This early difference between him and his partner has affected the overall scope of his parenting, with her solely responsible for liaising with other parents about playdates or birthdays, for example. She also deals with appointments with health and parent-support professionals, having established routines of doing so during her maternity leave. Nevertheless, Scott looks forward to his days at home with his son, feels the arrangement has been good for him and his family, and reflects on the confidence he has gradually developed as a caregiving father and his strengthening emotional bond with his son. Though it already connected with some of his initial values, it is evident that the experience of sharing care has changed his skills, outlooks and understanding of himself as a man and a father.

The role of fathers in early years caregiving has become an increasingly visible part of public discourse in recent years. Images of fathers wearing baby slings or changing nappies have become commonplace in advertising, articles and social media discourse, while discussions about dads as early caregivers, driven by charities, politicians and others, permeate news columns and have diffused into wider discourse. Such content varies significantly, of course. On social media, discussion ranges from the substantive reflections of involved fathers on the nature of their experience, to popular debate on masculinity and baby slings. In the realm of advertising, content ranges from sympathetic, yet restricted, television depictions of fathers taking a one-off turn at caregiving to cover for their partner (for example Amazon Alexa, 2018), to global PR campaigns oriented to increasing fathers' access to paternity leave (for example Dove (healthcare brand), 2019). In the UK, policy-related conversations also have centred on the issue of paternal leave in recent years, following introduction in 2015 of a Shared Parental Leave policy that afforded couples the right to share leave between them flexibly and a 2019 government consultation on potential enhancements to the policy.

Yet, despite the apparent visibility of discourse that alludes positively to early years fatherly involvement, the overwhelming burden of responsibility for caregiving in the first few years of children's lives in countries like the UK continues to fall on the shoulders of mothers. Studies have shown, for example, that the take-up of the UK's Shared Parental Leave scheme by fathers has been low, at between two and eight per cent of eligible couples, as a result of a range of financial and practical factors as well as enduring understandings about gender and early years care (Twamley and Schober, 2018, see Chapters 2 and 3). Importantly, there are equally few signs that significant numbers of men are adopting flexible or part-time work patterns after having children in order to share care for their children (ONS, 2018a). The aforementioned Amazon Alexa father, it might be argued, captures and plays to the broader societal situation seamlessly, his willingness, competence and caregiving intimacy celebrated, but only in the context of his role as temporary stand-in who is in need of guidance.

Like the overwhelming majority of fathers, when it comes to the responsibilities and practicalities of caregiving, this father excels at the often-mooted role of 'being there', both practically and emotionally. Yet such terminology (accurately) implies a role that remains secondary, centring on availability and support while the baby's mother occupies the unquestioned role of primary caregiver and expert.

Though it has substantial implications for their experience and potential, this book is not about fathers who are breadwinner-supporters, notwithstanding how involved, engaged, committed or intimate their parenting may be. It is about men who, like Scott, have stepped out of dominant frameworks by taking on caregiving responsibilities for babies or young children that approximate or go beyond an equal share with the child's mother. Through detailed attention to what unusual levels of fatherly caregiving involvement can look like in practice and how such arrangements are experienced by fathers and their families, we hope to enhance understanding of the prospects and possibilities for men to move beyond 'being there' and towards taking on equal or primary responsibility for early years care. Specifically, we explore, in the pages that follow, the circumstances that prompt fathers to take on such substantial caregiving roles when so many of their peers do not, as well as the nature of their arrangements and experience as care-sharing fathers, and the challenges they face. We also attend to the implications of such fathers' caregiving experiences for the development of their fatherly identities over time and the future of their families. Through doing so, we identify the factors that might enable greater numbers of fathers to share care, the ways society might make caregiving easier for those who do, and the significance of their involvement for individual journeys and societal futures.

'Involved' fathering, care-sharing and gender equality

For decades, research has demonstrated that the increasing participation of women in labour markets has not been matched by a reciprocal movement of men towards an embrace of domestic work and childcare. Instead, such work is delegated to low-paid and overwhelmingly female paid workers and/or retained as an unpaid burden on working women, whether through parental leave, flexible working or what Hochschild (1989) famously referred to as the 'second shift'. Crucially, as well as leaving women torn between work and domestic responsibilities in a practical, everyday sense, such a situation creates an ongoing mental burden of responsibility that has long-term implications for identity, priorities and ambitions (Christopher, 2012; Miller, 2017). At no time are such responsibilising pressures on women more acute than in the years after having a baby, prompting even the most career-centred of mothers typically to take far more time, energy and investment out of their working lives than do fathers. Not surprisingly, the impact of this on broader inequalities between women and men is substantial. In 2018, the UK's Annual Survey of Hours and Earnings indicated a gender earnings gap of 'close to zero' between the ages of 18 and 39 years transforming into a difference between men and women of 20–25 per cent in the years that follow (ONS, 2018b). As well as time off taken as part of maternity leave, such a disparity connects closely to the juggling of work and care by mothers thereafter. Not only are 51.8 per cent of employed UK women with dependent children in part-time work, as compared with ten per cent of men in the same situation (ONS, 2018a) but it is safe to assume that, even for many mothers who return to work full-time, the burden of having primary responsibility for children continues to substantially affect their labour market competitiveness in myriad ways (Christopher, 2012).

For Nancy Fraser, the solution to such inequalities involves a greater role for fathers in the home and, particularly, in caregiving. Her 'universal caregiver model' envisages the sharing of care between mothers and fathers on a substantively equal basis, which enables them, in turn, to participate on a similarly equal footing in paid work (1996). Fraser seeks to move away from what she terms 'caregiver parity models' that prioritise the provision by societies of entitlements and rewards that elevate the value of women's care work, whether in the form of more generous and better paid maternity leave and/ or longer-term caregiver allowances. While such approaches address the exploitation and lack of reward to which women caregivers are often subject, they reinforce the labour divisions between men and women. Fraser also questions the rewarding by societies of those who can most effectively delegate caregiving responsibilities onto external others (whether paid or unpaid). The latter approach, which Fraser refers to as the 'universal breadwinner model', may have been effective in enabling women to participate more effectively in labour markets but devalues the significance and value of unpaid caregiving in favour of traditionally masculine career-centred notions of life success. It also does little to challenge the ultimate delegation of caregiving responsibility to women in any case. Instead, Fraser endorses an approach that would recognise, value and facilitate the caregiving responsibilities of both men and women, as well as resisting cultures centred on excessive paid work hours and pressures. As with Rosemary Crompton's (1999) notion of the 'dual-earner, dual carer' society, instead of merely moving women towards traditionally male priorities, such an approach would involve men moving towards the traditionally female domain of care. As Gornick and Meyers (2004) put it, 'mothers and fathers would essentially meet in the middle in their in their allocation of time between the market and home'. Crucially, then, such an approach also would imply a fundamental undoing of family gender roles (Deutsch, 2007), whereby the various facets of caregiving and breadwinning become disconnected from gendered subjects (Ranson, 2010; Hodkinson and Brooks, 2018).

Consistent with such ideas, there is increasing agreement among academics, policymakers and others that when fathers adjust *their* work to take on a greater share of caregiving responsibilities, this has the potential to enhance the balance and orientation of their own lives at the same time as helping address broader gender inequalities. And, partly in response to this agenda, academic scholarship on fathering has developed significantly over the last two decades, covering a range of themes and topics, but often revolving around questions about levels of involvement, styles of caring and gendered understandings. Prominent UK studies of secondary carer fathers by Tina Miller (2011, 2017) and Esther Dermott (2008) have highlighted how expectations and self-understandings increasingly place value on fatherly involvement, intimacy and 'being there', but without substantial challenges to fathers' underlying status as breadwinners and supporters. And, as we show in the next chapter, UK research on 'involved fathering' recently has expanded somewhat, with a particular focus on examining the factors that affect fatherly involvement in care (Norman, Elliot and Fagan, 2014) and the nature of the barriers that are preventing fathers from taking up parental leave entitlements, for example (Twamley and Schober, 2018).

With one or two exceptions (West et al., 2009; O'Brien and Twamley, 2017), however, UK fathering research has rarely focused in detail on the circumstances and experiences of those fathers who *have* taken on care roles for young children that challenge breadwinner/support models by seeking to match or exceed the responsibilities of their partners. And while an increasingly significant body of such research exists in North America (Doucet, 2006a, 2009; Ranson, 2010, 2015; Chelsey, 2011; Kaufman, 2013; Solomon, 2017) and mainland Europe (Merla, 2008; Brandth and Kvande, 2018b) – research we draw upon extensively in the chapters that follow – much of the focus for such work has been on primary carer fathers (particularly stay-at-home dads) and those on temporary parental leave. As well as being one of the first UK projects to examine caregiving fathers in depth, this book makes a particular contribution by examining not only families in which traditionally gendered roles have been reversed (for example stay-at-home fathers) or where fathers take temporary periods of leave, but also those where care responsibilities are being shared more equally between mothers and fathers alongside paid work responsibilities on an ongoing basis (see Deutsch, 2001; Ranson, 2010). Through taking such a focus, we explore a range of different arrangements that involve care being divided in ways that challenge established gendered approaches, including many that, through the sharing of both breadwinning and caregiving, put into practice the aforementioned universal caregiver or dual-earner, dual-carer models.

The Sharing Care study

Drawing extensively on existing literature and a detailed examination of relevant policy, our primary aims in studying UK fathers who took their care roles beyond support for their partners revolved around achieving a concentrated and in-depth qualitative understanding of what such arrangements can look like, how they come to be and how they play out in practice. The intention was to contribute to ongoing conversations about policy and support, while developing sociological understandings of early years care, fatherhood and masculinities through close examination of a range of care arrangements that (apparently) defied established approaches to gender and parenthood through the extent of the father's involvement. We wanted to understand the circumstances and decision-making that had enabled fathers to take on such unusual roles and examine how the initial transition worked for them and their partners. We sought to outline the different kinds of temporary and ongoing care-sharing arrangements that fathers and their families engaged in and how these tied in with work and careers. And we aimed to understand in detail what the experience of care-sharing was like for such fathers and their families, with a particular focus on the distribution of responsibilities, everyday routines and styles of caring. A key part of this was understanding how fathers felt about the different stages and aspects of their caregiving, including in relation to challenges and difficulties they had faced and how these had affected their journeys. A further aspect that became important was the ways in which the experience of sharing care had contributed to the development of the men's orientations and understandings of themselves as fathers. Through learning about the detail of the experiences, perspectives and journeys of such fathers, we sought to move discussions forward by outlining what would help care-sharing fathers and their families address the challenges they face, what might enable more men to take on such roles and what the impact of early years care-sharing might be for the longer-term orientation of such men and their families.

Importantly, the project includes what we see as three key categories of caregiving fathers: 'parental leavers', which refers to those taking extended periods of temporary paternity leave; 'primary caregivers', who had taken up longer-term arrangements that involve them taking on a greater proportion of caregiving than was their partner; and 'equal care sharers', who were sharing care more or less equitably with their partners (see Chapter 4). Our decision to place the latter group at the heart of the project reflected the comparative neglect of equal sharer fathers by much existing research and a desire to understand alongside one another the range of ways fathers can move beyond a secondary or support care role vis-à-vis their child's mother. Such a focus also enabled us to explore our particular interest in the notion of care-sharing and the variety of forms this can take, including in relation to how care, work and day care are negotiated. It therefore enabled an alignment of the research with models that centre on the sharing of both care and paid work by men and women, such as those proposed by Fraser (1996), Crompton (1999) and others. Following much consideration we decided to focus solely upon fathers in heterosexual partnerships. While there could have been a good argument for including a greater diversity of family types, including separated or single-parent fathers, or fathers in same-sex relationships, our specific aim was to examine how care is shared by fathers in circumstances where a mother is also present within the relationship and household. Our interest, then, was in the particular interactional dynamic between men and women in heterosexual relationships with respect to what responsibilities are taken by whom and the ways these play themselves out in such a circumstance.

We carried out in-depth interviews with fathers in heterosexual dual-parent households who regarded themselves as the primary caregiver or as sharing care equally with their partners. While we relied to a significant extent on fathers' own understanding of their roles, we also set out parameters for what we meant by primary or equal caregiver in an information sheet as well as using a set of initial screening questions to help gauge the extent of their responsibilities. The parameters centred on whether the fathers were spending an equal or greater time than their partners were on childcare, but we also emphasised an interest in changes to paid work in order to facilitate care. Examples we provided included periods of parental leave, adjusted hours, working flexibly or part-time, changing job or becoming unemployed – though we also flagged an interest in those taking on equal or greater care responsibilities alongside more standard full-time work arrangements. Finally, we specified that 'for this particular research we are *not* looking for fathers who contribute extensively to care but less so than their partner'. Interestingly, this prompted one father, who had made very substantial adjustments to work in order to care for his child on two full days per week, to drop out of the project on the basis that his partner was doing three days. While some others interpreted the parameters more liberally – and in cases of doubt we acceded to their self-definition – all had made or experienced adaptions or changes to their paid work (though these varied in their extent) and had, in our understanding, taken on care roles that appeared to be comparable to or greater than those of their partners, in terms of their involvement in daily caregiving tasks. Inevitably, however, such estimations were imprecise and a few of the fathers who regarded themselves as equal carers and were included in the study ultimately seemed to be doing slightly less than their partners overall, even though their responsibilities, adjustments to work and sole care on weekdays comfortably exceeded those of most fathers of young children.

Fathers were recruited through a range of advertisements in a variety of online and offline locations, including children's centres, nurseries, parenting support websites and posts on social media. We also relied upon a snowballing approach whereby existing participants were asked to pass on details of the research to anyone else they were aware of who met our criteria. Volunteers were asked to email us initially, at which point they were sent the information sheet for the project and some brief preliminary questions about themselves and their caregiving responsibilities. The final sample of 24 fathers was concentrated in the south east of England but included a minority of participants from the midlands and north of the country. More importantly, there was considerable diversity in terms of caring arrangements, including a majority who were sharing care (more or less) equally with their partner, a third who regarded themselves as the primary caregiver in their household and two who were on extended parental leave (though three others had taken extended parental leave prior to their current arrangement). As we outline in Chapter 4, the main 'equal' and 'primary' caregiver categories entailed a variety of scenarios with respect to paid work, from a minority of unemployed 'stay-at-home dads' to, in the case of most, different approaches to part-time or flexible working hours. In spite of its diversity with respect to care arrangements, however, the sample was more homogenous in terms of social background and age, with all of the fathers white and most beyond their 20s and either currently or recently in professional occupations. This may partly reflect a greater propensity for older, middle class fathers to share care for babies and young children (Lilius, 2016; Johansson and Andreasson, 2017), but may also be an outcome of our approach to recruitment and, in particular, a reliance on participants putting themselves forward. The limitation of our project, in this respect, is not unusual in recent studies of fathers and highlights a collective need to do more to find ways of including minority, younger and more working class fathers (Dermott and Miller, 2015; Gatrell and Dermott, 2019).

Interviews typically lasted between 60 and 90 minutes and were audio-recorded, fully transcribed and anonymised. Where we could, we carried out the conversations in person and this was possible for half of the sample. For the other half we used online video chat software, something that enabled us to include fathers from a range of locations and to accommodate their complex and busy schedules more easily. There is increasing evidence that, rather than being an impediment to interview rapport, remote video-enabled interviews have significant potential as a viable alternative to face-to-face interactions (Deakin and Wakefield, 2013; Lo Iacono et al., 2015). The ability to be interviewed in a place comfortable to you, such as your own home, at a time suitable for you and without the need for the researcher to be physically present, may sometimes have the potential to substantially increase convenience and reduce interactional anxiety (Das and Hodkinson, 2019a). In line with this, we did not discern any consistent differences in the interpersonal dynamics of remote video interviews as opposed to those we carried out face-to-face. The main difficulty we occasionally experienced – perhaps predictably – took the form of technical issues with connections dropping, which could cause unhelpful breaks in the conversational dynamics and occasional short sections that were inaudible, but in most cases these issues were minor and easy to negotiate.

All interviews were semi-structured and based on a detailed topic list, but varied in their order and organisation. While some followed the topic list fairly closely and in the order envisaged, others developed into freer-flowing exchanges with the topics acting as guidance but the order depending as much on the interviewee as the researcher. We began all the interviews by asking the fathers to summarise their care arrangements and then go into detail about what they and their partners were responsible for, including a range of routine tasks and more irregular events such as caring for children if they were sick or accompanying them to hospital. The role of childcare and extended family as part of routines was of importance here also. We asked in detail about the motivations and circumstances that had enabled and led up to their care-sharing arrangements as well as how well they and their partners had adjusted to these. Fathers were also asked to describe in detail an average day on which they were the main carer and then compare their approaches to caring with that of their partners, parents and friends. We asked them to reflect in particular on aspects of caring, or of the arrangement in general, that they had found easy and difficult, enjoyable and challenging, and on how their experiences and sense of themselves had changed over time. We also probed about a number of other specific topics we felt might be of significance, including the role of employment and employers, relationships with health and parenting support institutions, and interactions with other parents. Amidst these primary topics a wide range of different issues and further questions emerged; as is often the case in qualitative research, the eventual data went significantly beyond our expectations and agenda.

Interviews were transcribed in full by a professional transcriber. Transcripts were coded thematically in a manner that was informed by existing concepts and questions at the core of our thinking, but centred on allowing themes and understandings to emerge from the data. Patterns across the coded material were identified and explanations developed. Each of us analysed and coded the interviews independently in the first instance, before refining key themes and explanations together. About a year after the original interviews, participants were contacted with a summary of our key themes and findings, complete with an invitation to comment, which two of them took up, albeit briefly and in order to affirm the relevance to them of what we had presented. In order to protect their identities, all interviewees were given a pseudonym (including Scott, referred to earlier) and these pseudonyms are used wherever we refer to or directly quote from their accounts. In addition to the protection of the fathers' identities, the project closely followed established protocols with respect to the use of information sheets, consent forms (completed electronically in most cases), opportunities to ask questions, and an emphasis on the fathers' right to decline to answer questions and/or withdraw from the study at any time up to a specified date.

A short note is warranted on our own position as researchers of care-sharing fathers. We both gravitated towards an interest in the sociology of fathers and fathering, having established track records and reputations in different areas of sociology – education studies in the case of Rachel and youth cultures for Paul. And this gravitation has, for both of us, connected to our own experiences of having and bringing up children. Rachel is the mother of three children aged 11, 15 and 20 and has juggled being her children's primary carer – including three periods of maternity leave – with a full-time academic career that has included significant periods in the role of head of department and faculty associate dean as well as co-ordinating extensive cross-national research projects. Paul is also primary carer for his children, six and eight. After their first baby, he and his partner opted against splitting parental leave between them because of the costs involved, but struggled in their traditional post-natal roles. For their second child, Paul took four months of extended paternity leave after their baby was six months old. When his first child started school, he switched to a part-time contract in order to spend more time with the boys on weekdays. As a consequence of our different positions, we both find ourselves personally as well as academically invested in the questions we explore in the pages of the book. And, while it is difficult to be certain how our respective positions affected our interactions with the fathers, we both shared aspects of parental identity and experience with them and sought to be reflexive and pragmatic about our similarities and differences from them. Rachel benefited, at times, from familiarities relating to her role as a parent and, sometimes, from the greater willingness men can sometimes have to open up about their lives to women (Miller, 2019). In a different way, Paul's experiences as a caregiving father seemed sometimes to help facilitate an atmosphere of comfort and openness, with overt forms of masculine performance unusual, for example. Like Jonathon Ives in his research on men's transitions to fatherhood, Paul inserted limited aspects of his own experience as a care-sharing father into the conversations where it felt natural to do so, something which seemed to help establish the setting as a safe space for disclosure and to place participants at greater ease (Ives, 2019). While there were some differences in the style, structure and pace of our interviews, it was difficult to discern consistent contrasts in what the men felt comfortable to discuss with each of us and, contrary to stereotypes of men as inherently uncomfortable discussing intimate aspects of their lives (Ives, 2019), the fathers were, in general, forthcoming, enthusiastic and, so far as it was possible to tell, as open as we could have hoped for about their experiences, successes and struggles.

Fatherly care horizons

A recurring theme throughout our discussions of care-sharing fathers in this book is our interest in the nature of the journeys such fathers navigated as they took on, negotiated and developed their care roles, and the various factors – structural, institutional, cultural or circumstantial – that may have shaped or influenced such trajectories at different stages. Drawing on existing work that focuses on the temporal development of fatherly identities (for example Shirani and Henwood, 2011; Henwood et al., 2015; Neale et al., 2015; Neale and Davies, 2015), we sought to foreground, then, what fathers' accounts told us about how their lives, approaches and outlooks had shifted through time. From what it was that prompted their initial take-up of care-sharing, to the ongoing development of their experiences, we explore how their identities and practices as fathers and as men were reinforced, developed, transformed or held back. And, as part of this, we examine how such practices and identities are enabled or constrained by myriad factors – both small and large-scale, private and public, everyday and longer-term. In our efforts to make sense of this in relation to our research, we bring together and develop some different bodies of theory.

First, our discussion connects to existing academic discourse about the doing and undoing of gender, discourse that already forms a significant feature of literature and research on fathers and fathering. Such understandings date back to West and Zimmerman's (1987) seminal contribution to debates about the social construction of gender, which extended Goffman's (1976) understanding of gender as performance and display, towards an emphasis on the ongoing, all-encompassing, everyday sets of interactive practices through which distinct male and female forms of being are generated and regenerated. But it is specific later emphasis on the ways what can be reinforced through practice can also be challenged through practice – or *undone* (Deutsch, 2007) – that has provided a valuable conceptual tool for those examining the significance of families with unusual divisions of gendered responsibilities. For Deutsch, greater emphasis is needed on the potential importance of everyday interactive behaviour as a site for gender resistance – or 'undoing gender', as she puts it, including the daily activities of parents who share care and domestic duties between them. And, as we explore in Chapter 2, more recent examinations of fatherhood have taken up Deutsch's challenge, in centring their enquiries on how the adoption of unusually involved care roles by fathers may entail the gradual erosion of dominant gender roles through practice. Sometimes operating in tandem with notions of doing or undoing gender in this body of work – and also of significance for this book – are specific understandings about the ways dominant forms of masculinity may themselves be subject to challenge or transformation through the adoption of unconventional roles and practices. Drawing on Connell's hegemonic masculinity framework (2005), whereby dominant and marginal/resistant versions coexist and are subject to struggle and change, Karla Elliott (2016) theorises the potential for the development of what she terms *caring masculinities*, centred on a rejection of domination and an embrace of care, emotion, dependence and relationality. In this book, we utilise, at different points, notions of the challenging of gender through practice, and consider the development of caring masculinities among the fathers in the study.

In order to make sense of fathers' journeys of practice and identity over time, and to illuminate the ways that practice integrates with institutions and structures, we combine these concepts from gender studies with understandings that originate in the study of life course transitions. In particular, we adapt conceptual tools developed by Phil Hodkinson and Andrew Sparkes (1997) as part of their work on career trajectories and decision-making. Drawing on Bourdieu's notion of habitus (1977) and Giddens' understanding of structure and action (1984), Hodkinson and Sparkes (1997) develop the notion of 'horizons for action' as a way to understand the range of possible pathways that individuals can envisage for themselves. A little broader in scope (as we see it) than notions such as 'imagined futures' (see Shirani et al., 2016; Thomson and Holland, 2002), horizons for action refers to an individual's vision of what is possible, available or appropriate for them at any moment in time or in the future – and highlights the ways such understandings can enable certain decisions, directions or pathways and prevent others. Rather than being determined purely by structural position, or by autonomous individual choice, horizons for action, for Hodkinson and Sparkes, reflect a range of inter-related factors, including the broader socio-cultural habitus in which we find ourselves (and the orientations and beliefs that may connect to this), the structuring of opportunities by wider policy, markets or institutions and the ongoing events, circumstances and interactions we may encounter. Because of this diversity of shifting factors, horizons for action may be structurally constrained but also are subject to change. Hodkinson and Sparkes' understanding can be seen, then, as a middle way between structural determinism and individualistic understandings of agency and choice. In this respect, it shares with Deutsch's notion of undoing gender an emphasis on how underlying structures may be challenged through practice and over time.

In this book, we adapt this notion of horizons for action as part of our attempt to make sense of fathers' pathways into and through their care-sharing roles. Specifically, we develop the notion of 'fatherly care horizons', as a way to conceptualise fathers' understandings of their parental roles, their masculinities and their broader sense of who they are and what is appropriate or feasible for them as fathers. Starting with what prompted their initial decision to share care and moving onto different aspects of the experience, we explore how fatherly care horizons are affected by ongoing or shifting actions and vice versa, focusing on the role of different long- and short-term factors as part of such processes. Here, drawing on existing fatherhood research that is attentive to temporality and transitions (Shirani and Henwood, 2011; Neale et al., 2015), we attempt to bring insight into the parenting journeys on which the fathers found themselves, highlighting key moments, or 'turning points' for them, as well as more gradual development of their competences, identities and masculinities through ongoing caregiving practice and experience. As part of this, we identify barriers and limits to their development as caregivers and the transformation of their masculinities but also show how far the practice of sharing care had shifted their horizons and challenged established ways of doing gender.

Outline of chapters

The organisation of the book's chapters reflects our desire to set out in detail the social and policy contexts in relation to the sharing of care by fathers, before providing a thorough analysis of experiences of the fathers in our study.

Chapter 2 places the Sharing Care study in the context of existing literature and knowledge on fathering, starting with broader understandings of fatherly involvement before going on to examine the insights of existing work on involved or caregiving fathers specifically. We outline what has and has not changed in relation to fathering practices and ideologies, identifying in particular a range of barriers to the practical mass take-up of care-sharing. We go on to look at what existing studies tell us about the motivations and experiences of fathers who become heavily involved in caring, how gender relations within such families play themselves out and what difficulties and limitations caregiving fathers can face. We particularly highlight those aspects of existing literature that we take forward in the chapters to follow.

Providing a substantive examination of the context in which care-centred fathers operate, Chapter 3 focuses on developments in family policy that are designed to encourage fathers to take a greater share of caregiving for young children. The chapter begins by highlighting enduring national differences in the ways in which fathers are supported – or not – by the state with respect to caregiving roles, and considers what can be learnt from other countries (particularly the Nordic states) that have taken steps to move closer to Fraser's universal caregiving model. The chapter then moves on to focussing on UK policy more specifically. We examine how it has shifted over the past 50 years, and the extent to which a 'maternalist' emphasis endures. The final part of the chapter considers how state policy can be mediated by workplace cultures and practices, and the operation of various social norms. Making links to our own sample, we suggest that greater attention needs to be given, by both policymakers and researchers, to flexible working policies – as it appears that the ability to work flexibly had helped to facilitate the sharing of care for a number of the fathers in our study. We also suggest that, while UK family policy was seldom explicitly mentioned in the fathers' explanations, the discursive shift in policy, evident over recent years, may have helped to validate the decisions they had taken for other reasons.

Chapter 4 begins our in-depth examination of the lived realities of fathers who take on care-sharing roles. We introduce the diverse care arrangements of the fathers in the study, who (as noted earlier) we divide into shared parental leavers, primary caregivers and equal care sharers. The chapter goes on to explore what it is that prompted fathers and their families to adopt their approach and, in particular, whether such a role lay within existing orientations or expectations or represented a transformation in these. In exploring this we develop further the notion of fatherly care horizons to explore whether becoming a primary or equal caregiver lay within what fathers could see as possible or feasible for them at different stages and how this came to change. While an implicit amenability to the possibility of sharing care was a prerequisite, we show how practical factors such as finances or the career prospects of themselves and their partners had often helped open up the possibility for horizons to change. The chapter goes on to outline how fathers' transitions to their new care roles worked in practice, placing emphasis here on the extent of the practical transformation of roles and identities involved and the challenges that came about as a result.

In Chapter 5 our attention turns to how the fathers talked about the detail of their care arrangements, with a particular focus on how different roles were allocated to themselves and their partners and their changing identities and orientations as parents. We show how many had come to think of themselves as largely interchangeable with their partners with respect to the different facets of caregiving, indicating an ongoing shift in their care horizons. We also discuss the styles of parenting developed by the men and how they compared these with those of their partners. While identifying considerable evidence of the embrace of interchangeable parental identities – and also of caring masculinities – we show how certain aspects of parenting had often continued to be dominated by mothers. Drawing on existing literature on mothering, we develop some explanations for these limits to many of the fathers' caregiving responsibilities and, potentially, to the further broadening of their care horizons.

A set of particularly significant limitations on fathers' caregiving identities and horizons are explored in greater depth in Chapter 6, which centres on fathers' tendency to feel out of place within daytime public spaces outside the home and the difficulties they experienced when it came to interacting with other parents. We ask why caregiving fathers tend to avoid or feel uncomfortable in some daytime public spaces and what the implications of their comparative isolation might be for their wellbeing and for the prospects of their becoming able to take on enduring care-sharing orientations or identities. We provide some detail on the anxieties and difficulties experienced by fathers within feminised daytime spaces, from shopping centres to playgrounds, and examine fathers' struggles with the dynamics of parent and baby events. We also note the absence of contact with other fathers for many we spoke to. Caught between feminised daytime spaces and traditionally masculine fathers' groups, the fathers frequently found themselves feeling out of place, we suggest, with significant implications for their caregiving journeys.

In the final chapter of the book, Chapter 7, we bring together the key strands from the preceding chapters, drawing empirical and conceptual conclusions from the Sharing Care study as well as developing practical and policy recommendations centred on improving the experience of care-sharing fathers and enabling more men to take up such roles. Beginning with a brief exploration of fathers' overall reflections on their experience and visions for the future, we outline the striking extent to which many of their identities and masculinities had transformed through their everyday caregiving practice, while also identifying the limits to their caregiving journeys, the uncertainties in their futures and the underlying endurance of notions of default maternal responsibility in the environments around them and, sometimes, their own understandings. We go on to outline what might be done to prompt more men to share care with their partners and how we might make the experience of care-sharing easier for those fathers who do take on such roles.

2

Extended Fatherly Involvement: Development and Understandings

Introduction

This chapter provides a critical examination of what we already know about fathers' involvement in the care of their children. It is structured in two parts. Part I focuses on the now quite extensive literature on fatherly involvement in general, exploring the extent to which approaches and understandings have changed over recent years. We start by outlining the emergence of a pervasive cultural ideal of the 'involved father', associated with a shift away from seeing fathers as primarily breadwinners and towards an understanding of fatherhood that is based instead on emotional closeness and a greater sharing of caregiving. We then show how such ideals are not always played out in practice, and explore some of the reasons why, within many families with heterosexual parents, mothers continue to bear the primary responsibility for childcare, and devote considerably more time to care than their male partners. Here we consider: the pull of paid work for fathers; the pressures associated with 'intensive parenting' and retaining 'executive responsibility' that fall particularly heavily on mothers; and the positioning of fathers as 'supporters' or 'secondary parents' by healthcare professionals and others. Underpinning all these areas is the operation of traditional gender ideologies, which we consider in the final part of this section.

Part II shifts the focus to the minority of fathers whose practices go beyond what might be expected of a secondary caregiver or supporter, considering the growing literature on stay-at-home dads, fathers who take extended periods of parental leave (some of it caring alone), and those who share care more or less equally with their partners. We explore what existing work suggests about their motivations for taking on such roles; their experiences of caregiving in this way; and the impact of their atypical decisions. We also consider in some detail existing debates about the extent to which such men can be seen to be transforming gender identities or, in Deutsch's (2007) words, 'undoing gender'. Throughout this section we also highlight the ways in which our own data articulate with such debates, and signal key arguments we will develop in greater depth in subsequent chapters.

Part I: Continuity and change in contemporary fatherhood

The emergence of the 'involved father'

Studies from many countries of the Global North have documented how, over recent years, there has been a cultural shift towards a more involved model of fathering (for example Dermott, 2008; Farstad and Stefansen, 2015; Johansson and Andreasson, 2017). In many cases, this represents a significant change from patterns established during industrialisation, in which fathers often were marginal figures in family life, and their role as primarily a 'provider' for their children was reinforced (Cheal, 2002). Contemporary fatherhood, it is argued, is associated with greater emotional closeness between fathers and their children, and a greater role for fathers in caregiving. Indeed, Dermott (2008), drawing on her research in the UK, contends that contemporary fatherhood should be conceptualised primarily in terms of an intimate relationship, as this emphasises the aspects of fathering that the fathers in her study considered the most important, that is their emotional connection with their child/children; the expression of affection within this relationship; and the exclusivity of the father–child dyad. Changing conceptualisations of fatherhood have also affected norms and expectations associated with early parenthood. Miller (2011), for example, has shown how men anticipating the birth of their child often expect to be closely involved in childcare, with new fatherhood 'envisioned as an opportunity to "be there" for their child(ren) in emotionally and practically involved ways that are qualitatively different to their own experiences of being fathered' (56).

As already noted in Chapter 1, such ideals are also often reflected in the media and in wider societal discourse, in which involved and present fathers are celebrated (Solomon, 2017). Johansson and Andreasson

(2017), for example, note that popular representations of fathers tend now to emphasise physical closeness (for example, through showing fathers holding a child) rather than bodily distance, which was more common in depictions of fathers in the 1950s and 1960s (typical representations focussing on, for example, fathers playing football with their children). Moreover, their analysis of the way in which fatherhood is discussed in blogs from around the world suggests that many such outlets place considerable emphasis on caring practices and often highlight the fulfilling nature of establishing close relationships with children.

Tensions between ideals and practice

Nevertheless, it is also clear from extant research that there are limits to the extent to which fatherhood – as it both understood and practised – has changed, and also differences with respect to both nations and social groups. In many countries, there are still a considerable number of men who have not embraced the 'involved father' cultural ideal, continuing to focus on their role as breadwinner and viewing childcare as largely the responsibility of women. This is evident even in families where the mother is highly educated and, prior to childbirth, had held a high status job (Orgad, 2019). Indeed, although the couples in Orgad's London-based study described their partnerships as egalitarian, she contends that they 'described divisions of labour where the husband was largely absent during the week and often far too tired to contribute to childcare at the weekend' (2019: 124). In such cases, 'involved fathering' practices were not seen as a necessary prerequisite for an ostensibly equal relationship.

Other scholarship has highlighted how, even when fathers do subscribe to the 'involved father ideal', there is often a notable difference between beliefs and practices. Dermott (2008) for example notes, with respect to her aforementioned UK research, the common tension between the discourse of 'intimate fatherhood', on the one hand, and enduring differences by gender in childcare work, on the other. The shift in the nature and quality of emotional relationships, then, is not necessarily associated with a similar change in the responsibility for childcare: 'because caring responsibilities flow from an emotional connection rather than from in themselves constituting the fathering role, the practicalities of "intimate fatherhood" are fluid and open to negotiation' (2008: 143). Similar patterns have been observed elsewhere. Johansson and Andreasson (2017), drawing on cross-national data from Nordic and Anglo-Saxon countries, also emphasise the disparity between the commitment of men to the ideal of an involved and caring fatherhood and their actual family practices. Moreover, fathers continue to be far less likely than mothers to take up parental leave after the birth of a child where it is not tied to some kind of 'quota' system – in which a proportion of leave is allocated to the father, and is lost to the family unless taken by him (Eerola and Mykkänen, 2013). (This is discussed in more detail in Chapter 3.)

Studies of time devoted to childcare and other related tasks have also revealed significant ongoing gender disparities. Although there is now a reasonable consensus that men's participation in childcare and housework has increased gradually, and that fathering has become a more important part of their lives (Doucet and Lee, 2014), studies from across the Global North have demonstrated that, in a range of different national contexts, mothers continue to spend more time on childcare and related domestic duties than fathers (Norman et al., 2018). For example, analysis of time-use data from Australia, Denmark, France and Italy has shown that, in all countries, mothers did a significantly higher proportion of care than fathers, even in the most egalitarian household types (judged in this study to be dual full-time earners) and the most egalitarian country (Denmark) (Craig and Mullen, 2011). Similarly, data from the Norwegian Time Use Survey conducted in 1990, 2000 and 2010 indicated that, for heterosexual couples with at least one child under the age of 20, women continued to do more 'family work' even when both partners worked full-time (Kitterød and Rønsen, 2017). Here, there are clear parallels with what Arlie Hochschild found in the 1980s, in her seminal work on the 'second shift' carried out by many working mothers in the US (Hochschild, 1989). In families with school-age children, mothers are also much more likely than fathers to take on the associated 'educational labour', such as ensuring homework is completed and managing other school-related activities (Gottzen, 2011; Park, 2018). More generally, qualitative studies in the UK have indicated that mothers continue to be positioned as the 'primary parent' – not least by fathers (Dermott, 2008; Miller, 2017).

The pull of paid work for fathers

In explaining these enduring differences, scholars have pointed to a variety of factors. Central to many accounts is the role of paid employment. In general, parenthood tends to lead to mothers reducing their hours of employment (or leaving the labour market entirely) to take on the bulk of childcare and domestic work, and fathers increasing their hours of paid work – to manage the reduction in household earning and the increase in expenditure (Norman et al., 2018; Orgad, 2019). Fathers' involvement in childcare is thus frequently contingent on what they believe can be accommodated within their work schedules (Norman et al., 2014).

Various qualitative studies from across the world have shown how this prioritisation of paid work is played out in practice, often despite an awareness of, and sometimes commitment to, ideals of 'involved fathering'. Miller's (2011) aforementioned longitudinal study of 'first-time fathers' in the UK shows how her respondents, although anticipating – prior to the birth of their child – playing a full role in childcare (sometimes on an equal basis with the mother), quickly revised their plans in the post-natal period when they found themselves thrust into the role of primary breadwinner. Childcare typically came to be something fitted around paid work, rather than foregrounded as it was in the case of the mothers (see also Miller, 2017). Although Miller acknowledges that the care provided by the fathers in her study tended to be more emotionally engaged and involved than that documented in previous research, 'paid work and strands of heteronormative discourses continue to shape, in sometimes powerful and dramatic ways, these men's individual choices and practices of involvement' (Miller, 2011: 192). Indeed, she notes how some of her respondents were caught between acknowledging the importance of parenting and their difficulty giving it priority, given the expectations and social status attached to engagement in paid work and its enduring association with masculinity. Moreover, she argues that the fathers had fewer constraints on their choices than mothers and so were able to 'move more easily – and less guiltily – in and out of paid work and the home' (Miller, 2011: 154).

Even in Nordic countries, where significantly more men take parental leave (see later discussion and Chapter 3), fathers continue to be more able than mothers to: decide on the terms of their participation in childcare; take parental leave less often; and work significantly more hours outside the home (Eerola and Mykkänen, 2013). Indeed, Eerola and Mykkänen (2013) argue that, in Finland, the dominant social narrative with respect to early fatherhood is that of the 'decent father'. Such fathers have a strong sense of responsibility for their family and participate in nurturing activities with their children, but also understand the roles of mother and father as largely distinct. The authors argue that 'The mother's primacy in childcare and house-keeping and the father's in wage work were narrated as conventions that both parents agree with, in parallel with Finnish parental leave statistics' (11). Although their research also identified two additional and competing narratives – that of the 'equal father' (which emphasised a gender-equal approach to parenting and a rejection of the male breadwinner role) and the 'masculine father' (in which the fatherly role was defined in largely traditional terms associated with breadwinning and male-specific nurturance activities) – the 'decent father' narrative was by far the most common among their interviews with first-time fathers in heterosexual relationships.

Fathers' continued prioritisation of paid work, as documented by these various studies, can be seen as a consequence of material factors (such as pay differentials between men and women, and differences between maternal and paternal leave schemes), workplace cultures (in which it is often easier for women than men to ask for a reduction in hours) and, perhaps most importantly, gender ideologies. We discuss the impact of this last point in more detail in the final section of Part I.

Intensive parenting

While the pull of paid work is significant in explaining the reasons why the practices of many men do not accord well with the cultural ideal of the father sharing care equally with his partner, a reciprocal set of influences operate upon mothers, which encourage them to retain primary responsibility for care and associated domestic work. Many of these coalesce around the concept of 'intensive parenting' (Hays, 1998). Intensive parenting is commonly understood as a highly demanding, child-centred approach to childrearing that involves considerable investment of time, energy and money, and which is frequently positioned not just as one of several possible approaches to parenting, but the moral choice, the way one *ought* to parent (Faircloth, 2013; Vincent, 2017). It is based on what is sometimes called 'parental determinism', that is the prioritisation of 'nurture' over 'nature', which has the effect of increasing the pressure on parents to make the 'right choices' for their child. It thus constructs parenting as a potentially risky endeavour, and expert guidance as a means of avoiding these risks (Shirani et al., 2012).

The pressures of this approach have been shown to fall more heavily on mothers than fathers as the ideal of the 'good mother' continues to be associated with physical presence and close involvement in all aspects of children's lives. Indeed, empirical research in the UK has suggested that fathers may be less likely to adopt such 'intensive' approaches in their parenting. Shirani et al. (2012) argue that the fathers in their study were more insulated from the demands of intensive parenting than their female partners partially because they were able to draw on what they call 'resources of masculinity', such as an emphasis on autonomy and self-reliance, which enabled them to reject pressure to follow expert advice. Similarly, Jensen (2018) has argued that social discourses related to 'parent blaming' fall unequally on mothers and fathers. She contends that while discourses of 'bad fatherhood' tend to focus on being either 'absent' or 'feckless', 'the vocabularies that are available around mother-blaming are rich and complex; there are so many ways for mothers to fail' (18). She notes that although the precepts of contemporary 'good parenting' have been extended to fathers, they are typically presented as a special case, 'implicitly framing them as less capable, more distant and less burdened by parenting' (17). While such evidence may seem more relevant to the parenting practices of mothers rather than fathers, we argue in Chapters 5 and 6 that such differing pressures may be responsible for some limits to the otherwise pervasive sense of parental 'interchangeability' articulated by our participants.

'Executive responsibility' and maternal gatekeeping

The pressures and expectations that fall on mothers, which are associated with intensive parenting or, more specifically, intensive *mothering*, can lead to mothers retaining control of various aspects of childcare, even when they engage in full-time paid employment and have partners who are willing to share caregiving. Ranson (2010) contends that, even in some couples where mothers play as great a role (or even a greater role) in breadwinning as fathers, they sometimes retain 'executive responsibility' for care. By this she means that such mothers co-ordinate the delegated care, and assume the role of main decision-maker for key medium- and long-term choices about care and other aspects of their child's life. Ranson also suggests that, in such cases, fathers can appear willing to assume the role of 'assistant' rather than 'manager' with respect to the responsibility for childcare. She notes other examples from her research on 'non-traditional couples' in which executive responsibility was shared more equitably, however. Similarly, Miller (2017) indicates that, even in families where practical child-related tasks were shared more between mother and father, giving up the mental work of caring and the associated 'executive responsibility' was often seen by the mothers as 'a step too far' (150). We engage with debates about executive responsibility in some detail in Chapter 5 when we consider the extent to which the highly involved fathers in our study took on such roles equivalent to those of their partners.

While the concept of executive responsibility refers primarily to the retention of particular co-ordinating duties and burdens, scholars have argued that inequalities in the division of care can also come about through processes of 'maternal gatekeeping'. This refers more specifically to mothers' ability *actively to restrict* fathers' involvement with their children. By being reluctant to give up their role as 'primary parent', mothers can make it more difficult for fathers to take on a significant caring role (Gattrell, 2007; Dermott, 2008). Some researchers have suggested that maternal gatekeeping is closely related to perceived paternal skill: Fagan and Barnett (2003) have argued that mothers in the US tend to exclude fathers from being involved with children when the mother perceives the father as having less parenting competence. Scholarship on maternal gatekeeping has, however, been criticised for failing to recognise the complex factors that shape attitudes and practices in this area. Miller's (2017) work, for example, provides a rather more nuanced account of how both maternal and paternal gatekeeping are played out in UK families. She writes: 'across the data there was evidence of gatekeeping or "blocking" behaviours being described in the narratives of the mothers and the fathers, especially in relation to claims of competency and incompetency' (155). Claims of paternal incompetence could be deployed by mothers keen to retain responsibility for particular aspects of childcare, but also by fathers to free them up from an activity. Building on Miller's approach, we explore later in the book how mutual, interactive processes whereby roles were both claimed and ceded, sometimes could contribute to the endurance of some aspects of gendered parenting even within families that in many respects were challenging established roles.

Healthcare provision and advice

The uptake of more 'involved' caring practices, on the part of fathers, can also be impeded, research has suggested, by the ways in which healthcare professionals interact with them – both in the antenatal period and after the birth of the child. Fathers in the UK, for example, have reported feeling alienated by the way in which information is given to them by midwives, health visitors and others (Featherstone, 2009), and have often viewed birth- and child-related services as being run largely by women for women (Lewis, 2013). Such perspectives can also be complicated by fathers' beliefs that mothers have a 'natural authority' over their pregnancy. This is articulated well by Ives (2014) in his longitudinal study with fathers-to-be over a nine-month period covering the birth of their first child. He suggests that the transition to fatherhood is a period of uncertainty, in which men experience the pressure of norms that are associated with the role of expectant fatherhood, but in which their sensitivity to the privileged position of their partners, and sometimes an effective marginalisation by healthcare workers, can lead to uncertainty and confusion about precisely what their role is, and even the appropriateness of claiming a defined role for themselves that is independent of, and unmediated by, their pregnant partner. (1015)

Somewhat similar tensions are discussed by Das and Hodkinson (2019c) in their research on new fathers and mental health. They note that, even amidst a broader context of new fatherhood discourses that stress the importance of active involvement in a wide range of areas, fathers typically find themselves addressed as 'supporters' (of the mother) in literature oriented to expectant parents and in ante-natal courses. They are thus positioned, from the start, as secondary carers, at the periphery of early caregiving (see also Thomas et al., 2017). Such differences continue, for many couples, to be played out in the post-natal period, too, with health visitors and other professionals often assuming that the mother is the primary parent (Featherstone, 2009; Lewis, 2013), something we explore in Chapter 5 with respect to the experiences of the fathers in our study.

Ideologies of masculinity

Many of the trends in fathering discussed so far, and in parenting more generally, are related to particular understandings of gender. Indeed, it is widely held that parenthood 'creates gender' more thoroughly than any other experience in people's lives (Eerola and Mykkänen, 2013). While some studies have argued that the birth of a child can act as a site for the development of new masculinities, which include provision, protection and caring (Enderstein and Boonzaier, 2015; Ranson, 2015; see discussion in Part II), others have argued that the extent to which an individual adheres to masculine norms can have a significant effect on the way in which they father. Petts et al. (2018), for example, found on the basis of a study of 2,194 fathers in the US that strong adherence to traditional masculine norms significantly reduced the likelihood of embracing the new 'involved fatherhood' ideal, while those fathers for whom the attachment to such norms was noticeably weaker were more likely to become closely involved with their child and foreground their father identity. Research that discusses the endurance of traditional masculinities – for example, fathering approaches that privilege breadwinning rather than childcare, rationality rather than emotional attachment, and presence in the public sphere rather than the home – often draws on the concept of hegemonic masculinity. This is the theory that at any one time there is one form of masculinity that is culturally dominant and most desired, and that men who do not exhibit this form are subordinated or marginalised (Connell, 2005). Typically, hegemonic masculinity in contemporary society is associated with physical strength and control, achievement within the workplace, heterosexuality, and domination over women (Medved, 2016). While few men can live up to the ideals of hegemonic masculinity, it operates as a powerful normative force (Connell, 2005), and often a strong counterpoint to 'involved father' ideals. Analyses of male and female parenting have also been influenced by studies that emphasise the importance of *practices* – many of which have been underpinned by West and Zimmerman's (1987) concept of 'doing gender'. As outlined in Chapter 1, this posits that each of us constructs gender by engaging in activities that are accepted by others as feminine or masculine, and we act with an awareness that we will be judged by others according to what is deemed appropriate masculine or feminine behaviour (Deutsch, 2007). Thus, fathers may sometimes be reluctant to take on substantial caregiving roles because such roles lie outside of established masculine expectations and may be perceived negatively by friends, employers, family or other parents.

Nevertheless, it is important to note that the relationship between fathering practices and gender ideologies is not uni-linear. There is now a growing body of work that has pointed to the ways in which the involvement of men in caring practices can help to reconfigure masculinities along non-hegemonic lines (Deutsch, 2007; Ranson, 2010; Elliott, 2016; Brandth and Kvande, 2018). Such arguments have been made primarily in relation to men who have taken on substantial caring responsibilities in the home, and we explore these in some detail in Part II. Other scholars have suggested, however, that the gender identity of fathers is not always stable over time, with some men enacting both breadwinner and involved father cultural scripts simultaneously (Humberd et al., 2015; Andreasson and Johansson, 2016; Coles et al., 2017), and others moving between traditionally masculine and feminine positions at different points in time (Doucet, 2006). This complexity is captured well by Doucet and Lee (2014) in their contention that: 'men's practices and identities of care-giving go beyond current conceptions of masculinities and femininities and may reflect philosophical and political concepts of self, identity and subjectivity that embrace varying degrees of dependence, independence, and interdependence' (363). A key question for both scholars and policymakers alike is whether a change in ideology leads to a change in practice, or whether it is changes in practices that result in ideological change. We return to this question in our discussion of the impact of family policy (in Chapter 3) and at various points in our exploration of the experiences of the fathers in our study.

Differentiated practices

While the discussion in this chapter to date has focussed primarily on the broad commonalities in fathering we see across the Global North, it is important to note that practices are differentiated, influenced by both national-level policies and norms, as well as social characteristics such as social class. As Doucet and Lee (2014) have argued, it is difficult to paint one clear picture of fathering (see also Meah and Jackson, 2016).

Comparisons are drawn within a number of studies of fathering between the more involved practices commonly seen in the Nordic countries (Iceland, Norway, Sweden and Denmark) and the less progressive forms of fathering evident in many other nation-states (for example Craig and Mullen, 2011; Johansson and Andreasson, 2017; Suwada, 2017). Indeed, there have been various attempts to quantify these national differences through, for example, the Fairness in Families Index (Fatherhood Institute, 2016) and the Parental Leave Equality Index (Castro-García and Pazos-Moran, 2016). The Fairness in Families Index compares nine indicators considered to be important in promoting gender equality in families, grouped into three main areas: institutional frameworks, such as the way in which parental leave policies are designed; social and economic indicators of women's participation in the public sphere; and the current distribution of unpaid work between men and women. In explaining why Nordic countries have been more successful than others in promoting greater gender equality in parenting, most researchers have pointed to specific social policies, such as non-transferable paternal leave, sometimes referred to as the 'daddy quota', which incentivise men to spend time caring for children and women to engage in paid work (see Chapter 3 for further details). Moreover, the greater number of men around during the working day, in countries where relatively generous paternal leave is available, can help to normalise fatherly caregiving. Indeed, Boterman and Bridge (2014) have argued that, in Amsterdam, the figure of the dad and his child on a cargo bike has become a potent symbol of urban egalitarian parenting (see also Lilius, 2016). (We return to these themes in our discussion of public space in Chapter 6.)

Nevertheless, the history of fatherhood in the Nordic counties suggests that changes can take considerable time to take effect and that, as some of the examples discussed earlier attest, such policies do not affect all men in the same way; even in Scandinavian countries, some aspects of traditional fathering practices endure. Moreover, understandings of fatherhood are clearly not *determined* by welfare policies – as this book will show, there are fathers in the UK (as well as in many other countries with less progressive policies than the Nordic states) who are highly involved in the care of their children.

Differences in fathering practices are also evident *within* individual nation-states, particularly in relation to social class. It is more common, for example, for fathers from higher socio-economic groups to take parental leave, and for them to be more present and involved in the lives of their children (Lilius, 2016; Johansson and Andreasson, 2017). This is largely explained by the greater economic resources they can draw upon (to help fund a period of parental leave, for example) and the greater flexibility they often have in their jobs (Lilius, 2016; Johansson and Andreasson, 2017). (As we note later, though, working class shift patterns can sometimes facilitate shared care, as can periods of unemployment.) Farstad and Stefansen (2015) provide an interesting example of how such social class differences are played out in the Icelandic context. At the time of their research, parents in Iceland were entitled to three months of non-transferable leave each, plus a further three months to divide between them, all with a high rate of financial compensation. They note that all the fathers in their sample put a high premium on some 'involved' parenting practices such as 'being there' for their children and establishing a close emotional bond. However, they also discuss the different conceptions of being a father held by their middle class respondents and their working class counterparts. The former placed considerable importance on establishing a primary caring role soon after the child's birth while, for the latter group, bonding was not seen as determined by being involved in infant care but as something that emerged more slowly over time. Farstad and Stefansen note that both groups show traces of a more inclusive masculinity – evident in the overall orientation of the middle class fathers and, for the working class fathers, their willingness to learn from mothers how to care for their child. They also, however, identify enduring elements of a more traditional approach to fathering in both – the importance of caring on their own terms, and the devaluing of mother's care work, on the part of the middle class fathers, and a willingness to opt out of care entirely, if it is practically possible, for the working class group. Research has also shown that approaches to fathering can differ depending on the age of the child(ren). Coles et al.'s (2017) analysis of Australian survey data indicated that fathers with young children typically spent more time on childcare (irrespective of hours in paid employment) than fathers of older children. Moreover, ethnicity, sector of employment, and education level (of partner) have all been shown also to affect the extent of involvement in childcare (Salway et al., 2009; Lilius, 2016; Coles et al., 2017).

Part II: Primary caregiver fathers

Over recent decades a growing body of work has examined the motivations, experiences and impact of fathers who – in contrast to some of the patterns discussed so far – *do* take on extensive caring responsibilities for their children. Such studies have focussed particularly on 'stay-at-home dads' and others who have assumed primary caring roles within their families, as well as fathers on extended parental leave shortly after the birth of a child and those who have sought to share childcare more or less equally with their partner. Not all three types of arrangement have, however, received the same degree of scholarly attention. While there is now a sizable literature on stay-at-home dads and primary carer fathers and, to a lesser extent, men on parental leave, equal-sharers have tended to be overlooked in the literature (Deutsch (2001) and Ranson (2010, 2015) are important exceptions).

Although there are some significant differences between the three models of care, they also share many important features, not least the fact that fathers discussed in such studies are likely to be caring *alone* for a sustained period of time. As we will discuss further in due course, this time alone with a child has been considered key for strengthening the bond between father and child, enabling the father to develop new care-related skills and his self-confidence (Brandth and Kvande, 2018). All three models of care also challenge the notion that fathers should be positioned as secondary carers to mothers. This part of the chapter first explores what existing work tells us about the motivations of fathers taking on such roles within their families, before moving on to examine their experiences and the impact their care has had on them, their families, and wider society. While a key aim of this section is to provide a detailed overview of our extant knowledge in this area, we also signal how we will be taking forward specific debates in the subsequent chapters of this book.

Motivations

For some fathers, it is important that their decision to take on significant caring responsibilities is seen by others as a definite *choice*. Indeed, the

Australian stay-at-home dads in Stevens' (2015) study were highly critical of media representations that suggested they were forced into their situation by, for example, having lost their job. They emphasised that it was very much their own decision, often influenced by a variety of personal values and financial factors. This was also the case for the American fathers involved in Solomon's (2014, 2017) research. They stressed, for example, that while they may have moved into full-time caring after having been made redundant, it was still an active decision not to look for another job. An important counterpoint to this emphasis on choice is the situation of the stay-at-home fathers in Hong Kong discussed by Liong (2017). All the respondents in his research had assumed their role because of some kind of crisis, such as their wife leaving them and their children, or health problems that made it impossible for them to continue with their jobs. Here, the cultural context appears significant. Indeed, Liong argues that it is unlikely fathers in Hong Kong would take up such roles under more benign circumstances – because of the strength of the breadwinner ideology in Hong Kong (and the correspondingly low status accorded to care), and the other forms of support that can usually be drawn upon to provide childcare, including grandparents and hired foreign domestic workers. Nevertheless, research suggests that, even in other contexts, caregiving fathers' keenness to emphasise the importance of choice sometimes can mask the significance of a range of financial, work and other circumstances.

As alluded to earlier, media representations of fathers who have assumed primary caring roles sometimes imply that money is the main motivating factor (Locke, 2016), suggesting that such arrangements are much more likely in families where the mother earns more than the father. Some empirical studies offer support for such assumptions. For example, O'Brien and Twamley's (2017) analysis of the families who took advantage of the UK's Additional Parental Leave scheme (the predecessor of the Shared Parental Leave scheme), under which fathers were able to take up to 26 weeks' additional leave after the mother had returned to work) demonstrated that, although ideals about fairness played a role, economic circumstances were key. In all the cases they studied, the mother earned more than or the same as the father, and thus the reduction in the father's income over the period of leave was not seen to be any more problematic than the loss that would have been incurred if the mother had taken the leave instead. Similarly, in Twamley's later work on the Shared Parental Leave scheme, the main reported barriers to making use of this were the financial implications and concerns that it would have a negative impact on the father's career (Twamley and Schober, 2018). Twamley and Schober (2018) thus conclude that this represents a 'culture-policy' gap in the UK, in which increasing cultural acceptance of the principal of shared parenting is in tension with policies that encourage the mother's role in care work via a poorly remunerated maternity leave transfer mechanism. We explore these policies further in Chapter 3.

With respect to decisions to take on long-term primary care roles, Chelsey's (2011) US research also points to the influence of financial and work-related factors. Indeed, she notes that in 21 of the 31 families in her study of stay-at-home dads, the father's job conditions were key influences, contending that: 'The common thread across the interviews is that without some sort of shock to the man's job (for example job loss) or men's job dissatisfaction, many of these families would not have taken on an at-home father arrangement' (650). Similar motivations have also been articulated by fathers in Canada and Belgium who have taken on primary caring roles: Doucet and Merla (2007) maintain that, in their studies, the fathers had often occupied a weaker employment position than their partners, or had wanted to reconsider their career options (see also Kaufman, 2013). In addition, Doucet and Merla argue that, for some families, a decision for the father to become a stay-at-home dad is a response to the failure of social policy to help parents achieve an adequate work–family balance. For fathers who have taken on significant caring responsibilities but not withdrawn from the workforce entirely, research has pointed to the facilitative role of flexible work environments (see Ranson, 2010). Specific arrangements may also be inflected by social class, with working class fathers making the most of the opportunities for caring enabled by shift work, while their middle class counterparts tend to take advantage of the control they often have over the start and finish times of their work (Kaufman, 2013).

Other studies have suggested that while work and financial factors may not be the primary drivers of a decision for a father to take on significant caring responsibilities, they typically feed into nearly all such decisions (Merla, 2008; Solomon, 2014). The way in which these are played out can nevertheless differ considerably. Merla (2008), for example, distinguishes between, on the one hand, fathers who had distanced themselves from work and embraced caregiving because of poor career prospects and/or high levels of dissatisfaction and, on the other hand, those who had achieved all they wanted to in their careers and/or were unable to spend as much time with their family as they desired.

Choices are also often framed with respect to particular values. Kaufman (2013) argues that the 'superdads' in her research, who had made significant changes to their working lives in order to care for their children, were motivated primarily by an aspiration to be more involved fathers. This then led them to seek a better work situation to facilitate the desired level of care, which often resulted in quite extreme actions such as leaving their jobs or changing career. A commitment to sharing childcare responsibilities was also important to the participants in Risman and Johnson-Sumerford's (1998) study – some of whom had previously experienced unequal divisions of labour and had then consciously shifted to a more equitable arrangement. Moreover, couples who had taken advantage of Additional Parental Leave in the UK were often motivated by a desire to achieve 'fairness' in their relationship – in terms of both the 'joys' of being home with a young child, and also the burdens (such as the perceived possible negative impact on their careers) (O'Brien and Twamley, 2017). For other families, values (about childrearing, gender and/or quality of life) played a lesser, but still significant, role in decisions – often in combination with other factors. Some of the fathers in Solomon's (2014) research spoke of their long-held, but typically unspoken and unplanned for, desire to be a stay-at-home dad, and also their view that in most respects they and their female partners were largely interchangeable (see later discussion). Research has also highlighted the importance, to some couples, of having one parent at home with a child irrespective of whether this is the mother or father (Solomon, 2014). Here, a relatively conservative approach to childcare is combined with a more progressive approach to gender relations (Doucet and Merla, 2007; Merla, 2008).

Perhaps the most common perspective in the literature, however, is that a decision to take on primary or equal caring responsibilities is predicated on a multiplicity of factors – including those related to work and values as discussed already (Doucet, 2004; Locke and Yarwood, 2017; Merla, 2008), but also a range of others – such as the role of one's partner, experiences of particular models of parenting when a child, and a calculated assessment of the costs and benefits (understood not only in economic terms) associated with different courses of action. For example, a mother's willingness to work often played a decisive role in the American, Canadian and Belgian families studied by Doucet and Merla (2007) and Solomon (2014), as did a mother's insistence that her partner played a greater role in childcare (Merla, 2008). Other studies have shown how fathers' decisions to take on significant caring responsibilities are sometimes driven by a desire not to replicate the 'distant' parenting style of their own fathers

(Brandth and Kvande, 1998; Doucet and Merla, 2007; Merla, 2008) or, alternatively, by modelling the practices of their own stay-at-home parent (typically their mother) (Solomon, 2014).

In developing our concept of 'fatherly care horizons' (introduced in Chapter 1 and discussed fully in Chapter 4), we highlight the importance of taking into account the multiplicity of factors that may prompt the taking on of extensive caregiving roles to come within fathers' visions of what is feasible, appropriate, desirable or necessary for them. Paying attention to the complexity of fathers' lives, it becomes too simplistic to frame this debate in terms of a dichotomy between 'choice', on the one hand, and 'compulsion', on the other hand. Instead, we highlight a complex interplay of longer-term dispositions and shorter-term factors in fathers' decision-making, while noting the particular significance of practical circumstances in most cases. Moreover, we explore how, while some had envisaged taking on an equal or greater care role for some time, for many others, the taking on of primary or equal caring responsibilities constituted a turning point in their lives that shifted their identity and horizons as a parent.

Experiences and impact

Reactions of others

Much of the literature on fathers who have assumed significant caring responsibilities for their children focuses on the kinds of reactions they receive from others and the impact of these. In a minority of studies, the affirming role of positive reactions is key. Solomon (2014), for example, argues that the US stay-at-home dads in her research received many more positive than negative comments about their decision from family, friends and strangers – including envious remarks from other men about how they wished they could have stayed at home with their children. The validation from their own fathers, reported by some of her respondents, was valued particularly highly as it 'affirmed their place among fathers despite their non-traditional role' (63). In general, such positive reactions made the men feel like exceptional parents – part of what some scholars may consider the 'patriarchal dividend' reaped by fathers when they are perceived as 'heroes' for taking on roles and occupying spaces traditionally seen as female (Solomon, 2014). Liong (2017) also reports positive reactions by the media to caregiving fathers in Hong Kong. He notes that newspapers and other outlets tended to focus on both the sacrifices made by stay-at-home dads and the high quality of their parenting. However, his analysis reveals differences by social class. Working class fathers tended to be portrayed as vulnerable, with media discourses focussing on the difficulties they had encountered. In contrast, middle class fathers were positioned as loving and caring men who had been willing to give up successful jobs to care for their children, despite strong societal norms around male breadwinning. Liong also reports how the fathers in his sample, and particularly those from middle class backgrounds, were still connected to the public sphere – through, for example, writing blog articles, making money while at home, and conducting seminars. He thus concludes that the ideology of the breadwinner is ultimately not challenged but merely adapted to applaud the stay-at-home dads.

Pervasive assumptions about the association between breadwinning and masculinity also help to frame the more common negative reactions to primary carer fathers documented by a greater number of studies. Although scholars argue that there has been some change in public perceptions of such fathers – Ranson (2015), for example, talks of the 'slow drip of change' – the challenges identified by scholars at the turn of the twenty-first century are equally evident in many studies a decade and a half later. Stevens (2015) notes that father caregiving is often framed negatively in the media, contrasting the superior 'involved father' (who, here, is defined as being emotionally close to his children, but not having made any significant adjustment to his working patterns) with the inferior 'househusband' who is coerced into stay-at-home fathering and is incapable of nurturing his children.

More problematic for fathers' ongoing experiences of caregiving, though, are the less than positive reactions of those they may encounter on a day-to-day basis. These are also well documented in the literature, and can tend to reinforce perceptions that caregiving fathers are not engaged in an appropriate role – because of assumptions that childcare is a female prerogative, a man's primary role is as a breadwinner and/or that caregiving fathers are not masculine (Merla, 2008). Doucet (2004) reported that every one of her participants (over a hundred Canadian fathers) referred in some way to the community scrutiny they faced, the social pressure to be earning, and judgements about not being successful men. She also suggests that such judgements can be particularly harsh for men who are not perceived to have already achieved labour market success. She argues:

> In effect, the economically unsuccessful male caring for children represents a form of double jeopardy because he is judged as a 'failed male' (i.e. not a breadwinner) … and as a deviant man (e.g. a primary caregiver). On the other

34

hand, a male who is visibly providing economically for his family, can feel more accepted in his community as a caregiver and issues of male embodiment thus recede in their salience. (Doucet, 2006b: 708)

More recent studies have revealed similar reactions in other parts of the world (for example Solomon, 2017). In Locke and Yarwood's (2017) UK research, for example, one respondent regretted describing himself in public as a stay-at-home dad because of the negative assumptions about his masculinity, status and work that followed. The implicit – and sometimes explicit – contrast between the degree of comfort felt by fathers in public and private spaces (Ranson, 2010) is a key theme that we return to later in the book, when we explore the social interactions of the fathers in our sample, and the implications these have for the range of caregiving roles fathers felt able to take on and for the development of their fatherly care horizons. This is touched on briefly in Chapter 5 and then developed in more detail in Chapter 6.

Equally problematic, for some caregiving fathers, are the ways in which public spaces at particular times of the day can be experienced as highly gendered and exclusionary. Merla (2008) argues that, in playgrounds, parks and shopping centres, the presence of a man caring for a child – particularly during weekdays – can seem strange; fathers' visibility in this way can remind them that they are inhabiting a place and taking on a role that is seen by many as not gender-appropriate. Doucet notes that displays of close physical affection between father and child in public spaces can be misinterpreted, and remarks that the 'overwhelming majority' of her interviewees spoke about 'having felt a watchful eye on them, at least once' (2006: 703). The 'feminisation of neighbourhoods' through the presence of young mothers is also commented upon by Boterman and Bridge (2014), who contend that, as a result, a strong message is given that 'everything is done by mums' (257). They also, however, point to important national variation in this gender patterning, suggesting that in Amsterdam, for example, where 'daddy days' are almost as common as 'mummy days', the dominant presence of so many middle class mothers is not as striking as it is in London. Similarly, Lilius (2016, 2017) remarks on the Finnish 'latte dads' on parental leave who frequent city cafes. Indeed, she argues that the urban landscape of Helsinki is important to both mothers and fathers on parental leave as it provides opportunities for bumping into acquaintances (and thus avoiding isolation), as well as enjoying the architecture and other attractions of the city. National differences in parental leave schemes and, relatedly, gender norms, can thus have a significant impact on the extent to which public spaces are experienced as feminised and thus potentially hostile to caregiving fathers. This is explored further in Chapter 6.

Fathers can also experience exclusion from parent social networks. Over two-thirds of the Belgian stay-at-home dads involved in Merla's (2008) research had encountered difficulties integrating into local or school-based networks and mothers' groups, and similar findings emerged from the studies carried out by Snitker (2018) in the US and Doucet (2006) in Canada. Doucet remarks on how many of the fathers she spoke to felt like a threat to the 'oestrogen-filled worlds' they saw around them, noting that 'these are worlds populated mainly by mothers and mothering networks which sometimes cast suspicious scrutiny on male participants' (704). In such cases, having a woman act as a 'bridge' was often very useful – providing reassurance to other mothers that 'this guy is OK' (Doucet, 2006). The fathers in Doucet's study also felt awkward about meeting in women's houses, and talked of how this placed strains on them, their mothering friends and the women's spouses. Merla (2008) notes that a large majority of the stay-at-home fathers in her study had also found it hard to maintain their presence in *male* groups centred on sport or a hobby – because of the difficulty they felt of finding topics to talk about that were of mutual interest. While such experiences and/or fears of exclusion – from both mothers' and fathers' groups – can clearly lead to loneliness and isolation for *all* caregiving fathers, they are perhaps particularly acute for single fathers, who have no partner at home (Doucet, 2006).

Although Doucet (2009) notes that there have been significant changes in Canadian society over time, with social acceptance of highly involved fathers improving substantially, various contemporary studies raise questions about the generalisability of such claims. For example, O'Brien and Twamley's (2017) study of UK fathers taking Additional Parental Leave describes how they reported 'having few or no friends with whom to share their leave experiences, and frequently contrasted their experiences with those of their wives/partners, who broadly speaking had a far wider and closer circle of friends while on leave' (175). Moreover, during their time as a primary caregiver, none had met any other men who were also on Additional Parental Leave. Consistent with such literature, the relative social isolation of the fathers in our own study on the days when they were caring alone is a key theme that we develop in Chapter 6 in relation to literature on the potentially exclusionary nature of daytime public parenting spaces. Offering an explanation centred on fathers' feeling 'out of place' within certain daytime environments, we suggest that it is significant, not just for the wellbeing of fathers and the scope of their parenting, but also because of the potentially discouraging message it may send to other fathers considering taking on significant caregiving responsibilities in the future. We also argue that the visibility of non-traditional practices within the public sphere can be important for changing both attitudes and dominant practices.

Family relationships and caregiving competence

While caregiving fathers continue to face challenges outside the home, research suggests that their experiences *inside* the home are often more positive. As noted previously, there is now a significant body of work that indicates that paternal solo childcare – rather than overall involvement in childcare and housework – is key to forming close bonds between father and child (Ranson, 2015; Norman et al., 2018). Magaraggia (2012) has argued that the time when fathers are the only caregiver for their child marks a turning point in their relationship: 'This ... unmediated space of autonomous intimacy, is foundational to fathers [who] aim to be more present' (85). Such time is seen is qualitatively different from caring with the mother present (Brandth and Kvande, 2003). This is partly related to the necessity that fathers caring on their own disengage from the rhythms and routines of paid work and focus fully on child and family (Doucet, 2009). Time caring alone also enables them to develop skills and take responsibility in relation to a wide range of caring tasks, and thus develop confidence – facilitating a shift away from seeing the mother as the expert (O'Brien and Twamley, 2017). Sharing care in the early years of a child's life is thought to affect subsequent parenting patterns. Indeed, a shared and fundamental characteristic of the parents of older children, engaged in equal parenting, interviewed by Ranson (2010), was that both mother and father had had experience of solo hands-on care from the start.

Brandth and Kvande (2003) identify distinct differences in care practices between fathers caring at home alone and those who engage in care but with the mother also present. The former group, they argue, are more sensitive to the needs of the child, carrying out needs-orientated care practice, and letting the routines of childcare determine what they do during the day. They suggest that, in their research (of Norwegian fathers on parental leave), in the cases where the mother was also present, the father continued in the role of 'support person' rather than primary carer or co-parent. Rehel (2015) describes similar findings from her research with Canadian fathers on parental leave. The importance of solo care is also emphasised in Ranson's (2015) work.

She focuses, in particular, on the embodied nature of the hands-on caring work that fathers do when they are alone with their children. By learning care techniques in this way, she maintains that fathers become 're-embodied' as men and 'engaged, committed fathers, likely to remain involved for the long haul' (180). Moreover, a consequence of developing such embodied caring skills, is that mothers and fathers may become 'interchangeable' in their parenting practices (Ranson, 2010). We discuss this further in due course.

The provision of hands-on care by fathers is also associated with a range of benefits beyond the strengthened relationship between child and father. Indeed, the amount of time a father spends alone, caring for a child, during the first year of parenthood is associated with the stability of parental relationships up to seven years after childbirth (Norman et al., 2018). Norman et al.'s analysis of data from the UK's Millennium Cohort Study suggests that it is the solo childcare that is significant, rather the father's overall involvement in childcare and other domestic tasks (although it remains possible the previous orientation may have played a role, too). This complements other research that has highlighted the positive impact of fatherly caregiving on fathers' own wellbeing and mental health (O'Brien et al., 2016), and that of their female partners – partially as a result of the extra time it can free up for mothers (Norman et al., 2018) (although see study by Latshaw and Hale (2016) discussed later, which raises questions about the extent to which breadwinning mothers in the US benefit from such gains in 'free time').

Parenting styles

In exploring the parenting styles of fathers who have assumed primary or equal responsibility for the care of their children, scholars have identified a range of practices, which relate to the gender identities taken up by these men. Some researchers, such as Doucet (2004), have argued that caregiving fathers typically adopt approaches to care that help them to affirm their masculine identity, partly in response to the sometimes negative reactions they receive. The Canadian fathers she interviewed emphasised the more 'masculine' quality of their care, such as placing emphasis on physical and risk-taking activities, sports, and being outdoors. The fathers often explained these differences in approaches to parenting in terms of embodiment – suggesting that they had a qualitatively different relationship to their children because of their gender. The perceived more nurturing approach of mothers, they claimed, was underpinned by the closer physical bond women had with their children as a result of pregnancy, birth and breastfeeding (also see Doucet 2009). Similar findings have been noted in other national contexts (Chesley, 2011). The American fathers in Snitker's (2018) research also claimed that they parented in a different way from mothers, encouraging 'rougher' games, and placing greater priority on allowing their children to explore, take physical risks and move further afield. They were resistant to terms that constructed them as feminine (such as 'Mr Mom'), which informed their desire to create a role that they perceived as 'masculine and specifically for fathers' (219).

Other studies have, however, suggested that fathering practices do not always conform to this particular model. The Australian respondents in Stevens' (2015) research, for example, while placing emphasis on the importance of 'masculine care', also described gentler, more nurturing practices that they engaged in with their children. Moreover, they noted that rough and tumble approaches were not exclusive to fathers. The fathers in Solomon's (2014) US study also adopted nurturing approaches to childcare. Indeed, this group of fathers eschewed more 'masculine' approaches altogether, leading Solomon to observe that they 'focussed on gentle physical affection, emotional intimacy, shared leisure and being in tune with their children's emotional needs' (61) – and this was true for fathers of children of all ages. They typically saw themselves as the most important caregiver for their children in their family, and more emotionally connected to their children than were their wives. Rehel's (2015) analysis of Canadian fathers taking extended parental leave comes to similar conclusions, contending that when fathers experience the transition to parenthood in ways that are structurally similar to mothers, they come to think about and enact parenthood in ways that are also similar to mothers.

Developing this perspective, which suggests the differences between parents with respect to their styles of caring can be negligible, Ranson (2010, 2013) discusses 'interchangeability' on the part of mothers and fathers. She argues that 'going against the grain' (that is the assumption of primary or equal caring responsibilities on the part of fathers, while mothers engage in breadwinning) brought about – for many of the families in her sample – a 'functional interchangeability'. She maintains that this interchangeability is not about identities (that is whether fathers are becoming mothers or vice versa) but about *practices*; irrespective of what had prompted their unconventional divisions of labour:

> [T]he clearest outcome was that fathers as well as mothers learned to take care of children in a hands-on way and,

in most cases, to take responsibility for their children's overall wellbeing. Especially in cases where both parents were earning as well, this produced example after example of caring work shared in a way that defied neat gender categorisation. (2010: 177)

Each parent knew, on a daily basis, how best to meet their child's needs, and their shared involvement in the child's life gave them a common language with which to talk about and share caregiving experiences (Ranson, 2013). Ranson goes on to explain that the term 'interchangeability', as used in this case, requires that 'practices usually associated with mothering or with fathering be considered separately from the person conventionally associated with its execution' (2010: 178) and that, when this happens, it becomes more appropriate to refer to them as 'parenting' rather than 'mothering' or 'fathering'. We explore the concept of interchangeability further, with respect to our own data, in Chapter 5. We argue that the fathers in our study typically undertook a wide range of caring and domestic roles – based largely on expediency and ideas about gender-neutrality. However, unlike those in Ranson's (2010) study, this interchangeability was evident not just on a functional level; we contend that it often had a profound effect on how the men saw themselves and, ultimately, understood their identity as fathers and parents. We also, however, identify specific aspects of caregiving that sometimes continued to be dominated by the fathers' partners, drawing on the previously discussed literature on maternal caregiving and on its reinforcement in different spaces to make sense of these enduring areas of disparity.

Division of domestic duties and leisure time

While the majority of studies of caregiving fathers have tended to focus on the activities fathers pursue with their children and the reactions they receive from wider society, there has been some discussion about whether fathers caring alone also contribute to domestic duties in ways that stay-at-home mothers traditionally have done. Latshaw's (2015) research with American fathers has revealed substantial variation in practices. Indeed, she distinguishes between two groups – the 'resolute' fathers, who had taken on the majority of domestic chores themselves, and the 'reluctant' fathers, who spent less time than their (breadwinning) spouses on tasks traditionally carried out by mothers such as laundry and cleaning. When compared to the 'resolute' fathers, those in the 'reluctant' group tended to be younger, less well-educated and from households with lower levels of income; they also tended to have assumed a primary carer role for shorter periods of time. Latshaw observes that, despite these differences, both groups did 'masculine chores' more frequently than other types of domestic work. This clearly has implications for the leisure time available to mothers and fathers. Analysis of data from the US Time Use Survey from 2003 to 2013, conducted by Latshaw and Hale (2016), found that a significant proportion of stay-at-home dads and breadwinning mothers swapped domestic duties when the mother returned from paid work – in order for the father to have time to pursue his own interests. The authors observe that these stay-at-home dads typically enjoyed greater amounts of leisure time than breadwinning wives, stay-at-home mothers and even many employed fathers. Similar findings emerged from Brandth and Kvande's (1998) study of Norwegian fathers on parental leave. While these men saw themselves as active fathers, they rejected any suggestion that they may be akin to housewives, leading the authors to conclude that the fact that the majority of men exclude housework from their daily activities reveals their strength within their families – 'Relations on inequality and dominance are produced as they negotiate their domestic labour' (311).

While the majority of fathers in Doucet's (2006) research also tended to emphasise various masculine forms of domestic work (such as carrying out repairs), Solomon's (2014) US fathers made little mention of masculine tasks. They described, with considerable pride, routinely carrying out 'feminine' chores such as laundry, cooking, cleaning and meal planning, and viewed this as an important source of support for their partner. As we will explore further in due course, such positioning in relation to domestic chores feeds into wider debates about gender ideologies. The fathers interviewed by Doucet (2006) and the reluctant house-workers in Latshaw's (2015) study can to some extent be seen as reinforcing masculine norms (by pursuing tasks traditionally seen as masculine and rejecting those viewed as feminine). Latshaw suggests that, for these men, this may be an important means of neutralising what they may view (or at least be concerned that others view) as 'gender deviance'. In contrast, Solomon's (2014) interviewees and Latshaw's 'resolute' fathers are perhaps helping to reinvent masculine norms. We return to these themes later in the chapter.

Relationship with work

The study conducted by Ranson (2010) of what she calls 'crossover' families (that is, those where the mother was the breadwinner and the father the primary carer) and 'dual dividers' (where both work and caring were shared equally between the mother and father) suggests that, in the cases where mothers take on breadwinning roles, they act in rather different ways from breadwinning fathers. The female breadwinners in her research, for example, limited the demands of paid work in the interests of family life, and also devoted considerable effort to maintaining the close ties to their children that they had established in the immediate post-natal period. For the fathers in her study, the experience of taking on primary or equal responsibility for childcare led many of them to rethink their relationship to work, coming to prioritise their family responsibilities over paid employment, and being willing to make significant concessions in their working lives to achieve this. Similar changes are also reported in Merla's (2008) research. Many of the fathers in her study developed a strong critique of people's attachment to work, evident in much of contemporary society, and were quite explicit that, for them, work was not central to their identity; they placed emphasis on the quality of their relationships with others, rather than material goods.

However, this rejection of the importance of paid employment is not obvious in all studies of caregiving fathers. Scholars such as Doucet (2004) and Merla (2008) have illustrated how, in some cases, fathers can go to considerable lengths to maintain their attachment to paid work – or at least give the impression of doing so to reaffirm masculinist norms. Merla describes how the fathers in her study: often presented themselves to others as being between two jobs, rather than having made a specific decision to spend time caring for their children; suggested that the boundaries between paid work and domestic work are not always clear cut; and took up a range of activities outside the home that could be seen as conventionally masculine (such as undertaking repairs for others) and located within the public sphere (such as running community groups) (see also Doucet and Merla, 2007). Doucet (2004) outlines very similar patterns among the Canadian stay-at-home dads she interviewed, arguing that the 'long shadow of hegemonic masculinity' hung over them with respect to work. The overwhelming majority of participants in her research let it be known they were taking on self-provisioning work, such as landscaping and carpentry around the house, and/or doing community work, including repairs at their child's school and organising sports activities. On the basis of this evidence, she contends,

> what seemed very clear in most fathers' narratives was that they were quite adamant, from within their practices

and identities of caring, to distinguish themselves *as men,*
as heterosexual (with the exception of gay fathers), as
masculine, and as fathers, *not* as mothers. (2004: 292; italics
in original)

They were thus actively working to dispel some of the negative
assumptions about their masculinity that they had come across in
their interactions with others, by underlining their commitment to
activities viewed as stereotypically masculine. Liong (2017) shows how
the Hong Kong fathers in his research were also keen to affirm their
masculine identity through engagement with work and/or activities
in the public sphere, but that the opportunities available to do so were
often delineated along class lines. He argues that while the middle class
fathers took educational courses, wrote blogs and contributed to local
newspapers, working class fathers often did not have sufficient social,
economic and cultural capital to follow suit, and so were forced to
adapt to their role as carers. Liong maintains that these fathers typically
acknowledged the constraints they were under and were more accepting
of a caring identity than their middle class peers.

In the chapters that follow, we engage with questions about paid work
with respect to our own sample of fathers. We argue that, for many
of them (and in contrast to what is often suggested in the literature),
workplace practices such as allowing various forms of flexible working
were more important than parental leave in facilitating their caring
arrangements, a point we discuss with reference to family policy more
generally in Chapter 3. We also show, however, that dominant and
stereotypical assumptions about 'ideal workers' affected some of the
everyday experiences of the fathers. In Chapter 6, for example, we
argue that they sometimes felt out of place in daytime public space,
because of the perceived judgements and expectations with regard to
masculinity and work – and that evening or weekend dads' groups,
oriented to breadwinner fathers on the assumption they were in paid
employment throughout the week, had the potential to reinforce
this further.

Transforming gender identities?

A key concern of many of the scholars who have researched the lives
of fathers who take up the role of primary or equal caregiver is how
gender identities impact on these roles, and the reciprocal influence
that such caring practices can exert on gender identities. The majority
of work in this area has pointed to the complexity of such processes,

and that influences are rarely one-way or simple. Nevertheless, it is possible to distinguish between studies that have typically emphasised the steps caregiving fathers sometimes take to reaffirm distinctly masculine identities even amidst their somewhat counter-hegemonic roles, and others that have placed greater weight on the ways in which fatherly caregiving can help to develop new forms of masculinity, which include traditionally 'feminine' traits such as an emphasis on nurturing and establishing emotional closeness.

The research that has argued that key elements of traditional gender identities – and some associated inequalities – endure, even in families that are practising an unconventional division of labour, has pointed to the ongoing impact of both masculine norms about breadwinning and the pressure of 'intensive mothering'. In relation to the latter, Chelsey (2011) contends that the partners of the stay-at-home dads in her research commonly had a higher level of responsibility for and psychological involvement with their children when compared with breadwinner men they knew. She goes on to argue that 'This can lead to real behaviour differences between women and men, like working less, making less money, and doing more domestic work, that have the potential to support traditional gender divisions, in spite of breadwinner status' (653). The female partners also experienced feelings of guilt at their domestic set-up, leading Chelsey to speculate that this may, in general, make it harder for women to take on or persist in 'at-home father' family arrangements 'as long as women's status as "good mothers" conveys greater personal and social benefit than their breadwinner status' (654). Equally, the fathers in her sample tended to struggle with their 'deviance' from masculine ideals that stress the importance of breadwinning. As we noted earlier, however, pressures of breadwinning ideals can vary, not least by social class – with middle class men who are viewed to have been previously successful in their career often facing fewer tensions than their counterparts who have had different employment histories. Other studies, most of which have already been discussed in this chapter, also point to the ways in which stay-at-home fathers tend to reaffirm a conventional masculine identity by, for example, maintaining links to paid employment, participating in the public sphere, and/or engaging in 'masculine' forms of caregiving (emphasising physical activities and risk-taking, for example) (Doucet, 2004; Medved, 2016; Liong, 2017; Snitker, 2018). Doucet (2006) remarks on the evident contradictions in what she sees as stay-at-home dads' attempts to, on the one hand, distance themselves from the feminine and, on the other hand, reinvent masculine care to include elements of femininities.

This 'reinvention' is given more prominence in other accounts of fatherly caregiving (see Solomon, 2017). Indeed, various studies suggest that, in some circumstances, fathers who take on significant caring responsibilities can be seen to be 'undoing gender' (Deutsch, 2007) and developing what Elliott (2016) has called 'caring masculinities' – that is those that exclude domination and embrace the affective, relational, emotional, and interdependent qualities of care identified by feminist theories of care (252). Elliott argues that developing such caring masculinities is a critical way men can engage in gender equality, and thus offers the potential for bringing about significant social change and the reconfiguration of gender relations. Such contentions have found support in empirical studies. The fathers in Solomon's (2014) research, for example, discussed parenting in gender-neutral terms; stressed the interchangeable nature of men and women with respect to parenting (see also earlier discussion); and did not think of mothers as having a connection with their children that they would never be able to attain. Moreover, various other authors have also suggested that caregiving fathers come to understand caring differently, developing a much more acute sense of the hard work involved, and are thus more appreciative of others who also care (for example O'Brien and Twamley, 2017; Brandth and Kvande, 2018b; Lee and Lee, 2018; Tarrant, 2018).

Ranson (2015) goes further, suggesting that fathers caring on a primary or equal basis are reframing conventional understandings of fathering and masculinity. She notes that 'when fathers do become competent caregivers to very young children, they become different kinds of fathers' (177) – and help to establish what she calls 'equality masculinities' in which gender is done differently. Moreover, by explicitly contravening dominant expectations of mothering and fathering, couples in which the father has taken on substantial caring responsibilities have the capacity to change over time the nature of those expectations (Ranson, 2010). While the majority of the fathers in her research had committed to significant caring responsibilities on a long-term basis, Brandth and Kvande's (2018b) more recent work has suggested that similarly profound changes can be affected by parental leave. Their research with Norwegian men on such leave (typically of ten weeks' duration) demonstrates how values and practices of care can be integrated into masculine identities without 'degradation of masculine status' (72). They write:

> From having a low confidence in their care-giving abilities, the fathers in this study reported a growth in experience, as they acquired confidence and increased feelings of

self-esteem, thriving on being loved, and appreciated by the child, all of which seems to have provided their life with a new meaning and purpose. (86–7)

In contrast to work that has suggested fatherly caregivers often measure themselves against traditionally masculine norms, Brandth and Kvande (2018b) contend that, for these men, self-worth was not viewed in terms of social status or material resources, but rather the extent to which they had developed their own competence at caring, established a close and intimate relationship with their child, and contributed love and security to their family. While Brandth and Kvande maintain that such perspectives can be seen as broadly in line with Anderson's (2011) view of a more 'inclusive masculinity', they acknowledge that they may also be affected by the men's temporary status as primary caregivers. As they had not had to give up their job, Brandth and Kvande surmise that they were less likely to be challenged about their breadwinner identity.

Elements of 'transformation' in gender identities are also identified by even those who emphasise the endurance of dominant inequalities. For example, while arguing that some practices of stay-at-home dads can serve to reinforce gender divisions, Chelsey (2011) also notes that other practices can serve to undo them. She maintains that by spending a significant amount of time in a primary caregiver role, fathers not only develop a range of parenting skills more similar to their partner's but, if they return to the workplace, they are likely to value flexible working opportunities, be more family-friendly managers and, by talking about their children, can challenge stereotypes that it is only women who care about family. Furthermore, wives and partners of stay-at-home dads can develop a deeper sense of similarity with working men, and learn how to incorporate the idea of paid employment into understandings of a 'good mother' (Chesley, 2011). Despite evidence about inequalities in the sharing of domestic chores discussed earlier, the practical support offered by fathers can make life easier for women, and increase the likelihood that they will succeed at work. Indeed, liberating women from childcare, while encouraging men's contributions in the domestic sphere, was a key goal of second-wave feminism (Doucet and Lee, 2014; Medved, 2016) and underpins the 'universal caregiver' model of gender equality developed by Fraser (1996), which was discussed in Chapter 1. As Ranson (2010) maintains:

[E]quitable household arrangements realign the balance of paid work and family responsibilities by freeing mothers from the extra caregiving responsibilities that constrain their opportunities in the labour market and by freeing fathers from the workplace expectations that constrain their family involvement. (181–2)

She goes on to acknowledge, however, that these are not easy changes to make, as they often require mothers to give up some of the power and authority that they may view as central to their maternal identities, while fathers may have to forgo career aspirations and earning potential.

Developing a similar argument, Medved (2016) contends that caregiving fathers can bring about change through practices of resistance (such as adapting their career ambitions and placing emphasis on the importance of care) and transformation (by moving towards an understanding of caring/earning roles in gender-neutral terms). The extent to which gender identities are transformed may also be related to the social positioning of the families concerned. Liong (2017), as discussed at various points earlier in this chapter, shows how the working class fathers in his research were more accepting of a caring identity than their middle class peers, primarily because they recognised that they had very few opportunities to maintain a breadwinner identity. He writes:

> [T]hese men defined themselves in terms of being responsible for their families, and taking care of their children and performing housework duties … therefore, by re-orientating their field to the family, these working-class fathers showed acceptance of their caregiving role and demonstrated a longer commitment to caregiving. (412–13)

Change is also likely over time; indeed, writing over a decade ago, Doucet (2004) argued that various changes in Canadian society, such as the extension of parental leave and the increasing use of it by fathers, and the growth in the number of parenting centres will likely lead to an increase in the social ease around active fathering.

We engage with these debates, with respect to our own data, in the following chapters. We suggest that, notwithstanding complexities, limits and ambiguities in their accounts, the manner in which the fathers in our study became accustomed to a wide range of caregiving roles and the ways they reflected on this were indicative of a fundamental shift away from ideas around protection and provision to those that foreground interdependence, interchangeability (in terms of identities as well as tasks) and close, positive affectivity. Through considering such issues through our notion of fatherly care horizons, we explore both particular turning points in their perspectives and longer-term journeys of change with respect to both their practice and their parental identities and outlooks. While we dwell at length on significant challenges and limits to such journeys, we also point to the striking distance that many had travelled, undoing facets of dominant gender through their practice along the way, and moving towards the establishment of caring masculinities.

Conclusion

In this chapter we have outlined key themes of importance to this book from the literature on fatherly involvement in general and on the minority of fathers who have assumed extensive caregiving responsibilities. It is notable that, while there is now a large international literature on fathering, and a substantial body of work on those who are primary carers or on parental leave, the number of studies that have focussed on those fathers who share care more or less equally with their partner is still small. This book thus makes an important contribution to our knowledge in this area by focussing on these 'equal care sharers' as well as those who had taken on primary caring responsibility and/ or were on extended parental leave. As part of this, we also place particular emphasis on fathers who were engaging in extensive care roles alongside flexible or part-time work, and on the means through which care at home was juggled with day care. In this chapter, we have also signalled various ways in which we take forward the extant literature. This includes extending the notion of parental 'interchangeability' in relation to its significance for fathers' identities as well as their practices (discussed in Chapter 5); highlighting the enduring differences in the experience of public and private spaces for many caregiving fathers (Chapter 6); and integrating notions of the undoing of gender and caregiving masculinities with an examination of developing fatherly care horizons as part of father's journeys (throughout the empirical chapters). While much of our emphasis is on developments in fathers' orientations, we also extend literature on maternal care, executive responsibility and so-called 'gatekeeping' in developing an understanding of how assumptions of what we call 'default maternal responsibility' can continue sometimes to underlie arrangements that are in many respects egalitarian or role-reversed (see Chapters 5 and 7). Before this, however, we discuss in Chapter 3 the broader policy context in which families make their decisions about caring responsibilities, examining the extent to which national governments can incentivise more caregiving on the part of fathers, and the ways in government policy can be mediated by societal- and individual-level norms.

3

Developing Policy Support For Care-sharing: And Its Limitations

Introduction

Providing a substantive examination of the context in which unusually care-centred fathers operate, this chapter focuses on developments in family policy that relate to fatherly caregiving. We focus on policy, specifically, because it provides an important backdrop to the chapters that follow. Our discussion in Chapter 4 of the reasons why the fathers in our sample took on equal or primary responsibility for the care of their young children indicates that practical circumstances often were key, though longer-term orientations could also play an important role. The impact of policy levers may only have been directly visible for those who had taken parental leave, but others had likely benefited more indirectly from the statutory right to request to work flexibly introduced in the UK in 2003 and/or the broader cultural impact of the shift in UK family policy over the last decade. More importantly, throughout the coming chapters we show how the accounts of these unusual fathers draw attention, alongside international evidence, to the ways policy might be leveraged to encourage greater numbers of men in a broader range of circumstances to become more involved in caregiving and how it might render such experiences easier and longer-lasting. This informs some of the policy recommendations that we outline in Chapter 7, the Conclusion.

While some scholars have argued that social policy often lags behind social change because the assumptions that underpin specific policy measures are based on previous rather than current time periods

(Newsome, 2017), others have maintained that policy can *affect* significant change – through both incentivising (usually economically) specific types of behaviour, and helping to establish particular cultural norms and dominant discourses (Milner, 2010). Reflecting on family policies in Norway and Sweden, Bergqvist and Saxonberg (2017) contend that the state has established, either through action or inaction, 'national ideals of care' which inform families' decisions about care. They assert that, even without the provision of economic incentives, if the state makes it clear through its policies that it expects certain types of behaviour, this can influence individual decisions. By way of illustration, they outline differences in attitudes among parents in Sweden and Norway. The national ideal of care in Sweden, they suggest, is based on the assumption that parents should share care equally, whereas the Norwegian equivalent emphasises that both parents should contribute to care but does not prescribe that the contributions should be equal. Thus, when Swedish parents in their research did not share parental leave equally, they felt guilty and talked about not living up to the national ideal of caring. In contrast, in Norway, the fathers typically felt that they were doing their duty and supporting gender equality if they engaged in partial sharing – typically using the non-transferable parental leave that was specially assigned to them, rather than the longer period of leave that could be shared between parents as they saw fit. Bergqvist and Saxonberg (2017) conclude:

> Moral incentives matter: the state sends signals about what is expected, so the Swedish system of officially giving fathers half the leave time and requiring them to give mothers permission to use any part of 'their' time does in fact encourage fathers to share more time. (1485)

The chapter first considers the enduring relevance of *national* policies in a world where supranational bodies and various globalising pressures increasingly exert influence. It then moves on to consider the key lessons that can be learnt from legislation that has been introduced in countries other than the UK, with the aim of facilitating greater involvement by fathers in the lives of their children. Here, we draw particularly on evidence from Nordic nations, which are commonly seen as having been the most successful in implementing 'family-friendly' policies, moving closer to Fraser's (1996) 'universal caregiver' model (see Chapter 1) and securing quite significant behavioural change among parents. We then provide a detailed analysis of UK family policy, with a specific focus on how it has addressed fathers, over the last 50 years. This section is structured chronologically, as we argue that there has been considerable change over time, both in the language with which fathers have been discussed, and the government's willingness to intervene in what has historically been seen in the UK as a private arena. We maintain that while we have seen considerable policy activity in this area, and a significant shift away from the strongly maternalist orientation of policy evident in the late twentieth century, UK policy remains some distance away from promoting a universal caregiver model. Finally, we suggest that policy is not always translated into behaviour on-the-ground in a straightforward manner – and consider various ways in which government initiatives can be mediated by policies, practices and cultures in the workplace, and also by wider societal- and individual-level norms.

Enduring importance of national policy

Despite various globalising pressures with respect to social policy (Ohmae, 1995) and the intervention of supranational bodies such as the European Union in family policy (Gregory and Milner, 2011; Baird and O'Brien, 2015), studies of the ways in which families are supported by the state have documented very considerable differences by nation, and these are equally marked with respect to provisions to encourage fathers to share care (Ray et al., 2010). Indeed, on the basis of their analysis of parental leave policies in 21 European countries, Castro-García and Pazos-Moran (2016) developed a three-fold typology corresponding to dominant national assumptions about fatherly involvement. Their first type – countries that promote co-responsibility for children – is seen most commonly in the Nordic region. These nations, the authors argue, come closest to reaching an equal breadwinner/caregiver model (similar to Fraser's universal caregiver model outlined in Chapter 1), through the provision of non-transferable, highly-paid parental leave of considerable duration. The second type (evident in France, Belgium, Spain, Denmark and Poland) assumes that men are 'incidental collaborators' in childcare. Its policies provide either well-paid non-transferable parental leave but only for a short period of time, or leave of a longer duration but at a lower rate of pay. Castro-García and Pazos-Moran argue that the system in these countries 'has more to do with separating women from employment (partially or totally) during early child-rearing' (67) than promoting shared care, with fathers contributing only immediately after childbirth. The third type of country is that which, Castro-García and Pazos-Moran maintain, reinforces the gendered division of labour by offering fathers only a very small number of days of paid leave or none at all. Here, a 'modified male breadwinner' regime is prevalent, and men are not considered even marginally responsible for childcare. Examples include Hungary, Greece, the Netherlands, Austria, Italy and Ireland.

Although family policies have, in many nations, changed quite considerably over recent years, often moving closer to the Nordic model by introducing specific non-transferable leave for fathers, some historical patterns endure. Indeed, Karu and Tremblay (2018) suggest that significant differences remain between countries in 'old' (that is western) Europe, particularly the Nordic countries, on the one hand, and those in eastern Europe and outside Europe altogether, on the other hand. The Nordic countries expanded their parental leave policies to include fathers in the 1970s and 1980s, and were the first to introduce a non-transferable allocation of leave specifically for fathers (what is often referred to as the 'daddy quota'). Despite the intra-European variation outlined earlier, and Europe's diversity in terms of welfare models (Esping-Anderson, 1990), western Europe 'displays some homogeneity when compared to other world regions with respect to a more generous and well-compensated leave system for both mothers and fathers' (O'Brien, 2013: 559). Gender equality policies elsewhere in the world have been much slower to develop. In eastern Europe, for example, although under Communism women were encouraged to join the labour force and supported by plentiful state-funded childcare, since the fall of Communism there has been much less emphasis on policies to enable women to combine motherhood and paid employment. Governments have instead often promoted a male breadwinner model – closing childcare centres, providing long maternal leaves, and offering few incentives for fathers to take parental leave (Robila, 2012). Robila (2012) has shown how such strategies have been pursued in a wide range of eastern European countries, including Bulgaria, Estonia, Latvia and Romania. Within many Anglophone nations, including the US, family policies are still not always seen positively, because of an enduring assumption, held by many, that the state should not intervene in what are essentially private matters (Karu and Tremblay, 2018) while, across the globe, the figure of the father as economic provider-in-chief remains a dominant cultural force in many countries (O'Brien, 2013), sometimes militating against the introduction of policies to encourage fatherly care. Thus, while Nordic reforms are often seen as having led to cultural change in the affected nations, this suggests that, in other parts of the world, policy is more likely to follow, rather than lead, attitudinal change.

International lessons on parental leave

Various different aspects of family policy can help parents to balance work and caring responsibilities more equally. As we discuss in more detail later, with respect to the UK context, this can include: the right to take up flexible working practices; the provision of childcare and early education; and financial support for families with children (to help cover the cost of childcare). Nevertheless, the most commonly discussed policy area in facilitating fatherly care specifically is the provision of parental leave. Studies have shown that if fathers spend a considerable period of time caring alone for a child they are more likely to take on a more equal share of childcare responsibilities subsequently (Karu and Tremblay, 2018). Research from nations in which parental leave reform has been associated with significant changes in fathers' involvement in childcare has indicated there are two elements that are key to maximising take-up among fathers – that it is non-transferable (that is if the father does not use it, it is lost to the family as a whole) and financially well-compensated (Bünning and Pollmann-Schult, 2016).

Across the world, when parental leave is available to either parent (a so-called 'transferable' scheme), it is much more likely to be taken up by mothers. This is explained with reference to enduring gender norms about caring (discussed in Chapter 2) and financial factors. As men typically earn on average more than women (O'Reilly et al., 2015; Fortin et al., 2017), families often calculate that they will be better off financially if the mother forgoes part of her salary over the period of the parental leave rather than the father his (Haas and Hwang, 2019b). Thus, while transferable schemes can seem fair and equal in theory, they invariably lead to mothers interrupting their careers for longer than fathers (Castro-García and Pazos-Moran, 2016). To provide incentives for families to share parental leave in more gender-equal ways, various countries have, over the past few decades, introduced a non-transferable portion of leave for fathers, often referred to, as noted earlier, as a 'daddy quota'. Norway was the first country to introduce such a quota, in 1993, and was followed soon after by Sweden in 1997 and Iceland in 2001. (It is notable, however, that not even the Nordic countries have equal periods of non-transferable and well-paid leave for each partner (Castro-García and Pazos-Moran, 2016).) In general, the introduction of such schemes has had a significant impact on leave-taking patterns. In the province of Quebec in Canada, for example, non-transferable leave for fathers was introduced in 2006. By 2011, the Canadian General Social Survey revealed that, among couples where at least one parent took leave after the birth of a child, 75 per cent of fathers in Quebec had taken leave compared to 50 per cent elsewhere in Canada (Mayer and Le Bourdais, 2018).

The importance of non-transferable parental leave, even in cultures where gender equality is valued highly, is evident. In Norway, for example, the most common practice among families is that the father makes use of his 15 weeks of (paid) paternity leave and the mother takes up the rest of the available 12 months of parental leave (Lappegård, 2012). Recent policy changes in Denmark are also instructive. The Danish government first introduced a period of paid, non-transferable leave for fathers in 1997, which led to a substantial increase in take-up. More recently, it removed the non-transferable nature of the leave, believing that practices around fathers' leave had changed permanently and become an accepted part of Danish culture. However, once the leave became transferable between parents, the take-up rate among eligible fathers dropped by 22 per cent (Bloksgaard and Rostgaard, 2015). As Birkett and Forbes (2019) have argued, this case illustrates quite clearly that policy change, in itself, is rarely sufficient to alter fundamentally the culture around care; it also underlines, however, the necessity of policy in effecting ongoing behavioural change.

The level of financial compensation for parental leave is also considered, by many, to be crucial to increasing its take-up by fathers (Castro-García and Pazos-Moran, 2016; Karu and Tremblay, 2018; Haas and Hwang, 2019b). In Norway, for example, where almost all eligible fathers take their quota of 15 weeks of non-transferable leave, they receive compensation of 100 per cent of their pay (up to a specified ceiling). In general, fathers' rates of leave are higher in countries with higher rates of income replacement and, in countries where payments are low, this is often a key deterrent for fathers (Kaufman, 2018). This is linked closely to the gender pay gap evident in many nations: if parental leave compensation is paid at a low rate, it is often harder for families to forego the father's salary than the mother's because the reduction in family income over this period would often be higher. The importance of the level of compensation is illustrated well in the natural experiment that occurred in Iceland in the years following the banking collapse of 2008. In the five years prior to 2008, Icelandic fathers used on average three full months of parental leave. However, after 2008, the maximum payment for parental leave was lowered considerably and, as a result, fathers' use declined markedly, while that of mothers increased correspondingly (Sigurdardottir and Garðarsdóttir, 2018). The most dramatic change was among high-income fathers, whose payments were most severely affected by this policy change (Sigurdardottir and Garðarsdóttir, 2018).

Alongside highlighting the importance of the non-transferability and level of compensation of parental leave, international evidence has emphasised the value to fathers of having recourse to statutory provision and legal entitlements, even in contexts where the support offered by employers is generous (Haas and Hwang, 2019b). As noted earlier in this chapter, statutory policies can, in some situations, foster among fathers a sense of obligation to take leave and become more involved in caregiving. Drawing on research conducted with Norwegian fathers who had taken parental leave, Brandth and Kvande (2018) argue that the 'pre-negotiated' nature of the leave was significant, as fathers understood their 'daddy quota' as a collective right given to employed fathers and thus not something for which they had to seek permission from their managers (see also Nordberg, 2019). Moreover, they contend that the legal status of the quota, as well as compelling employers to allow it, puts pressure on fathers themselves to reject 'ideal worker' norms associated with long hours and the prioritisation of employment. Närvi and Salmi (2019) make similar arguments with respect to Finland. They argue that taking the 'daddy quota' has become normalised, and seen as the new standard of involved and caring fatherhood. However, they also point out that Finnish fathers typically do not feel a similar obligation to take up more of the parental leave than the non-transferable part, indicative, they suggest, of a taken-for-granted assumption that they are not equally responsible for childcare (see also Gregory and Milner, 2010). Evidence from the Nordic states and from other parts of the world such as Quebec, thus suggests that family policy can make a substantial contribution to bringing about the universal caregiver model of gender relations outlined by Nancy Fraser (1996) and discussed in Chapter 1. However, even in those nations that have introduced the most progressive policies, it is notable that patterns of leave-taking still remain patterned by gender to some extent: mothers continue to be more likely than fathers to take up portions of leave that are open to either parent.

Fathers and UK family policy

In this section, we focus specifically on family policy in the UK, to shed further light on the context in which the participants in our study were making their decisions and the potential lessons offered by their experiences. We highlight that, although UK policy – as far as it impacts on fathers – has changed quite considerably over the past two decades, it has, to date, failed to facilitate the kind of fatherly engagement in childcare in the ways that have been seen in the Nordic countries. We explore some of the reasons for this, and juxtapose the largely positive language that is used in contemporary policy documents about fathers taking on more caring responsibilities with significant limitations in the substantive content of policy. We begin the section, however, by examining how UK policy has changed over time, and how assumptions about the role of fathers have been slowly shifting. We split our analysis into three sections: policy prior to the election of the New Labour government in 1997; the period of New Labour policy between 1997 and 2010; and more recent initiatives – from 2010 to the present day. This last period includes the Conservative–Liberal Democrat coalition government from 2010 to 2015, and the Conservative governments from 2015 until the time of writing (2020).

Policy prior to 1997: Families as private spheres

In general terms, the UK lagged behind much of Europe in the development of its family policies, particularly with respect to parental leave, until the end of the twentieth century (Lewis and Campbell, 2007; Kaufman, 2018). In common with many other countries, public policies in the aftermath of the Second World War were predicated on the assumption that families would comprise a full-time male worker and a full-time (home-based) female carer (O'Brien, 2013). Moreover, in the UK, family policy was also informed by a liberal model of welfare, which assumed that the family was a largely private arena, in which the state should not intervene (Milner, 2010). Thus, during the 1970s and 1980s, UK governments did little to either encourage or discourage mothers' involvement in the labour market or fathers' breadwinning, and were reluctant to develop any explicit family policies (Lewis and Campbell, 2007). Maternity leave legislation was first introduced in the UK in 1975, as part of the Employment Protection Act – but, because women had to have been employed for relatively long periods of time before they were eligible, until about 1990 only about half of women were able to take any such leave.

Reflecting on this period, Daly (2010) argues that while financial and support services were in place for families, and child benefit was paid on a universal basis, policies oriented to the protection and support of the family as a social institution were not developed (in contrast to many other European countries). Moreover, as late as the mid-1990s, government ministers claimed that it was the responsibility of mothers and fathers to reconcile, within their family unit, paid work with the unpaid work of care (Lewis and Campbell, 2007). Within this context, fathers were the subject of policy intervention only when their behaviour was deemed problematic. A notable example was the 1991 Child Support Act, which was intended to enforce the requirement that parents liable to pay child support to their partners should do so. It was seen as a means of addressing the perceived problem of non-resident fathers shirking their financial responsibilities (as well as lone mothers drawing money from the state). In relation to 'family-friendly' policies (rather than punitive measures), government interventions in this period were largely limited to sponsoring research and encouraging employers to consider the advantages to their business that might result from introducing schemes to promote work–life balance (Lewis and Campbell, 2008).

1997–2010: Work–family balance and enduring maternalism

When the New Labour government was elected in 1997, the UK lagged behind all of its western European counterparts in terms of family-friendly legislation, and was still characterised by a reluctance to take action with respect to what were seen as largely private family matters (Kaufman, 2018). However, over the decade or so that followed, there was a significant shift in the government's willingness to intervene in issues related to parental care. Featherstone (2009) argues that this change was related to a broader reorientation of social policy towards supporting a 'social investment' state. While the post-war welfare state (in the UK and elsewhere) sought to protect people from the insecurities of the market, the social investment state took a more proactive role in facilitating the integration of people into employment (Featherstone, 2019). This was underpinned by the belief that, as economies had become more open as a result of globalisation, the priority of the state needed to shift 'from seeking to maintain stable employment in a relatively closed national economy to the need to enhance competitiveness through increasing flexibility and ... innovation ... by intervening on the supply side' (Featherstone, 2009: 129). Supporting both men and women to engage in the labour market was a key part of such supply-side interventions, and led the government to develop a more explicit family policy. The family came to be seen by New Labour not only as an economic agent but also as an important facilitator of social integration and inclusion (Daly, 2010). Such perspectives converged with longer-standing feminist arguments about the importance of women's participation in the labour market. A further and associated change under New Labour was a willingness to use legislation normatively, to encourage what the government viewed as positive family practices, and discourage those that it deemed undesirable (Milner, 2010). As a consequence, issues of work and family received attention from several government departments, and public expenditure increased significantly (Lewis and Campbell, 2008).

From 1997, a series of radical reforms were introduced, 'bringing about a paradigmatic change in the goals of policy and giving the state responsibility for work-family matters' (Windebank, 2017: 59). Some of the key reforms of this period that impacted on families are summarised in Table 1. As Daly (2010) has argued, these policies were focussed on six main areas: education, care and wellbeing of children (for example expanding early education services); provision of financial support for families with children (for example the introduction of tax credits); establishment of specific services for families with young children (for example the 'Sure Start' programme); activation of parental employment (through tax credits, and the promotion of employment among lone parents); promotion of work–family reconciliation (through extending maternity leave, introducing paternity leave and giving all workers the right to request flexible working patterns); and expectations that parents will act in a responsible manner.

Nevertheless, while the New Labour agenda represented a significant departure from that of previous administrations, it was also characterised

Table 1: Key aspects of New Labour's family policy (adapted from Daly, 2010: 20)

Area of intervention	Key policy change
Early education and childcare	Expansion of childcare and early education services Universal early education guarantee (for three- and four-year-olds)
Financial support for families with children	Introduction of tax credits Increased level of financial support for families with children
Services for young children and their families	Expansion of family-related services under Sure Start Localism, and community development orientation (also under Sure Start)
Employment activation	Introduction of tax credits Promotion of employment among lone and other parents
Work-family reconciliation	Extension of maternity leave Introduction of paternity leave Right to request flexible working
Parental responsibility and behaviour	Greater intervention into family life generally

by some key elements of continuity, which had the effect of limiting its impact (Daly, 2010; Windebank, 2017).

Notable among these continuities was a strong maternalist orientation, evidenced by the extensions to maternity leave that were introduced in this period, and increases in maternity pay. Here, key elements of Fraser's (1996) 'caregiver parity model' (see Chapter 1) are evident, extending support for women providing care, but failing to address – and possibly even worsening – men's lack of participation in care and women's disadvantage in the labour market. Paid maternity leave was extended from 14 to 18 weeks in 1999, from 18 to 26 weeks in 2002, and then to 52 weeks in 2005. The level of maternity pay was increased as part of both the 2002 and 2005 reforms. In contrast, although paternity leave was introduced for the first time in 2002, this was of only two weeks' duration, and paid at a low flat rate. Some scholars suggest that the medium-term impact of these policy interventions has been significant in reinforcing maternalistic assumptions in the UK. Indeed, reflecting on these developments a decade later, Baird and O'Brien (2015) suggest that 'the legacy of a long mother-centred leave has been resilient and to some extent has hindered design innovation in the UK ... the power of a maternal template has been strong' (209). We return to these arguments later in this chapter, when we explore contemporary family policy.

With respect to fathers, specifically, Kilkey (2006) contends that their position in policy shifted somewhat over the New Labour years. She argues that in the very early period of the administration, there was little explicit focus on fathers, and policy tended to use the gender-neutral language of 'parents'. Moreover, many of the policies themselves were ostensibly gender-neutral, focussing on, for example, rights to emergency parental leave, part-time working and overall working hours (Kilkey, 2006). Kilkey notes that 'It did not seem to matter that in the context of a deeply gendered labour market and family conditions, gender-neutral policies would in practice be anything but' (168). For example, research has shown that, because of the gender pay gap and inequalities in caregiving, women are much more likely to request flexible working than their male counterparts (for example Radcliffe and Cassell, 2015). When fathers' specific involvement in families *was* discussed, it was typically in relation to their role-modelling and mentoring, rather than actual care-work (for example, fathers were encouraged to read with their sons, as part of wider initiatives to tackle boys' alleged 'underachievement' in schools). They were also sometimes problematised in policy, in the ways discussed earlier in relation to the 1980s and early 1990s (Radcliffe and Cassell, 2015). In 2000, however,

Kilkey argues that a shift occurred: fathers were referenced explicitly within policy and, for the first time, were discussed in relation to their contribution to childcare. In 2002, paternity leave was introduced and discussed widely in the press, with much speculation about whether Tony Blair, the prime minister, would take paternity leave after the birth of his child in 2003. Nevertheless, the limited nature of this leave (two weeks), and the language within which the policy was couched – emphasising the 'choice' fathers now had to spend time with their new-born child – constructed care as something fathers may choose to opt into (see Miller, 2011), rather than assuming a desire to care was universal (Miller, 2011) and/or something with which they had a responsibility to engage.

Alongside a pervasive maternalism and an ambivalent position with respect to fathers, New Labour policy has also been critiqued for failing to tackle meaningfully gender inequalities more broadly. Indeed, gender equality was rarely mentioned as an explicit goal of family policy, as compared to, for example, the desire to develop a social investment state, the improvement of fertility rates (by providing more support for women workers), the tackling of child poverty (by encouraging more parents, particularly lone mothers, to work), and the promotion of child development (by providing high quality early education) (Lewis and Campbell, 2008). When gender equality *was* discussed within policy it was primarily in relation to facilitating women's participation in the labour market, and in recognising their social contribution through the substantial increases in both length of maternity leave and the rate of maternity pay. Indeed, the position of men was, as Lewis and Campbell (2008) note, 'addressed much more cautiously' (535). They write:

> [W]hile the desire of fathers' groups for more time with children has been frequently noted in the policy documents, the decision not to tackle fathers' long-hours working, alongside a rather inflexible approach to leaves for fathers, that are also low-paid … makes it unlikely that UK government policy so far on balancing work and family will effect a major change in men's behaviour. (Lewis and Campbell, 2007: 23)

Moreover, feminist scholars have contended that New Labour's failure to acknowledge that the choices men take directly affect those available to women, alongside the use of gender-neutral language throughout much of relevant policies, did little to question wider structural inequalities in the division of care (Lewis and Campbell, 2007; Daly, 2010). For Daly (2010), despite the strong policy rhetoric about balancing work and family life, New Labour ultimately sought to strengthen traditional family relationships (through extending maternity leave, for example). Although a gender equality discourse was sometimes drawn upon, it was never the primary ideational frame (Windebank, 2017). Indeed, the extensions to maternity leave can be seen as broadly consistent with Fraser's caregiver parity model, while the emphasis on getting women into work once childbearing was over (purportedly to address the perceived problem of women staying at home at the taxpayer's expense), through initiatives such as the New Deal for Lone Parents (see Scourfield and Drakeford, 2002), had much in common with beliefs underpinning the universal breadwinner model (see Chapter 1). Ideas associated with Fraser's universal caregiver model, whereby fathers and mothers share caregiving and paid work, were notable by their absence.

Radical change was also constrained by the government's concern to protect the interests of employers, preventing far-reaching reform to workplace culture. A long hours culture in many UK organisations can make it extremely difficult for parents to achieve a good work–life balance, and can often have the effect of encouraging a traditional division of responsibilities within families, with women sometimes withdrawing from the labour force completely to care full-time for their children (Orgad, 2019). Nevertheless, the New Labour government allowed employers to opt out of the European Union's working time directive (which limited hours of work to 48 per week), while the introduction of a right *to request* flexible working patterns on the part of parents (and carers of dependent adults) provided an important first step towards recognising the importance of work flexibility (see Eek and Axmon, 2013; Bryan and Sevilla, 2017), but included no obligation for employers to agree to such requests (Fox et al., 2009; Daly, 2010; Milner, 2010).

Reviewing the various family-related policies of this period, Daly (2010) contends that New Labour was engaged in a process of repositioning rather than fundamental reform, in which parents and the family itself were 'located more closely in a market context' and 'the rhythms and exigencies of family life … [were] reframed in an activation mode' (442). This is evidenced not only in the substantive content of policies, but also the language used by the government in talking about them. Milner (2010) shows how, over the course of New Labour's time in office, the discourse of 'family-friendliness' shifted towards one of 'work–life balance'. This was associated with greater emphasis on the business case for introducing related measures, rather than foregrounding the impact on families and mothers' and fathers' caregiving practices. Moreover, she argues that the discourse of 'win–win' that was prevalent in government policy documents, which aimed to reassure business in order to secure their compliance in a voluntaristic culture of workplace relations, 'glossed over the gender implications of caring, with the risk of increasing women's double burden' (6). Developing this argument, Lewis and Campbell (2008) suggest that the use of the term 'work–life balance', while appearing to be inclusive, had the effect of obscuring the gendered division of unpaid work that, to a significant degree, underpins gender equality. Moreover, by focussing on individual choice, it did not acknowledge that an employee's decision is usually socially-embedded and frequently patterned by gender. Lewis and Campbell go on to argue that while the 'right to request' legislation assumed that individuals will negotiate with their managers, and placed a premium on individual control and choice, it failed to address group inequalities between men and women. They assert:

> Sharing care at the household level … poses particularly difficult issues, for there is a tension between the individual's real freedom to choose and gender equality. Historically, men have chosen not to do carework, which is bound to affect women's choices about care and employment. (535)

It thus did little to tackle the gender inequalities within the home, and tended to reinforce male breadwinner/female caregiver norms (or 'caregiver parity' in Fraser's model – see Chapter 1).

2010–present: Shared parental leave and greater focus on gender inequalities

By the second decade of the twenty-first century, there was a further change in family policy in the UK. By 2008, the New Labour government had recognised that the parental leave system that had been put in place over the previous decade was in quite significant ways gendered, with only mothers having the right to an extended period of leave after the birth of a child (Windebank, 2017). Thus, before it left office, it had discussed the merits of a transferable leave arrangement (influenced by what Baird and O'Brien (2015) call the 'Nordic turn' in family policy), and outlined plans for an 'Additional Parental Leave' scheme, which was subsequently implemented by the

Conservative and Liberal Democrat coalition government, which came to power in 2010.

The debate about Additional Parental Leave represented the first time in which an economic rationale had been used to justify giving fathers more time out of the workplace to care (Kilkey, 2006). Government discourse drew on ideas associated with the social investment state, discussed previously. It argued that children were the citizen-workers of the future, and that they were best served when both their mother and father were involved in their care (Kilkey, 2006). The government consultation paper that addressed the introduction of Additional Parental Leave argued that:

> When mothers work during the first year of their child's life and fathers play a greater role in bringing up their children, this can lead to strong, positive educational effects later on in the child's life ... The new law enabling mothers to transfer a proportion of their maternity leave and pay to fathers will help give children the best start in life by supporting fathers' involvement in their care. (DTI, 2005, quoted in Kilkey, 2006: 172)

Nevertheless, while the language used to talk about fathers had shifted considerably, recognising their potentially substantial role in childcare, emphasis often remained on what was best for children rather than what was best for the mother and/or father, or for promoting gender equality more generally. There were also important limitations to the Additional Parental Leave policy, which had an adverse impact on take-up.

As noted in Chapter 2, the Additional Parental Leave scheme allowed mothers to transfer some of their maternity leave (up to 26 weeks of the 52 weeks total) to their partner, and provided fathers with up to 26 weeks of leave in addition to their already guaranteed two weeks of paternity leave. However, fathers could not begin their leave until at least 20 weeks after the birth of the child and were only eligible if their partner had unused maternity leave. Fathers whose partners were not eligible for maternity leave, or who did not want to return to work before the end of their maternity leave were unable to take advantage of the scheme (Kaufman, 2018). Moreover, the rate of financial compensation was low – paid at the statutory weekly rate or 90 per cent of average weekly earnings, whichever was lower (Kaufman, 2018). Ministers claimed the policy would enhance fathers' engagement during the first year of their children's lives, yet they anticipated a very limited uptake of between four and eight per cent of eligible fathers (Baird and O'Brien, 2015). In practice, even these low figures proved to be optimistic – with under one per cent of fathers taking advantage of the scheme in its first year (Kaufman, 2018).

Within only a few years of Additional Parental Leave having been launched, the policy was amended and legislation for a new 'Shared Parental Leave' scheme introduced in 2013, available to fathers from 2015. Under the revised scheme, the 52 weeks of maternity leave and two of paternity leave were retained. However, mothers could transfer up to 50 weeks of their leave to their partners after a much shorter period of time (two weeks rather than 20), and the transfer was no longer contingent on the mother returning to employment. Thus, mothers and fathers could, if they wished, spend time on parental leave together looking after their child. Although the introduction of this scheme attracted more public discussion and debate than its predecessor, the take-up has again been extremely low. As noted in Chapter 1, current indications are that only a very small proportion of eligible fathers have taken advantage of Shared Parental Leave with estimated take-up rates ranging between two and eight per cent (Twamley and Schober, 2018; Walker, 2018).

Despite the poor take-up rate, the shift to a system of transferable parental leave in the UK, from 2010 onwards, can be seen, in some respects at least, as a fundamental change in family policy. It represented further significant movement away from the liberal model of minimal state intervention in family matters that had characterised the UK until the late twentieth century. This was perhaps particularly surprising given the wider economic conditions and the government's desire to cut public spending because of the global recession (Windebank, 2017). A change was also evident in some of the underpinning cultural assumptions about the orientation of leave. Windebank (2017), for example, contends that, taken together, Additional Parental Leave and Shared Parental Leave 'can be viewed as the beginnings of a paradigmatic shift away from maternalism and towards an adult worker model of work–family reconciliation' (63). Baird and O'Brien (2015) explain this shift with reference to the confluence of external and internal demands that had come to bear on the UK government. The former included pressure from the European Union, which had, since the 1990s been developing policies to promote work–family reconciliation policies, female employment and gender equality (Fox et al., 2009; Baird and O'Brien, 2015), while the latter included shifts in societal expectations (about the desirability of mothers of young children engaging in paid work) and an increase in women's levels of education. Indeed, the government chose to couch some of its case for transferable leave to business specifically in terms of the need to secure a return on the education of women through their greater labour market participation (Baird and O'Brien, 2015).

Nevertheless, in examining why take-up of both schemes has been so low, scholars have argued that while both Additional Parental Leave and Shared Parental Leave did represent a significant shift for the UK, neither ultimately replicated key aspects of the Nordic schemes – namely reserving a substantial non-transferable portion of leave for fathers, and ensuring that the rate of financial compensation was high. Fox et al. (2009) argue that parental leave policies typically focus on developing either an 'encouraging' or 'mandatory' approach. While the former provides certain incentives to encourage families to share leave more equitably between mothers and fathers, the latter commonly introduces a non-transferable period of leave 'with the intention of producing normative guidelines for fathers' behaviour' (315). As we explained earlier, there is strong evidence from the Nordic countries that it is leave that is *non-transferable* that is the more successful in facilitating fathers' involvement with the children (Fox et al., 2009). Without such an allocation specifically for fathers, take-up typically remains low (Fox et al., 2009; Baird and O'Brien, 2015; Boyer et al., 2017). Empirical research has shown quite consistently that, where leave is transferable, mothers tend to take the vast majority – linked to a range of gendered assumptions about, for example, care work and maternal bonding (Kaufman, 2018). Kaufman's (2018) analysis of the reasons why British fathers do not take parental leave concluded that, after the birth of a child, 'both mothers and fathers "fell back" into gendered roles that emphasised the naturalness or ease of caring for mothers and earning for fathers' (321). Without stronger policy incentives, many of the established gendered assumptions about familial roles discussed in Chapter 2 continue to shape post-natal family practices.

The government's decision not to introduce a non-transferable period of leave – despite the solid evidence from the Nordic countries that this is necessary if significant numbers of men are to be incentivised to take parental leave – has been explained in terms of the government's adherence to an ideology of free choice, opposition from the business lobby, and insufficient pressure from the wider UK electorate (Windebank, 2017). It can also be linked to an enduring maternalist emphasis in policy, evident in statements such as the one that follows from Jo Swinson, a former employment minister, when discussing the introduction of Shared Parental Leave. Although recognising that 'Parenting is a shared endeavour as we want to encourage full involvement from fathers from the start', she went on to state: 'The next step is introducing shared parental leave in April 2015, *giving mums and adopters real choice* about when they return to work and dads more time to bond with their children' (Department for Business, Innovation and Skills, 2014, n.p., italics added). This statement is significant in revealing that the government saw the choice as primarily the mother's – consonant with its reference to fathers taking up 'unused maternity leave' later in the same document. Mothers are positioned as primarily responsible for care, while fathers are constructed largely as supporters (see discussion in Chapter 1) – provided with the opportunity to spend time with their children but not expected to be ultimately responsible for them. This is a theme we return to later in the book when we consider the extent to which what we term discourses of 'default maternal responsibility' continue to affect the extent to which primary or equal carer fathers consider themselves, and believe they are seen by others, as fully interchangeable with their female partner. The emphasis on choice in the quotation from Jo Swinson also indicates a lack of awareness of some of the barriers families may face in being able to take up Shared Parental Leave, not least the financial burden it may place on many couples.

The level of wage compensation within the UK parental leave schemes is indeed also significant in explaining the very low take-up rate. As discussed earlier, the Nordic experience suggests strongly that to ensure such schemes are attractive to fathers, they need to be paid generously. Within the UK, families can be financially disadvantaged if Shared Parental Leave is taken up during the high income replacement period (the first six weeks) of maternity leave (Baird and O'Brien, 2015). At the time of writing, mothers are paid 90 per cent of their average weekly earnings for the first six weeks of their maternity leave and then £146.68 or 90 per cent of their average weekly earnings (whichever is lower) for the next 33 weeks. In contrast, Shared Parental Leave is paid at the latter rate (for the first 37 weeks before it becomes unpaid), whenever it is taken. Moreover, the significant differences by socio-economic status in take-up of parental leave schemes by fathers attest to the impact of financial factors. In Koskowski and Kadar-Satat's (2019) research, for example, of fathers who had taken any leave around the time of their child's birth (paternity, parental or annual), 20 per cent of those in the highest income quintile had taken parental leave (rather than other forms) compared with only 11 per cent of those in the lowest income quintile. The impact of a family's economic resources on propensity to take up parental leave has also been demonstrated in a number of other countries, too (see Lappegård, 2012, for example).

While the earlier discussion has focussed primarily on policy design and the nature of the particular measures introduced in the UK, gender is clearly deeply implicated in these issues. Traditional gender norms about caring and breadwinning go some way to explaining why families will not often choose to take up schemes such as Shared Parental Leave unless there is a discernible benefit (through a non-transferable component for fathers, for example), while the enduring gender pay gap helps explain why a substantial reduction in a father's income, through a period of parental leave, may be harder for a family to absorb that a reduction in the mother's income. Moreover, assumptions about the 'ideal worker' – as committed to their place of employment (through working long hours and/or being 'always available') rather than the home – are often imbued with masculinist norms, making it harder for fathers to step away from work for a period of parental leave. Indeed, Kaufman (2018) notes that many of the fathers she interviewed believed that longer periods of leave would not be supported within their places of work, even when this was not based on actual workplace policies.

In addition to encouraging fathers to play a fuller role in childcare immediately after the birth of a child, UK governments since 2010 have taken various other steps to promote 'family-friendly' practices. The right to request flexible working, first introduced in 2003 and available only to parents of children under six years of age, was extended in 2014 to cover all employees (who have worked for their employer for at least 26 weeks) (Boyer et al., 2017). Although the government has argued that the extension of this right 'sends a clear signal that the Government supports individuals trying to balance work with commitments at home' (Department for Business, Energy and Industrial Strategy, 2017: 2), men remain considerably less likely than women to make a request and more likely to have their request rejected when they do (see later discussion). (Research by Tipping et al. (2012) showed that while 28 per cent of female employees in their sample had requested flexible working, the comparable figure for male employees was 17 per cent.) 2014 also saw the introduction of a new right for fathers and partners to take unpaid time off work to attend up to two antenatal appointments. Again, though, there is evidence that employers may make it difficult for fathers to exercise this right (see later). Moreover, because the leave is unpaid, it has been taken up more frequently by fathers from higher income households (Tipping et al., 2012). While these various measures indicate an increased willingness on the part of government to intervene in family life and promote close involvement of fathers in the lives of their children, to date their impact appears limited.

Despite these limitations, family policy in the period since 2010 has tended to position fathers in a positive manner, emphasising the important contribution they can make to their child's development and emergence as a citizen-worker. Recent pronouncements have also signalled explicitly, and in contrast to many previous statements, that government sees policy as a means of addressing gender inequalities. For example, the government department responsible for much family-related policy stated that:

> The division of roles and responsibilities for childcare in the home affects employment outcomes amongst men and women with dependents. The gender pay gap can both affect the division of roles, and can follow as a result. We want to enable families to share caring roles more easily and equitably to deliver positive employment outcomes. (Department for Business, Energy and Industrial Strategy, 2017: 1)

It went on to make specific reference to the role of fathers, noting that their greater participation in childcare was beneficial not only for them and their child, but also for women, in helping to facilitate greater equality in the workplace:

> The involvement of fathers in childcare is important, not just for the child, but also to enable mothers to participate fully in the labour market. Government is keen to progress towards equality of the roles of men and women at work and at home, and to enable fathers to fully utilise the rights available to them. (Department for Business, Energy and Industrial Strategy, 2017: 2)

Such comments represent a significant shift in discourse from the first decade of the twenty-first century and earlier, in which gender equality is now referenced much more explicitly. It is notable however that the labour market is still used to frame such debates (echoing New Labour's emphasis on the social investment state), rather than the presentation of gender equality in the home as a desirable social goal in itself. Moreover, across family policy in general, stark distinctions continue to be drawn between, on the one hand, the 'good dads', keen to be involved in the care of their children, and valorised in parental leave and flexible working policies and, on the other hand, those who are viewed as not making a sufficient commitment to their children. Indeed, Neale

(2016) argues that, since 2010, an increasingly moralising and divisive public narrative has been developed by politicians, castigating 'feckless' and 'run away' absent fathers in a manner strongly infused with class stigmatisation (also see Tarrant, 2017). David Cameron, the former prime minister, is quoted as having said that it was 'high time "runaway" dads were stigmatised and the full force of shame heaped upon them' (quoted in Neale, 2016: 79). Here, despite various significant shifts in policy, documented earlier, continuity with some assumptions of the 1980s is evident.

As we have alluded to previously, there is also often a substantial disconnect between the language that is used about fatherly involvement, and the substantive content of policy. While political rhetoric typically emphasises the importance of fathers being engaged with their children and sharing care with their partners, the policies implemented, to date, have signally failed to achieve this goal. In acknowledgement that Shared Parental Leave – the flagship family policy of the past few years – has been taken up by very few families, the government launched a 'Share the Joy' campaign in 2018, to raise awareness of the scheme, publicise the stories of those who have benefitted and encourage greater take-up. It has employed digital website advertising, social media, and adverts in train stations and on commuter routes, and set up a new website providing information and guidance. Extensive use is made of testimonials from couples who have taken Shared Parental Leave, which typically stress the advantages to both the mother (in terms of career progression) and father (with respect to stronger bonds with his child). They also aim to reassure fathers who may be concerned about the impact of Shared Parental Leave on themselves, by emphasising that it was not perceived negatively by the fathers' colleagues and had no negative impact on their careers.

Although it remains to be seen whether this campaign achieves its objectives, campaigning groups, academics and even a parliamentary committee have pointed to more fundamental problems with the policy. Indeed, the House of Commons' Women and Equalities Committee published a report in 2018 calling for substantial changes to family policy to facilitate greater fatherly involvement in caring, and gender equality in both the home and workplace. Notably, these included a call for the government to replace Shared Parental Leave with a well-compensated and non-transferable 12-week period of paternity leave – reflecting some of the key lessons learnt from other nations (see earlier discussion). Moreover, in the summer of 2019, the outgoing UK prime minister, Theresa May, launched a consultation on parental leave, focussing on ways in which the Shared Parental

Leave scheme can be improved. Echoing various points we have made earlier, she asserted:

> [W]e are not sending fathers the correct message when our current leave allowances give women 26 times more leave than men. Evidence shows that for fathers to take more leave it needs to be dedicated leave for them, and it needs to be better paid. (May, 2019, n.p.)

The consultation also covered whether employers should be required to publish their leave, pay and flexible working policies, and whether there should be a requirement for employers to consider advertising jobs as flexible. It closed in November 2019 but, at the time of completing this book (January 2020), the government had yet to publicise the nature of the public feedback or make a formal response.

Mediation of policy

While some types of policy can clearly, as the evidence presented earlier has shown, incentivise fatherly involvement in childcare, there is not necessarily a straightforward relationship between national-level family policy and the extent to which care is shared between parents. Indeed, a variety of factors can mediate this relationship, including those related to the workplace and wider societal norms.

Impact of the workplace

Scholars have suggested that the relationship between the workplace, national policy and individual-level decisions is often complex. Indeed, Gregory and Milner (2011) have argued that fathers' take-up of work–life balance policies is influenced by organisational and employment-sector characteristics as well as national 'fatherhood regimes' and their own individual attributes. They contend that influences are often two-way: 'the workplace provides an opportunity structure for the realisation of in-couple choices and preferences about the division of responsibility for childcare, but it also constrains such negotiations from the outset' (36).

First, at a general level, within the UK, there is a strong association between an individual father's level of pay and/or type of job and his likelihood of taking parental leave. Lower-earning fathers are less likely to be eligible for higher levels of non-statutory paternity leave pay, have less access to parental leave schemes, and are typically less knowledgeable about their rights to family-friendly working patterns (Boyer et al., 2017). Within Scotland, for example, Koslowski and Kadar-Satat (2019) have shown how propensity to take leave (paternity, parental and/or annual) after a child's birth is strongly correlated with both household and individual income. Fathers took leave in 90 per cent of the households in the top income quintile in their study, whereas the comparable figures for fathers in the bottom income quintile was 43 per cent. Similarly, 90 per cent of the fathers in professional, managerial or intermediate jobs took some form of parental leave, but only 70 per cent of those with routine or semi-routine jobs. Similar patterns have been noted in Finland, for example, with higher-earning fathers more likely to take their allocated period of non-transferable leave (Närvi and Salmi, 2019). Such differences in take-up are clearly likely to be more marked in countries such as the UK where the level of compensation during parental leave is low. Highly skilled and prestigious jobs are also positively correlated with access to flexible working patterns. Analysing the European Company Survey, Riva et al. (2018) found that there was, across the 29 countries in the sample, a strong relationship between the skill profile of the employees (that is the percentage in highly skilled jobs) and the provision of flexible working hours in the workplace (that is the proportion of employees entitled to adapt, within certain limits, the time when they begin or finish their daily work, according to their personal needs or wishes). Similarly, within the UK specifically, less well-off fathers have been shown to be less likely than their more affluent peers to take up their right to attend antenatal appointments with their partner – largely because this leave is unpaid (Tipping et al., 2012). (It is, nevertheless, important to note that working class fathers can become involved in childcare through other means. As discussed in Chapter 2, this can include shift work – which can increase their availability during the day – and sometimes periods of unemployment.)

Workplaces also exert influence of their own, not just through the levels of pay they award. There is evidence that, while many workplaces promote fathers' rights to statutory paternity leave, they are much less good at publicising other policies that facilitate fatherly caring, such as fathers' rights to attend antenatal appointments and take unpaid parental leave to cover a child's sickness, for example (18 weeks per child under the age of 18 is available for such purposes) (House of Commons Women and Equalities Committee, 2018). Moreover, UK studies of flexible working have indicated that while nearly all employers, when questioned, say that they do offer some kind of flexible working, only a small minority of 'quality' jobs (defined in this case as paying over

£20,000 per year) are advertised as open to some kind of flexibility (House of Commons Women and Equalities Committee, 2018). With respect to parental leave, Koslowski and Kadar-Satat's (2019) research in Scotland is important in demonstrating the ways in which non-statutory schemes (that is those offered by employers, which are not *required* by law) can have a significant impact on take-up of statutory schemes. They argue that such schemes are especially important in countries such as the UK where statutory schemes are not particularly financially generous, and can thus play an important top-up role. In their research, the provision of such benefits varied hugely from organisation to organisation – from 39 weeks on full pay for fathers taking parental leave, to allowing only the two weeks of statutory paternity pay. Their interviews with fathers indicated that the level of financial compensation was, as discussed earlier, of great significance in their decisions about type and duration of leave. Moreover, they note that fathers with higher average incomes (itself correlated with propensity to take leave) were also often the ones who had access to the more generous workplace benefits – a situation that exacerbates socio-economic inequalities in leave take-up and possibly, as a consequence, fathering practices more generally. While workplace schemes can help to offset relative state passivity in this area (as is the case in the UK), scholars have suggested that, in nations with more generous statutory provisions, the strong role of the state may allow organisations to absolve themselves of responsibility for measures to promote work–life balance (Gregory and Milner, 2011).

Other structural aspects of organisations and their dominant cultures can also affect fathering practices. Although research suggests that few Norwegian fathers experience problems within the workplace when taking leave after the birth of a child (Brandth and Kvande, 2019), Norway is unusual in this respect. The vast majority of studies – even when conducted in countries such as Sweden and Finland, with generous statutory provision – have highlighted the various workplace constraints fathers often face, which can prevent them sharing the care of their newly-born child (for example Haas and Hwang, 2019a; Närvi and Salmi, 2019). Experiences can vary, however, by the nature of the workplace. Studies have suggested that, in general, public sector organisations tend to be more facilitative of parental leave than those in the private sector. This is thought to be because the latter are more concerned with the costs of replacing staff on leave and potential loss of profits, and are also often more male-dominated, so have less experience of dealing with leave requests than organisations with a greater proportion of women (Lappegård, 2012; Haas and Hwang, 2019a). Moreover, Nordberg's (2019) research in Norway indicated that managers in public sector law firms were much less likely than their counterparts in the private sector to see paternal leave as a problem – because their staff typically worked on longer-term projects, and thus managers had more capacity to postpone work if a father was absent for a few months. Workplace cultures may also be related to the specific sector of employment. For example, Nordberg (2019) has argued that, in Norway, a strong sense of social responsibility pervades the police force and extends to taking parental leave, which is viewed as a moral duty. Similar norms have also been noted within the rescue services in Finland (Närvi and Salmi, 2019). Furthermore, studies of flexible working have highlighted the importance of workplace norms, and how they can affect take-up. Borve and Bungum (2015) note that the approach of large transnational companies in their study was not conducive to working flexibly, as they typically demanded long working hours and extensive overseas travel. Moreover, in some workplaces, those who choose to work flexibly, in non-traditional patterns, can face significant stigma for their deviation from 'ideal worker' norms (Radcliffe and Cassell, 2015), and embrace of approaches that some perceive as stereotypically 'feminine' (House of Commons Women and Equalities Committee, 2018).

Workplace size can also be influential, with larger organisations typically having more experience of running leave schemes than those smaller in size, and fathers in smaller organisations sometimes anticipating that their absence will place a significant burden on others (Lappegård, 2012; Koslowski and Kadar-Satat, 2019; Närvi and Salmi, 2019). As noted earlier, the gender balance of a workplace has also been shown to affect propensity to take leave: studies from Finland, France and the UK have all pointed to the negative impact of male-dominated workplaces. This is typically explained in terms of lack of familiarity with leave-taking practices, policies and fathers' entitlements, and the absence of a culture in which taking parental leave is normalised (Gregory and Milner, 2011; Närvi and Salmi, 2019). Indeed, such cultural factors are highlighted in a wide variety of studies – from countries such as Norway and Sweden where norms about taking parental leave are well established, to other nations that have introduced parental leave much more recently and often without the individual, non-transferable allocation to fathers characteristic of the Nordic region. For example, Karu and Trembly (2018) have argued that across Europe – including the Nordic countries – it is only men who need to negotiate their leave-taking rights with their employers; for women it is often assumed that they will be taking leave, and negotiations are thus unnecessary. In relation to working hours, Gregory and Milner

(2011) have suggested that role-modelling by managers is important. In their study, if managers talked about their children and felt able to leave work at a reasonable time, others did too.

Empirical research has suggested that men often anticipate problems in asking for parental leave or flexible working, even when formal workplace policies are apparently supportive of such initiatives. Kaufman (2018) argues, on the basis of her research in the UK, that British fathers 'reported a sense that taking extended leave could potentially disrupt their workplaces even when this was not based on actual workplace policies' (321). She surmises that this may be a result of few of their male co-workers taking leave, or practices in the workplace that are perceived to marginalise those with children. Fathers in Koslowski and Kadar-Satat's (2019) research (in Scotland) expressed somewhat similar concerns, particularly beyond the period of extra-statutory wage compensation in organisations where that was available. They were concerned that being away from the workplace for a longer period may send managers a signal that they were not fully committed to their careers. This has also been played out in Nordic countries, but in relation to the period of statutory (transferable) parental leave instead. Närvi and Salmi (2019) note on the basis of their data collection in Finland: 'The workplace interviews suggest that even at workplaces that are supportive of their employees balancing work and family life, taking leave not explicitly understood as "for fathers" can appear unthinkable' (38). They go on to argue that this suggests that, while the fathers now accepted the non-transferable leave allocated to them as the new standard of involved fathering, they also took for granted that mothers would assume primary responsibility for childcare. Moreover, in some of the workplaces in their study, the 'ideal worker' was still conceived of by respondents as masculine and fully committed to their job, irrespective of outside commitments (see also Stropnik et al., 2019). Similarly, even in Swedish workplaces, men taking parental leave is not always normative. Haas and Hwang's (2019a) interviews with 56 employees across five large private companies suggested that the majority of the interviewees indicated that there were strong workplace norms about the job coming first, and that they believed leave should be taken in ways that reduce disruption to a minimum – at quiet periods, on a part-time basis and/or spread out across the year. Haas and Hwang (2019a) conclude:

> While Swedish policy obligates employers to allow fathers
> to take parental leave, our study suggests that policy does
> not change company expectations for working fathers nor

encourage flexible working practices that would make it feasible for fathers to take substantial parental leave. Several important aspects of traditional workplace culture and work structure were reported to set meaningful limits to fathers' ability to take even the two months of non-transferable leave granted them by legislation, let alone share care equally with mothers. (72)

Moreover, it appears that – as a result of some of these cultural issues – fathers are more likely to take advantage of flexible working opportunities if they are not specifically framed in terms of childcare (and thus perceived as implicitly gendered). The UK fathers in Gregory and Milner's (2011) research, for example, made more use of informal flexible working arrangements and universal flexitime schemes rather than flexibility policies that were linked explicitly to parental responsibility. Indeed, they note that where flexible working was linked to childcare, it was often framed as primarily a mother's right. Nevertheless, as more fathers take advantage of flexible working, it is likely that these cultural norms will change. Indeed, Gattrell and Cooper (2016) maintain that, among UK fathers, a sense of entitlement to (and thus willingness to use) flexible working has increased over recent years.

Specific ways of organising work can also make it harder for fathers to take up the parental leave made possible in policy. This can include: high levels of specialisation and work intensification, making cover by colleagues more difficult; insufficient staffing levels; and lack of organisational infrastructure to support employees who want to take leave and put in place substitutes. In addition, some studies have indicated that mothers' workplaces can also affect the decisions taken by fathers. In Norway, fathers are less likely to take long periods of parental leave if their partner is employed in an organisation where there is little cost to her (financially and/or in terms of career progression) if she takes a long period of leave (Lappegård, 2012).

National and social group norms

In our earlier discussion of the impact of the workplace on policy, we noted the impact of cultural norms related to concepts of the 'ideal worker'. Such norms, circulating in wider society, not only places of work, can also serve to mediate the effects of policy. While the policies introduced over the past few decades in Nordic countries are believed to have had a significant impact on understandings of parental roles and relations between men and women, similar policies introduced elsewhere in the world have not always had the same impact. Estonia is an interesting case-in-point. Karu (2012) describes how, despite the government introducing a generous parental leave scheme modelled on the Nordic countries (with dedicated 'daddy quotas'), fathers' contributions to childcare remained minimal. Her research indicated that a large proportion of Estonian men had taken parental leave but not taken on substantial care responsibilities because their partners tended to remain at home throughout this period. The policy thus had little impact on fatherly practices or gender norms. Karu and Tremblay's (2018) analysis of fathers' rights and patterns in take-up of parental leave in 29 countries also concludes that the wider cultural context within which policies are implemented is significant. They note:

> We still do not have any examples to confirm that the fathers' quota in its Nordic meaning and design would lead to an immediate change in the behaviour of families and fathers the way it has in the Nordic countries where there had already been decades of gender equality policies in place. (357)

Developing a similar argument, Kremer (2007) has contended that there remain national 'ideals of care' – norms about who should care for children – that are typically reflected in family policy. She goes on to suggest that if policies go against these norms, parents do not always follow the policy imperatives, even when there are strong economic incentives to do so. Moreover, as noted earlier, even in the Nordic countries there is evidence that policies designed to promote gender equality in childcare can often be limited in their wider impact – because of enduring gender-traditional norms (Haas and Rostgaard, 2011; Bergqvist and Saxonberg, 2017). For example, in Sweden, where the parental leave scheme is one of the most comprehensive and egalitarian in the world, there remain stark inequalities between mothers and fathers in the number of parental leave days taken and their participation in a range of parental activities (Wells and Sarkadi, 2012). More localised social norms can also help mediate policy, notably what Duncan and Edwards (1997) have described as 'gendered moral rationalities' – related to social characteristics such as ethnicity and class, as well as gender. They argue that the expectations and beliefs shared by social groups often produce different notions of 'rational' action, even within the same nation-state or local area. The interplay of policy, societal norms and individual moral rationalities are explored in further detail when we consider, in Chapter 4, the reasons the fathers in our study took on equal caring responsibilities within their families.

Conclusion

In this chapter, we have discussed the ways in which social policy can affect the decisions taken by fathers and their partners about caring practices within the family. The relationship between policy and cultural change is complex and, as evidenced by some of the examples we have cited earlier, policy change is rarely sufficient on its own to bring about gender equality. Nevertheless, the chapter has drawn on evidence from the UK and across the world and, in particular, from the Nordic countries, to argue that there are various ways in which governments can intervene to help parents share caregiving responsibilities more equally. A key focus – both within the academic literature and in national policy – has been the provision of parental leave. Such leave tends to be most effective in facilitating fatherly involvement when it is well-paid and offered on a non-transferable basis. While family policy in the UK has changed considerably over recent decades, shifting away from the strong maternalist emphasis that had characterised many of the initiatives of the late twentieth century, to date its parental leave schemes have not taken on these key features and, as a result, take-up among fathers has been poor.

As we will go on to explain in the chapters that follow, for a number of the fathers in our sample the issue of parental leave was important. Sometimes this was because they had benefitted from the Shared Parental Leave policy themselves. For others, it was the absence of a paternal leave period that was significant – because their taking on extensive caring responsibilities only after their partner had ended her maternity leave had contributed to challenges they faced along the way (see Chapter 4 in relation to difficult initial transitions to care-sharing and Chapters 5 and 6 with respect to the establishment of children's emotional preferences and maternal parental social networks, for example). Nevertheless, many of our fathers had successfully taken on the role of primary or equal carer despite not having taken any extended parental leave. While our sample is of course relatively small, such experiences, we suggest, demonstrate *both* that paternal leave may be highly advantageous *and* that it is not necessarily a prerequisite for the establishment of more equal caregiving relationships. Indeed, what was crucial for many of the men was the ability to work flexibly and modify their work patterns – through reducing their total hours, compressing them into fewer days and/or working from home for certain periods of the week (see Chapter 4). Moreover, while broader evidence shows how workplaces can stigmatise men with significant caring responsibilities – who take extended parental leave, work flexibly and/or do not work long hours – it is of significance that the unusual group of men in our sample reported largely supportive managers and colleagues. While it can be harder for governments to intervene to promote flexible working and supportive workplace cultures than put parental leave policies in place, we will go on to suggest the former is an area that ought to be prioritised if greater numbers of men are to take on the kinds of roles of the fathers in our research.

Not surprisingly perhaps, the impact of policy only rarely figured explicitly in the father's accounts of how they came to take on their extensive care roles or how their experiences played themselves out. In teasing out what enabled their fatherly care horizons to encompass the notion of taking on an equal or greater share of care for their young children, we show that it was often practical circumstances that were the most prominent. Yet it remains likely that the changes in UK policy we have described in this chapter helped create conditions more conducive to what they were doing than those that existed in the past, whether due to specific measures relating to parental leave or flexible working or the broader change in language and orientation of policy and the cultural impacts of this. A symbolic or cultural shift in policy away from a strong maternalist orientation and towards one centred on fatherly involvement of care, in other words, may have played an indirect role in what they saw as feasible and, at the very least, helped to validate decisions that they had taken. More importantly still, we show throughout the remaining chapters, and particularly the conclusion, how the experiences of the fathers in our Sharing Care study can inform discussions on how further policy change might enable greater numbers of fathers to follow in the footsteps of those in our study, and – crucially – render aspects of their experience of doing so an easier one.

4

Shifting Care Horizons: Care-sharing Arrangements, Motivations and Transitions

Introduction

What kind of arrangements does care-sharing entail for fathers, and what prompts fathers and their families to take on their unusual approaches to early years care? To what extent does the adoption of such arrangements represent a transformation of roles and orientations and how do fathers and their partners transition into them? In this chapter, we begin our examination of the experiences of the fathers within the Sharing Care study by outlining the range of different care and work arrangements they had taken on, before going on to explore the circumstances and motivations that had precipitated these and the nature of the process through which they became a reality.

The study's inclusive approach to the notion of fatherly care-sharing enabled insight into a striking range of approaches fathers were taking to the adoption of either primary or equal care roles within the early years of their children's lives. In the pages that follow we show how, while a minority of those in the study had taken parental leave, most were currently in the midst of longer-term post-maternity-leave arrangements in co-ordination with different sorts of permanent or semi-permanent adjustments to work. We outline a range of approaches with respect to the division of caring and breadwinning between partners and to the balance of parental versus non-parental care. Notwithstanding the qualitative, non-representative nature of the study, such a diversity of approaches, we suggest, highlights a need to broaden our understandings of what some term 'involved' fathering in order to better understand the range of temporary and more permanent care-sharing arrangements it might involve. In particular, it flags a need to examine the practicalities of medium-term arrangements that involve both partners juggling family care, work and external care. It is important, we suggest, for the approach of practitioners and policymakers (see Chapter 3), as well as academics such as ourselves, not to render such post-leave care-sharing possibilities invisible or unsupported.

With respect to what it was that prompted fathers to take on their unusual care roles, we examine the comparative significance of pre-existing ideals and broader orientations as against developing practical circumstances. While broader orientations and specific moral drivers – such as a desire to share burdens and opportunities equally, to develop father–child bonds or to limit reliance on outside forms of childcare – played a substantial and sometimes pivotal role, it was often practical circumstances that seemed to have been the most direct prompt for fathers to take on a larger share of care. We go on to consider, in light of this, the extent to which the decision to take on equal or primary caregiving roles represented a continuation or transformation of orientation, expectations and identity for the fathers, and the interplay of factors that might affect this. While such a decision was likely made easier by their broader habitus and orientation, we suggest that, for many fathers, the decision to adopt such roles represented something of a turning point for them. It constituted, in other words, a change of direction, both practically and in terms of their parental outlooks and identities. It also often represented the start of an ongoing journey of development in their competences and understandings of themselves as fathers. Bearing this in mind, we explore how, in combination with broader orientations, the onset of particular sets of circumstances or events may have the potential to open up spaces in which dominant gender roles and narratives can begin to be challenged.

In the final section of the chapter we continue this theme of transformation through examining in detail how the fathers' care roles were taken up in practice. Here, we outline how, during the immediate post-natal period, most of the fathers found themselves in the fairly traditional role of primary breadwinner, while their partner took a substantial period of maternity leave. While illustrating the potential for couples who began parenthood in a traditional manner to transform their roles at a later point, the extent of this sharp transformation in roles, we contend, created challenges for the fathers and their partners. We explore the ways such challenges manifested themselves and suggest that some such challenges might be reduced if it were made easier for couples to share care from an earlier point.

Continuities, transformations and care horizons

As indicated earlier, a theme that runs through a good deal of the chapter is the extent to which the taking on of equal or primary care roles constituted a continuation or transformation for the fathers in the study. In other words, were these fathers already predisposed in various respects to sharing care at least equally with their partners, with all the potential this entails for the undoing of dominant gender roles (Deutsch, 2007), or did such an arrangement represent a significant change of direction? This is a question that connects particularly to our discussions of what it was that prompted fathers to take up their unusual arrangements but also to the process through which they took up such roles in practice. Its exploration relates to a combination of structural, subjective and circumstantial factors and, in order to make help us make sense of this, we return to the notion of 'fatherly care horizons' referred to in Chapter 1.

Through this concept, we seek to highlight the importance of fathers' shifting visions of what is conceivable or feasible for them with respect to their caregiving practices and identities – and the macro and micro, structural and circumstantial factors that might explain their perspectives. The concept represents an adaption of Phil Hodkinson and Andrew Sparkes' (1997) use of 'horizons for action' to theorise the ways different sets of factors affect the possibilities young people are able to envisage with respect to their career pathways. Careers, Hodkinson and Sparkes suggest, obviously are shaped and constrained by direct barriers of different kinds, but are also dependent on what individuals are able to see as possible or feasible. Horizons for action, they suggest 'both limit and enable our view of the world and the choices we can make within it' and, by way of example, they note that 'the fact that there are jobs for girls in engineering is irrelevant if a young woman does not perceive engineering as an appropriate career' (1997: 35). In extension of the work of Bourdieu, such horizons are understood not as a matter of individual choice but as rooted in our habitus and the ways this reflects our social position, upbringing and the established 'schemata' through which we filter and interpret events, opportunities and circumstances that we may encounter. Yet, crucially, for Hodkinson and Sparkes, horizons may not always follow deterministic patterns (a young woman may take on a job in a garage partly because, even though it lies outside of dominant gendered expectations, the particularities of her life history places it within her horizons for action) and, rather than being set in stone, they are in constant development, as a result of ongoing sets of interactions, institutions and circumstances. Thus, 'new information is constantly absorbed within the existing schematic framework, causing refinement and modification to the habitus and the horizon for action' (35). In other words, new encounters, events or interactions may, in some circumstances, prompt horizons to shift.

It is the concept's emphasis on the importance of what people are able to see and the ways this reflects a combination of embedded orientations and shifting circumstances that prompts us to find its adaptation to the situation of fathers taking on counter-normative care roles so useful. Thus, the caregiving horizons of fathers are liable to be heavily shaped by socialisation, life history and habitus – all of which are affected by structural position and more specific relationships and orientations. Yet more recent encounters and contexts may also play a significant role, from the orientation of policy or institutions (health providers, workplaces) that are encountered during the perinatal period, to the specifics of peer cultures and a range of significant and sometimes unpredictable practical circumstances. Recent encounters or events may often reinforce existing orientations and/or broader dominant understandings of what it is or should be to take on the role of father. But they may sometimes prompt shifts in habitus and fatherly care horizons, and it is this possibility – alongside the factors that may render such a shift possible – that interests us here.

Our examination of the possibility of such shifts in fatherly care horizons prompts us to borrow another concept from Hodkinson and Sparkes' discussion, that of 'turning points'. Initially developed by Strauss (1962) and comparable to Giddens' (1991) notion of 'fateful moments' and, more recently, Thomson and colleagues' (2002) emphasis on 'critical moments', this notion refers to periods during the life-course in which individuals go through a significant transformation of direction, orientation and identity. Turning points, argue Hodkinson and Sparkes, may be self-initiated or forced, may come about as a result of the impact of institutional or policy structures, ongoing interactions or events or a combination of these. And they both affect and are affected by an individual's broader habitus. In the discussion that follows, we discuss turning points in two different ways. First, we explore the extent to which the *decision* to take on a primary or equal caregiving role appeared to represent a turning point for many fathers with respect to their fatherly care horizons. Second, in our examination of the *practical transition* into the taking on of such care roles, we explore the nature and acuteness of the transformation involved for both fathers and their partners during this time, and the challenges that resulted from this. Notwithstanding their largely middle class, white and predominantly liberal broader orientations, for many of the fathers, we argue, the taking on of their unusual care roles did indeed represent a substantial turning point, both symbolically and practically. We go on to suggest that, while it opened up a variety of opportunities, the extent and rapidity of the change led to challenges for both them and their partners. Before beginning to develop this narrative, however, we begin our discussion by examining the striking range of care arrangements fathers had taken on and discussing the significance of these.

Fathers and care-sharing – a plethora of arrangements

As we have outlined in Chapter 1, the sample for the Sharing Care project, recruited through advertising on social media and in local nurseries and children's centres, was exclusively white and largely middle class and this has a bearing on our findings. As we explore, while most white, middle class fathers occupy the role of breadwinner-supporters, it seems likely that the broader habitus of the group we recruited and the salience of ideas about involved or intimate fatherhood and 'being there' (see Chapters 1 and 2) among this demographic, may have affected their willingness to countenance the possibility of greater care involvement, once it had emerged. Meanwhile, although the sample was limited with respect to race and class, the diversity of primary or equal caregiving arrangements among the fathers is striking (see Appendix). Unusual though it may be, taking fatherly care responsibilities beyond a secondary or support role entails a wide range of temporary and more permanent approaches. And, with respect to the latter, arrangements vary considerably with respect to two factors in particular: the split between partners of breadwinning and care work and the balance between parental and outside forms of care. In order to make sense of the range of scenarios we encountered, we have distinguished between three main categories of caregiving among the fathers in the study.

Parental leavers

For two of the fathers, their unusually high level of caregiving responsibility at the time of the research took the form of periods of leave taken through the UK's Shared Parental Leave system, which allows couples to split the family's leave entitlement between them taking periods at home together or separately (see Chapter 3). Joseph had taken advantage of the flexibility the scheme allows, by taking 13 weeks off together with his partner immediately after the birth of his son, prior to returning to work for three months and then taking off a further 11 weeks alone during which he was the baby's sole weekday caregiver. Chris, meanwhile, had taken the two weeks of standard paternity leave allowed in the UK before returning to his role as a research consultant for eight months and then taking a further seven weeks of leave via the Shared Parental Leave scheme when his partner returned to work. Three of the other fathers in the study had previously taken extended periods of parental leave prior to the adoption of more permanent equal or primary caregiving roles. It is noteworthy that, if we include all five who had shared parental leave with their partner at one point or another, in only one case (Chris) did this *not* look like leading to a longer-term shared care arrangement (see Chapter 7). While it is noteworthy, then, that only a small proportion of our sample had taken on extended periods of parental leave – and therefore that scholarly and policymaker attention on sharing care should not be confined to this dimension – there is some support for indications elsewhere that parental leave has the potential to form the first stage of ongoing fatherly involvement and the development of caring identities (Brandth and Kvande, 2018b).

Primary caregivers

A third of the fathers said that they had taken on the ongoing role of primary carer for their young child, following the conclusion of periods of parental leave in the first year of their baby's life. In all of these cases, the fathers' partner had returned to full-time work following a substantial period of maternity leave, but there were differences in how much weekday care the fathers were responsible for. Four fathers regarded themselves as full-time carers, were not engaged with paid work and were responsible for hands-on daytime care throughout the week. Such arrangements were consistent with what Ranson (2010: 46) calls 'crossover' couples, who had 'simply reversed traditional family roles' and with what more commonly is referred to as 'stay-at-home fathers' (Merla, 2008; Solomon, 2014). The other four primary caregiver fathers were engaged in significant part-time work, with caregiving on these days accounted for by paid childcare, grandparents or their partner. Timothy's two-year-old son, for example, went to nursery on Monday and Tuesday, enabling him to concentrate on his freelance events-management role on these days. In Patrick's case, it was his partner's flexible full-time working arrangement and her desire to retain some everyday caregiving involvement that allowed him to work one day a week as a restaurant supervisor: 'basically it's 100 per cent I do childcare except for the one day I'm working when my other half, who's full-time, is the parent for that day.' In these situations, then, rather than taking on the equivalent of a full-time housewife role, fathers were adopting a part-time working model – comparable to those taken by numerous women during the years following maternity leave (ONS, 2018a) – that involved juggling care with paid work and, sometimes, the organisation of paid or unpaid outside day care.

Equal care sharers

The majority of our fathers – just under two-thirds – were sharing care and paid work (more or less) equally with their partner. Somewhat neglected by existing literature on 'involved' fathers (see Chapter 2; and see Risman and Johnson-Sumerford, 1998; Deutsch, 2001; and Ranson, 2010 for exceptions), this group was also the most diverse, in terms of how care and breadwinning responsibilities were divided throughout the week, and the balance between parental and non-parental care. Referring to the equal sharing couples in her Canadian research, Ranson (2010) distinguishes between 'shift workers', who each adjust work to enable children to be cared for by either the mother or father at home every day, and 'dual dividers' who work full-time, rely on outside care during weekdays and share responsibilities equally at other times. While offering a useful starting point, this distinction did not fit particularly well for the arrangements of our equal care sharers, most of whom were located somewhere between the extremes. Notably, the families of these fathers were *all* using outside childcare for some of the working week but rarely for all of it, and there were a variety of arrangements that fell within this spectrum.

Robert and his partner were among those least reliant on outside childcare. Both were working part-time, three-day weeks, enabling each to care for their son for two days and him to attend nursery on the other day. As Robert put it:

> Well it is 50/50. We both work a three-day week, we're there [work] for one day overlapping where our son goes to nursery ... and the two days each that we don't work

is full-time care and then at the weekend we share things. (Robert, equal care sharer)

At the other extreme, Ryan and his partner both had been working full-time since she returned to work from her maternity leave but, through the use of compressed hours, she was able to care for their daughter on one full day a week and he was able to look after her on two afternoons. In other cases one or both partners worked freelance and the flexibility this provided enabled parental care on one or more days a week. While most couples had settled into fairly regular weekly routines, things were more unpredictable for Jeremy and his partner, both of whom worked freelance:

> It's constantly changing all the time … it depends who's around, who takes care of the children, how we work out who can take on a job … the last six months have probably been half and half … if one of us is working, the other one tends to be looking after the whole day, occasional half days but generally the whole days. (Jeremy, equal care sharer)

What this range of temporary and permanent approaches to sharing care suggests, we would argue, is a need to broaden our sense of what equal or primary fatherly caregiving can actually mean. As we established in Chapter 2, a good deal of recent scholarship on 'involved' fatherhood has centred on situations where traditional roles have reversed through the father taking on full-time (or close to full-time) primary caring responsibilities and the mother working full-time (for example Doucet, 2006; Merla, 2008; Chelsey, 2011; Solomon, 2014) or on fathers taking temporary parental leave (Almqvist, 2008; Rehel, 2015; O'Brien and Twamley, 2017; Brandth and Kvande, 2018b). And in Chapter 3 we showed how UK policy developments and discussions in relation to early years childcare and fatherly involvement also tend to be focused primarily on parental leave. Such attention is justified given the potential of parental leave to help set in train roles and responsibilities that may endure. Yet greater understanding and support also is needed with respect to primary or equal carer fathers who do not fit into the category of stay-at-home dads or parental leavers but are involved, alongside their partners, in juggling extensive caregiving duties with paid work and different forms of outside day care on an ongoing basis. Finally, the taking on of permanent or semi-permanent care-sharing roles by fathers *after* a period of maternal primary care is of significance, in indicating that the eventual taking on of such care-sharing represented a transfer or reversal of responsibilities – a point to which we shall return later in the chapter.

Motivations for care-sharing and fatherly care horizons

As we have outlined in Chapter 2, much has been written about why most fathers do not take on extended parental leave or equal or primary care roles (Almqvist, 2008; Norman and Fagan, 2017; Twamley and Schober, 2018). Knowledge about what it is that prompts a minority of fathers and their families to adopt counter-normative early years care arrangements, meanwhile, is developing quickly but remains patchy, particularly in the context of the UK, and for less visible groups such as those sharing care equally and/or juggling care-sharing with flexible working. Where existing work on primary carer fathers has touched on what prompted their unusual approach, a theme has sometimes been the extent to which men feel they actively chose to stay at home (Solomon, 2014) or, alternatively, found themselves taking up such roles in response to practical circumstances such as finances (for example Merla, 2008; Chelsey, 2011). It is sometimes suggested that class differences play a role here. Thus, although she notes the significance of circumstantial factors too, Solomon's emphasis on the ultimate importance of the active choice for the stay-at-home fathers in her study may partially have reflected her sample's highly educated and middle class orientation. In contrast, Chelsey's research, based on a more demographically mixed US sample indicates that it was only her most well-educated participants who said they had actively chosen to be their children's primary carer, with most others citing a response to practical circumstances as key (Chelsey, 2011). In most cases, however, it would seem that a variety of factors are at work, something indicated by isolated UK studies (for example West et al., 2009; O'Brien and Twamley, 2017).

The largely white and middle class orientation of our own sample limits our ability to explore holistically the role class or ethnic differences may play in UK fathers' decisions to take on extensive caregiving roles. In combination with the diversity of care arrangements they had adopted, however, this orientation offered a valuable opportunity to explore how it was that these fathers had taken pathways so different from the majority of white, middle class fathers, who tend to espouse broad notions of fatherly involvement or intimacy while taking up secondary care roles (Dermott, 2008; Miller, 2011). The organisation of our discussion connects to a distinction between longer-standing ideals or orientations and either long- or short-term practical circumstances. Our data show that, while such decisions always reflected a range of factors, the importance of circumstantial factors in prompting the arrangements taken up was particularly noteworthy. While the backgrounds and orientations of the fathers are liable to have rendered them more open to the possibility of taking up counter-normative roles, then, in many cases it seemed unlikely such roles would have been seriously considered in the absence of such practical circumstances. We develop, in and through this empirical distinction, an exploration of the extent to which decisions to become parental leavers, primary caregivers or equal care sharers represented something consistent for the fathers with their existing expectations and identities or, rather, a transformation of these. Through the notion of fatherly care horizons outlined earlier, we place emphasis on continuities and transformations in fathers' visions of what was conceivable, possible and appropriate for them with respect to their role in early years parenting – and the range of long- and short-term factors that may have had a bearing upon this.

Explicit prior beliefs and orientations

A few of the fathers said the decision to take on an unusual share of care responsibilities in their family had been primarily driven by existing values and ideals relating to either gender, relationships or childcare, with which they and/or their partner associated themselves. Occasionally, for example, the notion of gender equality was expressed as a broad social ideal to which fathers felt they were contributing. Here, the decision to make an extensive contribution to caregiving was presented as a reflection of participants' existing sense of identity as progressively-minded individuals (or couples) keen to change society for the better. For example, when John was asked what had prompted him to take on an equal caring role whereby he cared for his son one day a week, he focused particularly on his concern to contribute to broader gender equality:

> I tend to, I like to think I'm quite a sort of modern, forward thinking person in lots of ways ... my political leanings are very much sort of progressive, left wing, kind of green ... generally I think sort of gender equality is incredibly important ... gender pay equality is a, you know, a fairly hot topic, and I think people would think about that and you know obviously I just think it's ridiculous that a woman would be paid less than a man, but that is still the case in a lot of areas. (John, equal care sharer)

In other cases, fathers' emphasis on gender equality was expressed more narrowly, in relation to the way their own relationship worked, something that had prompted a decision to apply this principle to care for their young children also. Scott, who was sharing care equally with his partner following a period of shared parental leave, told us that 'when we talked about having a child, we ... wanted to do everything 50/50 anyway, we do in our lives anyway, and I just felt that ... childcare definitely would be exactly the same' (Scott, equal caregiver). In these cases, in spite of its apparent contrast with normal practice – and often with the expectations of friends, parents or others – the decision to adopt a primary or equal caregiver role was experienced as something consistent with the existing beliefs, roles and identities of the father. For a few of the fathers, then, such a course already formed a clear part of their fatherly care horizons, because it lay within the scope of their existing understandings of their place in the world and what was foreseeable for them within that.

A further variation of this in the sample involved emphasis on the specific value of fathers spending extensive time with their young children, something typically believed to be beneficial to both. Here, the discursive emphasis was on being a 'good dad', by taking on significant care responsibilities and having plenty of time alone with one's child in order to develop as strong a relationship as possible. As well as being connected with long-term benefits, this sometimes involved reference to immediate paternal wellbeing, with respect to direct enjoyment of caring time and/or the ability to experience and participate in their child's rapid development. This convergence between long-term ideals and a more immediate desire to spend time with his son was exemplified by Anthony, who cared alone for his 13-month-old son one day a week:

> I had a sort of strong desire that ... I would play as much of a role as I possibly could do ... definitely work-wise it's, I think it is the principle that has driven it all that we, you know, we wanted to be equal in our care, I wanted to be you know a good dad, the best dad I could be ... And I suppose slightly selfishly also just wanted that extra time with him, I mean that's you know just as ... an enjoyable experience of being able to spend that time together ... and just the two of us in a way. (Anthony, equal care sharer)

Once again, the decision to adopt a primary care role seems somewhat consistent here with Anthony's existing horizons.

While progressive ideals of gender equality or the benefits of being involved in care were sometimes of importance, beliefs about the significance of parental as opposed to non-parental care for young children also had at times played a role in the taking on of the fathers' unusual care arrangements (see West et al., 2009; Solomon, 2014). In the case of Patrick, who was the sole carer for his children four days a week, this parent/non-parent dualism appeared to have contributed – alongside other factors (which we outline later) – to his development of a gender-neutral understanding of the value of parent care:

> I think we are a better family for the parents parenting the children, I think that is the big strength of it … I don't think there is a specific advantage to the children that it's me doing it, but there's not specifically disadvantages, it's just this is the parent that's doing it. (Patrick, primary caregiver)

In this scenario, an unusual and progressive arrangement with respect to the gendered division of labour is partly prompted, not by a specific initial orientation towards this, but by the coming to prominence of a somewhat more traditional set of values regarding the undesirability of outside forms of childcare. And while they manifested themselves particularly strongly in cases like Patrick's, such sentiments were also expressed in weaker form, by fathers whose families *did* use outside care, but were keen to place limits on how much. James, for example, had taken on compressed hours in order to restrict the time his daughter spent at nursery to two days a week: 'we needed to find a way to make it work that meant [child's name] wasn't in nursery too much, because we didn't want her in all the time, and we wanted her to be home with us as much as possible' (James, equal care sharer). Here, it is a little less clear whether the taking on of an extensive care role lay within the existing orientation of such fathers or whether, instead, the coming to prominence of a different ideological priority (parents doing parenting) had had the effect of expanding their fatherly care horizons and enabling them to begin to see their gendered role as parents in a counter-normative way.

Yet values centred on the importance of parental rather than non-parental care do not always result in the opening up of opportunities for counter-hegemonic arrangements or understandings with respect to the doing of gender. More commonly, whether through ideologies of intensive mothering or attachment parenting, they can inflict extensive pressure on women to remain at home to care in order preside over a high-intensity and pro-active parental approach to children's early development and to nurture the closest of mother–baby bonds (Hays, 1998; Shirani et al., 2012; Miller, 2017). So why, in the case of some of the fathers in our study, did ideals about parental care have the opposite effect? In order to understand how beliefs in the importance of parental care also could open up opportunities for egalitarian care arrangements, we need to understand how such ideas coincided with other factors. And while these other factors sometimes included more specific existing beliefs about equality or fatherly involvement (as we have shown), they tended more consistently and directly to relate to unusual practical circumstances that had made it expedient for the father to play a greater role.

Crucially, this specific point connects to a much broader tendency across the sample – whether or not existing values and ideals were mentioned – for practical circumstances to play a significant part in the decision for fathers to take on their care-centred roles.

Circumstances, expediency and transformations

As noted earlier, it sometimes is suggested that working class caregiver fathers are more likely to be prompted to take up their roles in reaction to practical circumstances – such as redundancy, unemployment, shift working or similar – with their middle class counterparts more likely to understand fatherly involvement as an active choice relating to their educated, liberal values (Chelsey, 2011). Our findings on middle class fathers, however, suggest the division may not be so clear-cut. For, in spite of the importance vested in ideals and beliefs by a few fathers, it was practical circumstances that were cited most strongly and consistently across the sample as a whole. Often, then, fathers across the different care arrangement groups talked at length about the importance of finances, careers, job practicalities, locations and childcare issues. Even in those cases where conscious existing ideals and beliefs had been emphasised as key, practical circumstances often also appeared to have been aligned in a manner conducive to the arrangement. More often, though, rather than being premeditated and consistent with existing fatherly care horizons, the decision to take on extensive care roles appeared to have represented a notable change of direction, or turning point.

Most obviously, perhaps, a pragmatic approach to the current and potential earnings of each partner often played a decisive role. Specifically, as in some other studies (for example Doucet and Merla, 2007; Merla, 2008; O'Brien and Twamley, 2017), many of the couples were in the unusual position of the mother having equal or greater earning power, career potential or job security than the father. The decision for the father to take up an equal or primary caregiving role often was presented as a pragmatic response to such a situation. Jason, who had taken up the role of primary carer for his 20-month-old daughter, showed how an expedient approach to earnings and earnings potential had apparently led him towards the adoption of a somewhat gender-neutral understanding of parental caregiving:

> I think it comes down to just basic prioritisation in the end, people think, look, can you earn more, yeah, then go for it … I've actually, I've got no problem with it, as long as whoever's earning more brings it back, if you bring it back then that's great, if it's me, if it's her, it doesn't matter, because as long as we're getting it, then we're still together getting it. (Jason, primary caregiver)

In the same way that men's higher earnings often reinforce the likelihood of mothers sacrificing paid work to take primary responsibility for caregiving (see Chapter 2), our study suggests that, where this earnings circumstance is absent or reversed, this has the potential to contribute to the development of more progressive arrangements – a finding that confirms indications from some other studies about the importance of financial expediency to the decision of men to take on caregiving roles (West et al., 2009; Chelsey, 2011; Twamley and Schober, 2018).

Fathers also often emphasised that their partners were more ambitious and career-minded than they were, and that work was more pivotal to their partner's identity and wellbeing than it was to their own. Consistent with this, decision-making sometimes also hinged on the perceived aptitude and orientation to work of mothers, who were either considered more suitable/skilled as breadwinners or as having a greater need to focus on their career. In the case of Ed, who had taken on full-time weekday care of his two young children, it was a combination of earnings and his wife's greater perceived career orientation that had been key:

> She was earning considerably more than me, though I would say that … she also gets a lot more enjoyment from her work. She's a natural worker, she can put in twelve hour days, Monday to Friday, without blinking! And has got extraordinary stamina, extraordinary commitment and just gets a tremendous amount of satisfaction from working! Which I never actually did. For me, it was always very much a means to an end. (Ed, primary caregiver)

Sometimes such issues of earnings and career orientation were fairly established and had led to consideration of the possibility of the father taking on an equal or primary care role well before children had been born. Aaron, who was solely responsible for wrap-around care of his children throughout the week, told us that the ongoing discrepancy with respect to his and his partners' earnings had meant it always had been likely he would take on primary caring responsibility when they had children: 'since she [partner] started this job she's earned more than me anyway ... so I've always said, well if anyone's off, it's me, you're going to work because you earn more than I do anyway' (Aaron, primary caregiver). In this situation, although the earnings difference contributed to the opening up of an opportunity for Aaron and his partner to identify the possibility to take on counter-normative roles, the process seemed to have been a gradual one and did not represent a particularly sudden turning point. Rather, such an eventuality had begun to establish itself in his care horizons at an earlier point, even if the final decision to go ahead was taken later.

Often, however, particular sets of circumstances had emerged or been brought into sharp relief more recently, and consideration of unusual care roles had come about in response to these. Sometimes, the career orientation of mothers had been highlighted dramatically by significant pre- or post-natal mental health difficulties. William said that 'the whole process of being pregnant, being on maternity leave, [partner] found disempowering for a range of reasons ... So that isolation just kind of stayed throughout ... So that maybe shaped how we did things' (William, equal care sharer). In other cases, it was the father's situation as primary breadwinner that had become untenable, through frustrations with lack of progression, difficulties with colleagues or redundancy. Patrick, mentioned earlier in relation to his idealistic emphasis on the importance of parental as opposed to non-parental care, disclosed that the main trigger for him, rather than his wife, taking on the primary care role was that his job had been placed at risk between the birth of his first and second children, following a period during which both he and his wife had been struggling in their respective roles:

> My school was offering redundancies and my job was one of the ones that was on the possible redundancy list, so we just kind of ... sat down and over a period of a couple of months we said, no, we need a change, clearly life's not happy. (Patrick, primary caregiver)

In Chris' case, it was a combination of general financial difficulties and the sudden collapse of the company he was working for that prompted his partner to return to work full-time following her maternity leave for their first child, and him to take on the role of primary caregiver for a period of time. Once his orientation and horizons had been shifted as a result of this turning point, a more active decision was taken for him to take extended parental leave for their second child:

> It probably was ... primarily just expedience, I think ... we were running low on cash and we couldn't afford for her to be on maternity leave for very much longer, so it made sense for her to go back to work, and since the company that I was working for was kind of spiralling down into the depths of oblivion it made, it just made sense for me to ... to look after her while we, while I tried to find something else. I thought it was a valuable thing to have done and I felt ... I felt a lot closer to my daughter being the primary carer ... So second time around with our son there was part of me that wanted to repeat that if it was possible. (Chris, parental leaver)

In other cases, practical issues to do with work flexibility, location and/or childcare availability had prompted fathers and their partners to rethink initial plans. In James' case, a mismatch between the days his partner was going to be required to work when she returned from maternity leave and the days they could get at their local nursery was the main trigger for the decision for him to request flexible hours to care for his daughter one day a week.

> It was initially the hours that, or the days my wife was going to be required to work, so Monday, Wednesday, Friday, she had to either take those days or resign ... And then, so we, initially we were going to put [child] in [nursery] three days a week ... but there wasn't a space for Wednesday, so she could only do, we could only get her in on Monday and Friday, so we were like, right, how are we going to sort this out? ... And the only way to sort it out was for me to change my hours, when we discovered I could do that. (James, equal care sharer)

In other examples, mothers had hoped to return to work part-time but it had become clear that this was not going to be allowed by their employer, or would present an unacceptable barrier to career progression, prompting the father to investigate the adjustment of his own working hours instead. Or mothers' careers lacked everyday flexibility or involved long commutes or working hours, prompting fathers to become primarily responsible for wrap-around care or a day or two of care at home. In cases like these, then, changes in circumstances *after* initial post-natal patterns of care had been established had created the possibility of a turning point, prompting fathers and their partners to rethink their arrangements going forward.

It is important to recognise, of course, that elements of these men's existing life histories and understandings of the world may have enabled them to be more receptive to the possibility of sharing care (once it had emerged) than would other fathers faced with similar circumstances. While some had, as we have seen, an existing idealistic drive to take on extensive care responsibilities, even for the majority who did not, it remains likely that aspects of their habitus, relationships and orientation contributed to their capacity to consider and ultimately take up such a role when prompted. As well as having white, middle class and somewhat socially liberal broader backgrounds, the men were already comfortable with the general notion of 'involvement' in care and were in relationships in which, prior to the onset of children, there was some degree of parity with respect to the balance of career and home life. Fathers from different backgrounds, in different relationships or contrasting trajectories may not have responded to unusual earnings differentials, maternal depression, difficulties at work or childcare problems in the way that they did and, importantly, their partners may not have countenanced the sharing of care either. Yet, crucially, having the potential to have one's fatherly care horizons shift in so progressive a direction is not the same as such a shift actually happening, and it is here that circumstances such as those outlined seemed to have played such a significant role.

Coinciding and facilitating factors

Importantly, it usually was the coincidence of a number of factors that had prompted the taking on by fathers of their primary or equal caregiving roles, even if one or two had been pivotal. In some cases, one factor in particular had been identified as of primary importance, but it became clear that other considerations had also contributed to the decision. Notably, for some of the fathers who cited existing beliefs and identities relating to gender equality or the desirability of fatherly care as central to their decision, factors such as comparative earnings or career prospects also appeared to have played a role. In other cases, a series of coinciding factors and situations had coalesced with one another and it was the combination, rather than any in particular, that was key. Michael, for example, initially cited his own desire and comfort with regard to caring as central to the decision for him to become primary caregiver in his family, but also placed emphasis at different points in the interview on difficulties that had emerged with his work situation, his partner's higher salary and the prohibitive cost of putting both of their young children into childcare:

> I've ... always been good at you know dealing with children, they don't sort of scare me or daunt me in any way, and you now the stereotypical changing nappies and getting up early and all that sort of stuff doesn't, it wasn't something that even crossed my mind twice ... So I've always wanted to look after them ... And also at work, things weren't going very well, I had, I was signed off work with anxiety and stress, my manager wasn't doing a very good job with me...
>
> [Partner] took as much time [maternity leave] as we could afford for her to take at that point in time and ... because [partner] earns more than me, which is probably another little reason ... I mean I would be not taking home too much at the end of the day with putting both [the children] into childcare. (Michael, primary caregiver)

In this case, it might be argued that taking on a primary care role already lay within Michael's fatherly care horizons, and he clearly had envisaged himself as a heavily involved father prior to taking up his role, and yet a series of current practical circumstances clearly had also played a significant part in enabling him to actually go ahead and become his family's primary caregiver.

In addition to the range of factors they felt had directly precipitated their decision, fathers' accounts also included references to further additional factors that had helped facilitate their arrangements, even if they had not seemed key to the decision-making process. Such factors differed depending on the situation, but included having the financial means to absorb taking parental leave, working part-time or forgoing freelance work (though care did not always represent a financial loss due to the costs of day care or of the mother not working), being the one who worked closest to the children's day care and, crucially, having a partner who was willing to relinquish her own primary care role. Although it was not discussed explicitly by many fathers as a key factor, the latter point is, we would suggest, difficult to underestimate. As discussed in Chapter 2, ongoing pressures on mothers to embrace the role of primary carer in spite of the sacrifices this may entail are well-documented, and this – together with fathers' willingness to defer to such a situation and cede responsibility – sometimes can itself act as a barrier to greater fatherly involvement (Fagan and Barnett, 2003; Puhlman and Pasley, 2013; Miller 2017).

Another factor frequently emphasised by fathers was how lucky they felt to have a work situation conducive to the possibility of either parental leave or flexible working. Sometimes this took the form of the flexibility that was afforded by self-employment and/or homeworking. More often, it related to the perceived open-mindedness shown to them by their employer. Though some mentioned worries about the impact of caring on their career or inferred a lack of understanding of their responsibilities by colleagues, we were struck by the rarity with which significant difficulties with employers were mentioned by the fathers when it came to the negotiation of time off or flexible hours. And, while some attributed this to their employer having a generally progressive orientation, others felt they had specifically benefited from having immediate line managers who had children of their own and therefore were personally sympathetic to requests to adjust work to facilitate caregiving (see Gregory and Milner, 2011). Scott's account was fairly typical in this respect:

> One nice thing about ... my manager is that she's got an older daughter, but she's sort of gone through the whole kind of rigmarole of ... child-rearing as it were, so she was very empathetic towards it all, and very understanding, and they've been super, like so good and so flexible with it. (Scott, equal care sharer)

While it is difficult to be sure how unusual the largely positive experiences these fathers had with their employers was, evidence relating to why most fathers do *not* take on equal or primary caregiving roles often has cited a lack of flexibility or understanding among employers or within the workplace (see Chapter 3). Progressive employers, then, whether through overall organisational policies or the bespoke arrangements of sympathetic line mangers, had been a significant enabling factor for progressive care arrangements for the fathers in the study. This may suggest that making opportunities for flexible working more widespread, easier to access and less reliant upon idiosyncrasies, would be a valuable area for policy attention (see Chapter 7).

Shifting horizons

Responding expediently to financial or other circumstances does not always result in progressive arrangements when it comes to the establishment of care arrangements for young children. Indeed, parents and others frequently cite individual earnings disparities, alongside a range of other practical circumstances, as their primary justification for the adoption of traditional arrangements centred on the mother as primary caregiver (Orgad, 2015). What the experiences of the fathers in our study show is that the combination of contrasting circumstances with suitable existing orientations and understandings can open up possibilities for the consideration and adoption of counter-normative arrangements. Our adaption of Hodkinson and Sparkes' notions of horizons for action and turning points offers a helpful way to make sense of this, not least because of a recognition that the range of feasible opportunities individuals can see reflects a combination of existing orientations (through emphasis on cultural habitus and life history, for example), broader structural circumstances and ongoing (and sometimes unpredictable) events and interactions.

Consistent with this, the precise role of circumstances themselves as against participants' existing beliefs, orientations and broader habitus seemed to vary somewhat within the sample, as did the acuteness of the turning point represented by the decision to take on a primary or equal care role. In some cases circumstances comprised a factor in the final decision even when the taking on of extensive caregiving roles already lay clearly within the father's horizons. In such situations the extent of the turning point in their thinking may have been comparatively modest, because fathers already regarded sharing care as compatible with who they were or wanted to be. In other cases, the presence of beliefs about the importance of parental intimacy or 'being there' – which may have been longstanding or emergent – had contributed, alongside the development of unusual circumstances, to the coming into view of possibilities for more extensive involvement. And, importantly, even in cases where the significance of a priori beliefs and orientations was least apparent, it is likely that existing positionings, values or approaches to life held significance, in minimising resistance to the possibility of responding in the way they did to the circumstances in which they found themselves. Here, becoming an equal or primary caregiver had not initially formed part of fathers' care horizons but they still may have been more amenable to the possibility, once it emerged, than might others with different backgrounds or lifestyles.

Notwithstanding such receptivity, however, it is the circumstances themselves, we would suggest, that often had been the more direct impetus for the taking up of care-sharing, whether this already lay within fathers' horizons or not. Middle class and somewhat liberal-minded they may often have been, but no more so, in our estimation, than many other middle class fathers who express broadly progressive aspirations relating to fathering but do *not* countenance taking on an equal or greater share of care for young children (see Dermott, 2008; Miller, 2011, 2017). Even though some had already become used to and comfortable with progressive arrangements in their broader relationships, then, for most of the fathers the taking on of counter-normative caring roles represented a substantial additional step. Without the unusual practical circumstances described, there is little reason to think the idea of taking this additional step would have found its way into the horizons of many of the fathers, let alone be taken up. Rather, for men who had often begun their fatherhoods with relatively traditional role divisions and, often, an expectation these would continue, the emergence or exacerbation of particular circumstances had often opened up the possibility for a 'turning point' in their orientation, whereby existing identities and possibilities change and new directions became opened up. Or, as Chelsey (2011) puts it, by making it more difficult to do gender in established ways, financial and other circumstances may sometimes have opened up unexpected opportunities for gender to be undone – or at least to be done differently. Sometimes such circumstances were adverse, regrettable and difficult, of course, and yet, without them, the opportunity to adjust visions of feasible, appropriate or suitable parental roles may not have emerged.

Becoming a primary or equal caregiver

In the previous section, we explored how, for some of the fathers, the decision to take on an equal or greater proportion of caregiving had already formed part of their fatherly care horizons, while for many others it had represented a turning point in their conceptions of what being a father might entail for them. In this section, however, we show how – even in those cases where a significant caregiving role had been consistent with existing orientations or expectations – the practical taking up of such a role tended to represent a considerable reversal of arrangements. This is because, regardless of what had prompted their decision, all but one of the fathers had taken up their responsibilities only after a relatively long period during which their partner had become established as the family's full-time primary caregiver. This meant that the transition into new arrangements often entailed a practical turning point with respect to routines, roles and identities.

Maternity leave

In most cases, the care arrangements in the fathers' families in the months immediately following the birth of their children were relatively unremarkable in gender terms. Partners had taken between six months and a year of leave on their own and had, as part of this, assumed a clear role as primary caregiver. Consistent with this, even though some had provided extensive and crucial support to their partners during this time, the fathers typically found themselves in the role of primary breadwinner, in a manner comparable with the experience of many other fathers (Miller, 2011). As John explained, the adoption of an equal caring arrangement whereby he and his partner took one day a week off to care at home had come about only after a 'normal' period of maternity leave: 'yeah, we had the sort of normal mother-only maternity period and … once our son went to childminders … we decided that my wife and I would each work four days' (John, equal caregiver). Indeed, in some cases, fathers' role in paid work had intensified during this first year, as in the case of Timothy, who was eventually to take on caring for his son on his own for three days a week: 'She did, she actually took a full year of maternity leave, so the nine months' statutory, plus an extra three months at a reduced rate. During which time I took all of the work I could' (Timothy, primary caregiver).

This ordering of arrangements often connected to the fathers having not taken up their right to take extended periods of paternity leave. When we asked fathers whether they had thought about taking extended leave, it became clear that, with the exception of the five who had done so at one point or another, this had normally either not been considered at all or had been quickly dismissed. In those cases where specific reasons were given, these related to the priority the couple gave to breastfeeding, the perceived desire or need of the baby's mother to take a substantial period of leave alone following birth or the financial expediency of organising things this way – normally as a result of their partners' maternity leave benefits being more advantageous than those for their own paternity leave. The latter, which connects closely to policy debates about levels of compensation for fathers on paternity leave (see Chapter 3), was pivotal to Aaron and his partner:

> I mean [partner's name] was going to take nine months … she was working in [employer location] and the [employer] maternity pay for the teachers was really good … it was like 16 weeks or something like that, so we were basically getting full pay for four months. (Aaron, equal care sharer)

It is worth underlining that, even for a group of fathers who eventually took on unusually extensive caregiving responsibilities, the sharing of parental leave earlier in their babies' lives rarely had been considered. Partly, this is because the notion of taking on an equal or greater share of caregiving itself had often not initially formed part of fathers' care horizons. Significantly, though, the sharing of parental leave had rarely been a serious consideration even for those who *had* been considering taking on a greater role later on. In James' case, even after sharing care equally with his partner successfully for their first child, the option of shared parental leave had been quickly rejected for their forthcoming second baby, on the grounds that his partner actively wanted to have a full year of leave after the baby was born:

> We did, we thought about it [shared parental leave] but my wife's very keen on getting that full year with the baby at home, so … no, she doesn't want to do that, this is her choice, so I'll support that obviously. But I will still, at least I still get a day, one day, extra day a week that I'm still going to be at home. (James, equal care sharer)

Most of the fathers in the study, then, were fairly unexceptional in their approach to post-natal care arrangements and the reasons they gave for this. And, furthermore, even in the five cases where extended periods of paternity leave had been taken by fathers, these began – with the exception of Joseph (who took the first 13 weeks off together with this partner) – only once their baby was several months old and only after a significant period of exclusive weekday care by their partner. Robert and his wife's approach, prior to the eventual adoption of an equal caring arrangement, was typical in this respect: 'I think I … worked full-time during [partner]'s maternity leave, so we did, we split the parental leave equally, she did six months of maternity leave and then I did six months of paternity' (Robert, equal care sharer).

When fathers take on equal or primary caregiving responsibilities, then, it would seem there is a significant chance they will do so only after their partner has spent a period of time in the role of primary caregiver during the first several months of their children's lives. This is of significance for a number of reasons. First, such evidence demonstrates that, for all its value, it would be wrong to think of extended paternity leave as a prerequisite for fathers taking on extensive caregiving roles thereafter. The possibility of men taking on long-term equal or primary caregiving roles after beginning their fatherhoods in a somewhat traditional fashion is an important one and this sort of care trajectory needs to be understood and supported. Second, however, the lack of parental leave take-up – or consideration – by many in a sample of unusually care-oriented fathers – starkly confirms the extent to which exclusive maternal care in the first six months to a year after birth remains entrenched (see Doucet, 2009). And in the specific context of UK policy, it reinforces existing evidence that the prospects for significant increases in take-up of Shared Parental Leave seem bleak without radical changes to how this system works, particularly with respect to the issues of transferability and compensation (see Chapters 3 and 7). By extension, these first two points invite questions about whether, notwithstanding key practical issues regarding post-natal recovery and breastfeeding, it may be ideologically and financially more realistic for men in the current UK cultural and policy climate to take on an equal or greater share of caregiving for older babies and toddlers than for younger infants. Finally, while paternity leave may not be a prerequisite for fatherly care-sharing, the taking on by fathers of greater responsibilities only after a significant period of exclusive maternity leave is liable to involve an acute transformation of roles at a point where various approaches, relationships, routines and identities relating to caregiving have already been established. It is with couples' experiences of these sharp practical caregiving turning points that we now concern ourselves.

Transitions and challenges

Families had taken a range of different approaches to the transition of care arrangements following the mothers' extended periods of maternity leave. Sometimes, a period of overlap had occurred whereby the father would take on his new arrangement in the final few weeks of his partner's maternity leave in order to enable a period of time during which both partners were at home together. While in some cases this was pre-planned, in others it had come about as a result of particularly rapidly changing circumstances. In Michael's case, his problems with work and depression – which eventually were to result in voluntary redundancy – had prompted a period of leave that coincided with the end of his partner's maternity period, enabling both to be at home caring for a few months:

> The transition worked quite well because we both had quite a long period of time when we were both there. I … was signed off for work around the Christmas period, and then my employer offered me a sort of a couple of months' wages just to kind of disappear as it were. And so I took that, so it meant that from sort of mid-December through to was it February or March … [partner] went back, we were both at home full-time … So actually if we could have planned for a sort of take-over, that's how we would have done it. (Michael, primary caregiver)

For other families, such a joint period had not been possible and there was a more direct and immediate switch from maternity leave to the new arrangement.

In either case, in spite of broadly positive feelings about their roles, many of the fathers spoke about the anxiety they had experienced in the periods just before and after taking them on. Tellingly, such anxieties were not primarily centred on adjusting to new flexible paid work arrangements but on the challenges of taking on their caring responsibilities. With respect to the former, some did mention minor transitional issues relating to the challenges of them and their colleagues getting used to their more restricted working week, or a feeling that colleagues did not take seriously the extent of their home responsibilities. On the whole, though, most felt that their employers and colleagues had been accommodating. Worries were much more pronounced, though, when it came to the taking on of care roles and, in particular, the prospect and early realities of taking on caring for their child *on their own* throughout the day (see Brandth and Kvande, 2003). Even those who had been most heavily supportive of their partners during maternity leave had normally only taken sole charge for periods of a few hours prior to the transition to their new roles. Timothy, who had recently taken on sole daytime care responsibility for three days a week, recounted the challenge of coming to terms with the extent of the responsibility: 'there's a certain amount of shock initially from the, oh my God this thing is dependent upon me entirely – and I think that initial shock and adjustment is, was the biggest thing for me to get my head around' (Timothy, primary caregiver). Similarly, in reference to the time just before his period of exclusive parental leave, Joseph emphasised the anxiety he had felt about the challenges of approaching care in the right ways without the presence of his partner:

> I'm kind of thinking, well there's going to be all this responsibility for me to establish a routine and to stimulate him just enough and to provide certain levels, the right level, of experience and texture and stimulation, make sure he's sleeping at the right times, also wean him in a particular way and do all of that stuff and do that on my own. (Joseph, parental leaver)

Sometimes such anxieties persisted beyond the immediate transitional period. John went into some detail with us about the worries he was still experiencing every week prior to his one day in sole charge of his son, several months after he had taken on the role:

> So it's, at the end of the day, at the end of Monday I feel great about the time I've spent with him. But on Sunday, beginning of Monday I'm ... quite, well anxious about the day ahead because it's bloody hard work ... And so I enter every, every Monday with an amount of trepidation. (John, equal care sharer)

John went on to emphasise that, in spite of enjoying various aspects of his days with his 15-month-old son, he found such days to be substantially harder than every other day of the week. And when asked what it was, in particular, that led to his anxiety, he cited the length of the time during which he felt a heavy responsibility to expend all available energies on making sure that his son was happy.

As well as illustrating the particular challenges of taking on a greater caregiving role following a period when one's partner was the full-time primary carer, what such accounts also illustrate is how seriously the responsibilities of caregiving appear to have been taken by the fathers, as part of an active, intensive role whereby substantial energy is spent on ensuring their child had the best day possible, something that appeared sometimes to weigh heavily on them. While such feelings may not have been as intense, ongoing and all-encompassing as the gendered pressures of intensive mothering (Hays, 1998), or the anxieties and responsibilities experienced by mothers in the immediate post-natal period (Das, 2019), such worries may suggest these caregiving fathers were not quite as immune from pressures to parent intensively than, it is argued, are fathers in general (Shirani et al., 2012; Miller, 2017). Consistent with this, we found little evidence – in contrast to some other studies of primary carer fathers (Doucet, 2004) – that most of the fathers had planned or expected to focus significant parts of their days of caregiving on paid work, DIY or other extraneous activities. Rather, in most cases, their minds seemed intensely focused on and worried about offering the best possible care to their children throughout the day. Part of the reason for fathers' anxiety during the changeover period, then, was the seriousness with which they often understood their new roles and the weight of the responsibility this created. Once their care horizons and practical realities shifted away from normative patterns, it seemed these fathers had become less sheltered from dominant parenting ideologies and were experiencing at least some of the moral burdens that normally fall upon mothers.

Some of the fathers also faced particular practical challenges when they first took up their new roles. In the case of babies who had been exclusively breast-fed during the maternity leave period, bottle-feeding had sometimes been a difficulty in the first few weeks, leading to anxiety and, sometimes, a need to hastily arrange unscheduled partner meet-ups for a breastfeed. Such issues tended to have resolved themselves over time, but had clearly led to anxiety for fathers seemingly unable to deliver their children's most basic needs. Thomas outlined how difficult this was for him and for his partner, who had had to come home from work early to feed their son:

> the first day I was alone … he wasn't drinking from a bottle very easily yet, but I thought OK … it will be fine, and it proved to not be the case … he was still more used to the breast and yeah, so the first, the first few days were a bit … So my partner was coming home a bit earlier than what she usually does because the first few days I was not able to make [child] drink enough. (Thomas, equal care sharer)

In other cases, children had taken some time to get used to their mother's absence and this could make days at home particularly testing for fathers, both practically and emotionally. Ed, who had become a full-time primary caregiver following his partner's maternity leave for their second child, explained that his two girls' emotional response to his partner leaving the house in the mornings and repeated requests for her throughout the day had shattered some of his initial optimism about becoming a stay-at-home father:

> it has been really, really tough but … and mentally you
> know I've found it really challenging … my ideal scenario
> was you know, I'm, you know to kind of paint a picture
> you know, I'm sat at the table, you know having breakfast
> with the girls and mummy's kind of … waving and going
> off to work and everyone is happy and smiling … 'bye bye
> mummy, we're staying at home with daddy and we can have
> a lovely day' you know, mummy's happy … because the
> children are happy, the kids are happy because you know
> … we are getting much, much closer to that but, Jesus
> Christ, that's been a journey, it really has been a journey.
> (Ed, primary caregiver)

It is likely, of course, that sometimes the close, regular affective contact involved with breastfeeding or co-sleeping with the mother may prompt an emotional preference for her even in cases where fathers share parental leave from birth. Nevertheless, our findings show that the acute transformation of roles following exclusive maternity leave may often have created significant challenges in itself and that greater daytime involvement from the fathers at an earlier point may sometimes have reduced such difficulties. We return to this issue – and to Ed's situation – in Chapter 5, in relation to the ways emotional preferences had continued to affect caregiving practice and identities for some of the fathers even after their new roles had become established.

Transitional difficulties seemed sometimes to have been even more pronounced for the fathers' partners. Whatever the specifics of the situation, fathers' accounts indicated that most of the women had found the combination of returning to work *and* relinquishing their role as the family's primary caregiver a difficult one. In some cases, the mother's personal preference, according to their partner, would have been to have a greater number of days at home herself but she had been persuaded – either by practical circumstances or parenting ideals – to acquiesce to her partner taking on as much or more than her. While noting that, overall, things were now working well, Anthony talked at length about his partner's difficulties coming to terms with an arrangement where they each cared for their son on one day a week. Describing her acceptance of this as a 'sacrifice', he outlined some intense anxieties she had faced during the first weeks both because of her broader mixed feelings and the extent of the transformation of roles it had involved:

> I think in her heart of hearts, if she was completely honest
> about what she wanted to happen, it would have been that

she was three and a half days and I was five [at work] ... the first two weeks I think were really difficult for [partner] in terms of going back to her job ... it's just that was a ... shock to the system I guess in terms of that just as a change, but you know both just the reality of you know getting her head around what she does for a living sort of stuff and the practicalities. And also just losing that time with him, you know, actually that was a big change as well, the not being together all day, every day sort of aspect of it. (Anthony, equal care sharer)

As well as illustrating the strain caused by such a transformation of responsibilities, the anxiety and guilt for both mother and father here draw further attention to the way that the extent of mothers' affective and symbolic attachment to the role of primary caregiver and all the pressures entailed therein can sometimes act as a potential barrier to higher levels of fatherly care.

Even where mothers had been largely content with or actively keen on the arrangements themselves, they still often had faced anxieties about the implications for their maternal identities. Jeremy's partner's preference was for them to share care equally, but she nevertheless found the transition to that equal arrangement difficult: 'she's found it slightly more tricky and I think ... earlier on the burden was more on her, and when we did get more equal, she found it really difficult moving to the, having less time with the kids and working more' (Jeremy, equal care sharer). Similarly, Brian's partner was clear that she wanted to be at work, but felt a constant awareness of being judged by others, including her mother, as a result:

She has said this to me on a number of occasions, that you constantly feel like you're being judged and that you're being ... that everyone thinks that you're somehow failing your child by going back to work as a mum. On the up side, she has readily said to me on a number of occasions and has also said it to her mum, when this topic has perhaps come up and been slightly contentious, that she would go stir crazy if she was permanently at home with [name of child]. (Brian, equal care sharer)

These mothers were experiencing maternal pressures that are commonplace among women returning to work from maternity leave (Hochschild, 1989; Ranson, 2013; Miller, 2017). As Christopher argues, experience of the expectation to 'continually put the needs of their children above their own' typically creates irreconcilable tensions between home and work for such mothers and can result in their taking on responsibility for care and parenting co-ordination work, even when direct daytime caregiving is someone else's responsibility (2012: 75; also Miller, 2017). Such pressures, we would suggest, may sometimes become even more intense for women returning to work *and* transferring care responsibilities to the child's father. In this situation, after all, they are not only placing some degree of priority on their career but are also relinquishing the role of primary caregiver in their family, something at odds with decades of maternal socialisation (Bass, 2015) and, also, the initial establishment of roles in their own families prior to and/ or during maternity leave (Rehel, 2014; Miller, 2017). In the next chapter we will show how such pressures sometimes contributed to women continuing to take on considerable co-ordination and 'mental work' (Miller, 2017) of care, among other things, even when practical care delivery was being shared at least equally. And this also sometimes seemed to have been of significance during the transitional period. In Scott's case, his partner's anxieties during her transition at the end of maternity leave had become intensified by specific worries about the prospect of him taking over caring for their son during the day. This had resulted in what he regarded as the micro-managing of his caregiving during the first few weeks, something that, in turn, led to him feeling guilty about being at home while she was at work:

> I think there was sometimes, when I was transitioning over to looking after [child], I think my partner, like not intentionally … she was very worried about me taking over, just like I think we had a discussion one night when she was sort of saying how I need to remember this, this, this. And I think it was part of that, for her, that loss … And … I had a bit of guilt where I felt, oh am I taking this away from you and, but I want to do this … But it was fine, I think it was just her getting used to going back to work (Scott, equal care sharer)

Sometimes such difficulties during the transition were brought into particularly sharp relief by their contrast with the approach of peers or, in a minority of cases, disapproval from relatives. Only a few of the fathers said that they knew other parents who had taken on similarly equal or reversed roles and, while friends had typically been supportive, this did not negate the impact of taking on a set of roles that contrasted so much with those of others. Meanwhile, in a minority of cases, including Brian's partner (referred to earlier), the children's grandparents had expressed surprise or opposition to the unusual arrangements and this had exacerbated transitional anxieties.

Importantly, a number of the challenges faced by the fathers and their partners during the transition into their primary or equal caregiving roles had gradually eased with the passing of time and it was notable that most spoke in very positive terms to us about the experience overall (see Chapter 7). Equally, anxieties and difficulties probably will always form part of transitions away from periods of full-time leave and into longer-term arrangements, whatever the comparative contribution of mother and father. Nevertheless, we want to argue that, for the families involved in our research, concentrated maternal responsibility during the first six to 12 months of babies' lives – even in those cases where care-sharing already lay within fathers' care horizons – had often contributed to a particularly stark shift of roles and responsibilities when fathers took on a greater role thereafter. In turn, the acuteness of this practical turning point had sometimes led to challenges that might have been easier to manage had care responsibilities – and identities – been shared more from the start. Moreover, we will go on to discuss in the next two chapters how, in spite of their many successes, there were certain aspects of daily care that sometimes continued to be challenging for fathers or left primarily to mothers even beyond the transitional period focused on here. Alongside other factors, we will argue that the roles and routines set in train during maternity leave were continuing to play their part in reinforcing an endurance of what we call default maternal responsibility – and an associated holding back, in some respects, of transformations in fatherly care horizons.

Conclusion

In this chapter we have outlined the range of care arrangements with which the fathers in our sample were involved before going on to explore what it was that prompted these and, finally, the nature of their transition into becoming equal or primary caregiver fathers. Through doing so, we have been able to highlight the importance of post-maternity-leave care-sharing arrangements as an object for attention, the extent to which such arrangements are prompted by existing orientations or by changing circumstances and, finally, the challenges of transferring to a progressive caregiving arrangement *after* an extensive period of maternity leave. And knitting together the discussion has been the question of whether the adoption of unusual care roles represented a continuation or a transformation in the outlooks, or care horizons, of the fathers.

Fatherly caregiving involvement that goes beyond a secondary role, we have suggested, can take a variety of forms, may often not take place until after parental leave periods have ended and does not necessarily involve the relinquishing or suspension of careers. It may therefore be beneficial to broaden the focus of research and policy on so-called 'involved' fathering to include greater emphasis on permanent or semi-permanent post-paternity-leave arrangements that involve fathers taking an equal or greater share of caregiving while they and their partners' weekly lives consist of an ongoing negotiation between parental care, flexible or part-time paid work and outside childcare. In particular, greater attention might be focused on fathers who share care largely equally with their partners.

When it came to how and why the fathers' unusual care arrangements came about, we showed how, while some of our respondents regarded their ideals as pivotal, it was often practical circumstances and the families' willingness to respond in particular ways to these that seemed to have been key. Furthermore, the decision for fathers to share care at least equally had often been taken in response to developing events rather than being preconceived. Our use of the notions of fatherly care horizons and turning points, adapted from Hodkinson and Sparkes (1997), enabled us to highlight the importance of continuities and changes in what fathers see as possible, feasible or appropriate for them, something affected by a combination of factors relating to their habitus in the past and present, both structural and circumstantial. Thus, for only a minority of our sample, we suggest, did taking on equal or primary care roles represent something clearly within their existing vision of what lay in their futures. For the others, a combination of their initial broader habitus and the onset of particular sets of practical circumstances had created the space to enable their care horizons to extend, enabling a turning point in their roles and identities and the opportunity to take up counter-normative gender roles.

In the chapter's final section, we used the notion of turning point in a slightly different way. For, whether or not their decision to take on extensive care roles represented more of a continuation or transformation in their care horizons, most fathers faced a sharp practical turning point when it came to the taking-up of their roles. The rootedness of full-time maternal care in the first period of many of the babies' lives, even for such apparently counter-normative families, meant that, when fathers did eventually take on significant care responsibilities, this involved a dramatic transformation of responsibilities and identities and a challenging transition both for fathers and their partners. While it clearly is not a prerequisite, then, the sharing of parental leave from an early point in babies' lives would likely make the transition into more permanent care-sharing arrangements easier. In the next chapter, we will show how, as well as affecting initial periods of transition, exclusive maternity leave after babies are born may also play a role in creating limits to the scope of the caregiving of equal and primary carer fathers, even once their roles and routines have been established. We also outline, however, how far many of them had travelled with respect to the development of parental identities centred on notions of interchangeability and equivalence with their partners.

5

Developing Fatherly Roles and Identities: Towards Parental Equivalence?

Introduction

In this chapter we turn to the detail of how the sharing of care by fathers was working out in practice and the significance of this for their caregiving approaches, identities and horizons. In particular, we explore how roles and responsibilities were divided between the fathers and their partners, examine similarities and differences in their styles of parenting and outline how the fathers had come to view themselves and their roles. We already have established in Chapter 4 that, through taking on their unusually involved caregiving roles in the first place, the fathers had taken a substantial step outside of dominant understandings of early fatherhood and, often, one that also represented a turning point from their own early practices and expectations. In the coming pages, we ask what happened next, and how far the fathers' challenge to dominant ways of 'doing gender' in early parenthood went. Against the context of somewhat contrasting arguments in existing literature, we ask how comprehensive their caregiving responsibilities had become and the extent to which their identities and practices demonstrated a movement towards gender-neutral approaches to parenting. We also identify some barriers that sometimes placed limits on the scope of the fathers' caregiving roles and the transformations of their identities and horizons.

Fathers or gender-neutral parents?

As outlined in Chapter 2, indications from existing research on primary carer fathers are somewhat inconsistent when it comes to the extent to which their fatherly approaches and identities come to resemble those normally associated with mothers. For Andrea Doucet (2009), the ongoing significance of long-term gendered habitus prompts even those fathers who have taken on the most extensive practical caring responsibilities to reject the notion that their roles or identities resemble those of mothers (see also Doucet, 2006a). Doucet (2009) reports, for example, an overwhelming belief, even among full-time stay-at-home fathers, in a unique emotional and physical bond between mother and baby, something often connected with perceived differences between themselves and their partners in terms of approaches to care, comfort and nurturing. Consistent with this, primary carer fathers in some studies are reported to have emphasised a focus on traditionally masculine physical activities, risk-taking and playfulness, something they contrasted with the gentle, nurturing style attributed to their partners (Doucet, 2006a; Chelsey, 2011; Snitker, 2018). Such a narrative, in Doucet's understanding, 'allows fathers to distinguish their caregiving from that of mothering and to impart a form of masculine care, rooted in using physical embodiment, play, and adventure' (2009: 85). The retention of paid work as a key aspect of identity is also sometimes emphasised, whether through focusing on the importance of part-time work or presenting their current care-centred routines as a temporary 'career-break' (Brandth and Kvande, 1998; Merla, 2008; Chelsey, 2011). Doucet (2004) also reports a tendency to frame days at home in masculine terms by emphasising time devoted to stereotypically masculine forms of unpaid work, such as home-improvement projects.

Finally, questions have been raised about how comprehensive such fathers' taking on of caregiving responsibilities is, not least with respect to what Doucet terms 'community responsibility' and 'moral responsibility' as a parent (Doucet, 2006a). While the first of these refers to fathers' lack of engagement with networks of other parents and children, the second alludes to a tendency for women still to shoulder an ultimate sense of responsibility for children, including in relation to the judgements of others. A question is raised here about whether mothers sometimes continue to take overall responsibility for care, its co-ordination and the mental and emotional weight this equates to, even where fathers contribute heavily to its delivery (Christopher, 2012; Parke, 2013; Miller, 2017). The ongoing emotional labour of such moral responsibility is articulated in Ungerson's (2006) distinction between *caring for*, which equates to practical care tasks and *caring about*, intended to capture this all-encompassing affective and mental dimension. Without disputing the substantial challenge to dominant modes of fatherhood represented by fathers taking up primary care duties, studies such as these tend to place emphasis on limits to the transformations of masculinity and undoing of gender within such families (Doucet, 2006a Chelsey, 2011).

As we also have outlined, however, other studies have placed clearer emphasis on the gender-undoing potential of fathers taking on extensive caring responsibilities. Such studies highlight how the embodied process of discharging everyday caregiving can prompt the development of fundamentally transformed masculinities centred on nurturing, emotion, embodiment and relationality (Solomon, 2014; Ranson, 2015; Brandth and Kvande, 2018b). Competences developed through care practice, argues Ranson (2015), translated for the involved fathers in her study into long-lasting affective commitments to care that traditionally are the preserve of mothers. In Solomon's study of stay-at-home fathers, this also had contributed to largely gender-neutral understandings of parenting that challenged mother/father distinctions. The notion of parental equivalence between mothers and fathers has also featured in isolated existing studies that − like our own − include fathers who share care equally with their partners. Risman and Johnson-Sumerford (1998), for example, outline how roles and responsibilities were, in practice, distributed largely equitably in what they term 'post-gender marriages'. Research on 'equally shared parenting' by Deutsch (2001) also focuses on the prevalence of equality in the sharing out of tasks among such couples, though distinguishes between couples for whom the division was largely 'genderless' and others where the 'equality' relied on greater specialisation along gendered lines. Placing particular emphasis on the former, Ranson's aforementioned (Chapter 2) use of the notion of 'interchangeability' in relation to the practices of a range of non-traditional Canadian caregiving couples suggests a significant 'undoing' of established notions of mothering and fathering and their replacement with gender-neutral notions of 'parenting' that involve the 'fluid exchange of care-giving responsibilities and a frequent blurring of gender boundaries' (2010: 175). Ranson does still note the persistence of certain gendered differences of approach even among interchangeable couples but these are understood primarily as being a matter of parental 'style'. Here, men may sometimes parent more 'like a man' and women more 'like a woman', but the substance of parenting has, in her understanding, become practically interchangeable. As will become clear, Ranson's notion of interchangeability is of importance for our discussion of the experiences of the fathers in our study. We also draw, though – both here and in Chapter 6 – on the useful distinction she makes between fathers' experience of parenting inside and outside the home whereby, in the case of the latter, caregiving fathers may continue to face significant gender-related challenges and where traditional expectations can continue to weigh more heavily (also see Locke and Yarwood, 2017).

In the discussion that follows, we explore what we take to be a discourse of parental interchangeability in the accounts of many of the fathers in our Sharing Care study. Rather than emphasising their distinctiveness as fathers and their difference from mothers, we argue the fathers tended more often to present themselves as the equivalent of their partners, able to switch in and out of different caregiving tasks according to need. While part of our emphasis, following Ranson, is on an expedient and largely gender-neutral approach to the *practical* division and discharge of roles (what Ranson refers to as 'functional interchangeability'), we also focus on the symbolic significance of this perceived interchangeability for how fathers saw themselves as parents. We go on, however, to outline how the men's partners were sometimes continuing to bear a disproportionate burden for certain emotional, organisational and social aspects of care, drawing on our data and existing work on families and care to delve into the likely explanations for this which, we suggest, relate to both maternal pressures and paternal barriers.

'We feel like parents rather than mum and dad': interchangeable understandings

When the fathers discussed how they felt their roles had developed and how responsibilities were divided up in their household, there was some diversity in the sample, but we were struck by how consistently most inferred a degree of equivalence between themselves and their partners and their ability (and willingness) to switch in and out of a range of different caregiving roles. Anthony's response, for example, illustrated a sense of himself and his partner as having become equally able to undertake roles as the need arose and comparable in terms of his son's level of comfort with them:

> We really sort of settled down into a nice routine and I think we ... are sort of completely interchangeable as parents in terms of his [son's] ... care ... in terms of his you know

preferences or desires of parenting, he doesn't seem to be bothered (laughs) which one of us it is that does anything! (Anthony, equal care sharer)

The notion of interchangeability – used explicitly in Anthony's account – captures, we think, a sentiment expressed in many of the fathers' narratives, connecting to Ranson's use of the concept to understand situations in which 'practices usually associated with mothering or with fathering [are] considered separately from the person conventionally associated with their execution' (2010: 177–8). Importantly, our use of the term does not suggest the fathers felt that their caring practices were identical to those of their partner, that every task was split evenly or that their parenting was gender-free. After all, the sample entailed a range of parental leave, primary caregiver and equal care sharer arrangements with different divisions of roles and responsibilities in each case (see Chapter 4). Meanwhile perceived or actual differences between themselves and their partners did emerge in some of the accounts, as we shall see. What our use of interchangeability encapsulates, though, is how most of them presented themselves and their partners as similarly capable and willing to discharge most or all of the tasks associated with care according to need, and broadly equivalent to one another in much of their role as parents. While it was particularly noticeable among equal caregiver fathers, who comprised the majority of our sample, such an understanding also was regularly apparent among parental leavers and primary caregivers, even if they were doing a disproportionate share of daily caregiving at the time we interviewed them.

Consistent with such an understanding – and in contrast to some earlier studies of caregiving fathers – we did not encounter much evidence that the men were at pains to highlight their distinctiveness as male rather than female caregivers, or to play down the significance of caring itself in favour of a focus on their breadwinning activities, home improvements or other masculine pursuits during their days at home. Even though most of them were working either part-time or full-time, as we noted in Chapter 4, many placed emphasis on the seriousness with which they took their caring responsibilities and the weight of responsibility and pressure they sometimes experienced when caring alone during the day. John's descriptions of his Mondays at home with his one-year-old, for example, highlighted the amount of thought and worry involved in making sure the day was successful in caregiving terms, how emotionally invested he was in this and the extra sense of attachment between him and his son he felt this generated:

He's at that age where, and he's not, he's not very happy to be left on his own at the moment … it's just the constant nature of being on alert all the time, not being able to relax for a moment … wanting to make sure he's stimulated and having a nice time … it's the pressure of … keeping him entertained, keeping him happy, keeping him safe. And yeah, if I take him out, will he get upset and will I need to bring him home? And I guess the easiest part of the day … is when he's sleeping and he's, and it's nice because he's getting the rest that he needs and also I can have a sit down, I can tidy up and clear up and get ready for lunch … Or if I'm going out in the afternoon I can get, I've got a bag of everything, nappies and sun cream and hats and coats and you know toys and food and everything I need to put in a bag and I've got that ready now and … And oh yeah I'm going to sit down for a minute! The nicest part of the day is the end of the day when my wife comes home and he's happy … and he's happy because he's been happy with me … I think on Mondays at the moment, because he's been with me all day, I get a little bit extra of a kiss or whatever it is, a big smile and … and I think that, yeah, that's probably the nicest part of the day is the end of the day when I've done it, it's been fine and he's happy. (John, equal care sharer)

Meanwhile, even though careers often remained important to the men, rather than being at pains to talk about the importance of this, many, across the different care arrangements, accepted that paid work had become more pivotal to their partners' identities than their own, as here:

I love my job but I don't feel it's as big a part of who I am in the same way that it is for [partner], you know, if we're on a night out and we meet people, you know, oh what do you do, if someone asks what do you do, [partner] will be then still talking forty five minutes later. (William, equal care sharer)

While the extent to which this tendency to eschew career-centrism by the fathers preceded or followed on from the taking on of their care roles may have varied between them, their accounts demonstrate significant movement beyond the dominant binary that, regardless of the career situation of each, mothers ultimately privilege their maternal selves as core to their identity and fathers their career (see Doucet, 2006a; Miller, 2017).

In some cases, overtly gender-neutral understandings of parenting were explicitly endorsed by fathers from across the different care groups. Patrick, who was sole daytime carer on four days a week with his partner taking care responsibility on the other, explained that he disliked the label 'stay-at-home dad' because he felt it implied there was something distinct or different about being a father in such a role as opposed to a mother. His preference was to think of himself as a stay-at-home parent, without a reference to gender:

> Stop focusing on it as being a stay-at-home dad and just either parent can be the stay-at-home parent and just kind of normalising it into the middle ... all I am doing is parenting my children and fulfilling the role of the parent who keeps the house running ... that's all it is really. (Patrick, primary caregiver)

Such endorsements of the notion of parental equivalence may be regarded by some as unsurprising, particularly given that studies sometimes have indicated a tendency for fathers to exaggerate the extent of their contributions to domestic work and childcare and underplay those of their partners (Pew Research Center, 2015). We want to suggest, though, that these fathers' comfort with describing themselves as broadly equivalent to their partners is of some significance. This is because their emphasis on interchangeability rather than their distinctiveness as male or masculine carers indicates a shift away from the more clearly differentiated motherly or fatherly identities visible in many existing studies of both secondary (Dermott, 2008; Miller, 2011, 2017) and primary (Doucet, 2006a; Chelsey, 2011) carer fathers. It also suggests that, as well as having significant practical implications (Ranson, 2010), the notion of interchangeability can capture something symbolic and affective – how many of the fathers had come to see, feel and present themselves, not merely as contributing, but as substantively equivalent to their partners and able to discharge myriad tasks according to need. This is particularly striking when we take into account that most of these fathers began their parenthoods in the traditional role of primary breadwinner (see Chapter 4). As we also showed, the initial transfer of responsibilities that accompanied the taking up of their care-sharing roles often was accompanied by significant pressures, anxieties or difficulties. For many of the fathers to have shifted so much towards an understanding of themselves as interchangeable parents indicates that, as their practical involvement in care became more entrenched, this was accompanied by ongoing shifts in their identities and horizons going forward. While not all were as explicit as him, William's comparison of his and his partner's parental identities before and after the taking on of their care-sharing arrangement when she finished her maternity leave relayed clearly how he had come to see him and his partner as broadly equivalent: 'in terms of the status, [partner] was very much MUM [laughs] and now I would say, beyond maternity [leave], it's more like we feel like parents rather than mum and dad if that makes sense' (William, equal care sharer).

Sharing out tasks and roles

An emphasis on the eclipsing of traditional gender roles by a flexible, expedient approach also dominated fathers' detailed accounts of how daily tasks were distributed in practice. It remains possible, of course, that some exaggerated their contributions, as men sometimes have in the past (see earlier) but we think the level of detail we asked them to provide about different routines and tasks and our tendency to come back to such details at different points in the interviews may have helped minimise this. It also was evident that fathers *did* seem to be forthcoming about particular areas of limitation to their caregiving that they were aware of, as we shall see later. While our observations inevitably are reliant on their accounts, we were struck by how little evidence we could find that hegemonic masculinities and femininities were playing a substantial role in who responded to children at night, got them dressed, put them to bed, made them food, played with them, read to them or ferried them to and from childcare. Brian expressed this particularly starkly:

> It's whoever is closest to the door if she wakes up screaming ... it all kind of just falls into a sort of a natural rhythm of one doing one bit while the other's doing the other ... if one is getting her tea ready, the other would be playing with her in the garden, you know, one's running the bath, the other one's sorting out her clothes to go to grannie's the next day. (Brian, equal care sharer)

In most cases, of course, the situation was a little more complex than Brian's description, not least because the presence of both parents within the house at once during the daytime was normally confined to weekends. Rather than both doing care tasks simultaneously, it was more usual for one partner to be working on a given day while the other took responsibility for most or all of the care and domestic tasks that needed discharging, from getting children dressed and fed, to changing nappies, to cooking and cleaning, or facilitating play or learning. Not surprisingly, in the case of primary caregiver fathers it was they who more frequently took on this range of tasks during weekdays, while time was more evenly divided up for equal care sharers. Those responsible for care during a given day typically were responsible for morning duties, while evening caregiving tended to be shared or undertaken primarily by the partner who was at work during the day but, importantly, this often depended on circumstances relating to timings, locations and other aspects of the family's routines, including those relating to paid work. Some of the fathers also described how interchangeability extended to a flexibility with respect to stepping in for one another if it became difficult to discharge care duties according to the normal routine, whether through work commitments or, as James describes here, ill health:

James: There's been the odd occasion where I've been
                ill, on a day by myself and I think, God, how am
                I supposed to be ill and deal with her? And we've
                tried it a couple of times and I've just had to back
                out and call my wife home from work and say,
                seriously I can't do this.
Interviewer: Yes, and does that work the other way round as
                well, so …?
James: It has done, yeah, so yesterday morning for instance,
                my wife was feeling so unwell that I had to stay
                home for the morning and take half a day holiday
                and just sort things out. So yeah, it kind of swings
                both ways. (James, equal care sharer)

On days where both partners were at work, the sharing out of morning and evening responsibilities often was understood as relating primarily to availability, convenience and expediency. For the majority, who were in dual-earner households, such tasks often included logistics with respect to childcare arrangements. Nursery drop-off and pick-up duties were typically determined by issues of timing and location vis-à-vis home and each partner's work. For some of the fathers this meant that they were normally responsible for this, while in others the role alternated or was taken on by their partner. In Timothy's case, although he was regarded by himself and his partner as his children's primary caregiver, was their sole carer on three days a week and was nursery's first call in the case of an emergency, his wife had taken on responsibility for routine drop-off and pick-up from nursery on the other two weekdays because it was located conveniently on her way to work and, as such, she had become nursery's regular contact for routine matters.

A similarly expedient approach seemed to apply with respect to who would pick up and care for the child if they became ill while at day care. Thomas recounted how he had postponed work appointments to pick up and look after his son for a day, and that his wife had then taken the following day off:

> It was myself that went to fetch our son from the nursery ... I'm the closest to the nursery anyway, and because my wife, she works ... 45 minutes by bus ... So yeah, I fetch him and took that day off, the rest of that day off. So I arranged with my clients and then my partner took the other day. (Thomas, equal care sharer)

Likewise, when we asked who would normally accompany children to hospital if they had an accident or were seriously ill, the answer often hinged on which partner was at home or available. For stay-at-home dads or those on parental leave alone, this meant there was a greater likelihood that they would do this whereas, for others, it would depend if the need arose on one of their or their partner's days at home. Somewhat to our surprise, few fathers suggested their partner would be more likely to go than them, and proximity and availability seemed in most cases to be more important here than gender. As Jason put it, 'It would entirely depend on the situation, whoever's free ... I mean if she [daughter] needs to go, she needs to go and we'll organise to go there ... If my partner's free, she'll take her, if I'm free, I'll take her' (Jason, primary caregiver).

Significantly only two of the fathers were caring for children under a year old at the time of the study, meaning the impact of breastfeeding and of the particularly strong ideological emphasis on mother–baby bonding during this key period (Doucet, 2009) is underrepresented in the study. For the fathers on parental leave, it was clear that breastfeeding, in particular, played a role in differentiating maternal and paternal burdens, particularly in the first few months. In Joseph's case, in spite of initial intentions to share most tasks from the start, the centrality of breastfeeding together with the baby's difficulties with bottle-feeding had led to a disproportionate daily and nightly burden for feeding on his partner, even though they both were off work together for 13 weeks. What extended parental leave had enabled, in his case, was that, when faced with such a situation, Joseph took on as many other care and domestic tasks as was feasible:

> [Partner's] job has been sort of mainly to feed [child] and I've been mostly cooking, doing housework, carrying everything that isn't him and that sort of thing ... in the first few days he wasn't sleeping at night at all, and I was ending up sitting on that sofa at three in the morning, with him sleeping on me ... I am still getting up very early in the morning, taking him when he wakes up, he'll usually, he'll wake up, it could be as early as 5.30, it could be 7 o'clock this morning was quite unusual and then [partner] will give him a feed, at which point he'll be suddenly awake and I'll take him and I'll look after him downstairs, whilst [partner] can get an hour or two's sleep to recover, because she's been the one who hasn't been sleeping overnight. I change probably 95+ per cent of the nappies, which is only fair, given that I don't do any of his feeding. (Joseph, parental leaver)

The centrality of the mother to feeding and the regularity of feeding during this early period, then, made the notion of parental interchangeability difficult to achieve even where both parents were off work and contributing extensively. Nevertheless, Joseph and his partner had responded to the situation – like fathers in Ranson's work (2015) – by taking on an equal or often greater share of 'everything but breastfeeding'. And subsequently, when the baby was older and his partner returned to work, Joseph took on a further period of 15 weeks of parental leave, this time caring throughout the daytime on his own and including bottle-feeding.

What this may suggest, consistent with some of the data we presented in Chapter 4, is that the taking on of interchangeable parenting may become easier to do after the first several months of an infant's life. For, across the rest of the sample, the fathers' accounts tended, as we have seen, to indicate that the interchangeable self-understandings many had developed were largely aligned with distributions of everyday roles and responsibilities that were more centred on practical expediencies than on gender. In many cases, then, their symbolic and affective sense of themselves as interchangeable, caregiving parents, seemed to be connected to a 'functional' interchangeability whereby, as Ranson proposes, 'caring work is shared in a way that defied neat gender-categorising' (2010: 177–8) and where, we suggest, an expedient approach to practicalities was often understood as the primary driver of role allocation.

As well as demonstrating the distance travelled by many of the fathers and the extent of their involvement, it is worth noting that the emphasis on interchangeability of roles and tasks here, rather than a full maternal/paternal role reversal, for example, underlines our understanding of the fathers as engaging in care-*sharing*. In part, this reflects the nature of a sample in which the majority were equal care sharers and where half of the primary carer group were juggling care responsibilities with between one and three days of part-time work. It also illustrates, though, that even where men take on the greater proportion of childcare responsibilities and women take on the role of primary breadwinner, mothers often retain significant parental responsibilities and status, both practically and symbolically. Not surprisingly, the notion of interchangeability was least obvious among the small number of full-time stay-at-home fathers in the sample who were doing the vast majority of daily care work, but even here there were indications of significant ongoing maternal involvement or status. In Michael's case, although he was currently in the role of full-time caregiver, with his partner responsible for breadwinning, there was a sense of interchangeability between them in the longer term with respect to the possibility of him and his partner switching – or not – in the future:

> At the moment we've got some challenges because [partner's employer] are doing a restructure and it looks like possibly she's going to be made redundant … [partner]'s going to initially look for work, with me remaining as the, looking after the children, but if after a set period of time she's had no luck, then I will start looking again. (Michael, primary caregiver)

Here, in spite of a largely uneven split in practical duties at any one period in time, an interchangeable understanding centred on an apparently gender-neutral expediency was apparent with respect to the course that might be taken in the future – and, crucially, neither parent is regarded as inherently more suited to the role of main carer. What interchangeability indicates, then, is first, that care-sharing fathers took on an extensive range of responsibilities and often came to take on a somewhat gender-neutral understanding of themselves as parents as compared to their partners, and second, that even when fathers were placed in the position of primary breadwinner, their partners tended to still be understood as substantial contributors to caregiving, whether in the present or future, a theme to which we shall return.

Parenting styles

One of the areas of continuing parental gender difference most starkly highlighted in previous studies of caregiving fathers is the styles of parenting employed by mothers and fathers. As noted earlier, some studies (Doucet, 2006a; Parke, 2013) have observed an emphasis among primary carer fathers on traditionally masculine approaches centred on an encouragement of risk and on physical and outdoor activities. Consistent with this, about a third of the fathers in our study, in spite of the range of tasks they were taking on, made reference to imposing fewer rules than their partners, encouraging their children to play more independently or a propensity towards 'rough-and-tumble' or physical play. All these aspects came into Anthony's account, along with a recognition of the potentially gendered nature of such an orientation, though he was keen to outline the similarity of his and his partner's approaches in other respects:

> I don't know what the best way of saying it that doesn't make me seem like a neglectful parent, but him sort of pushing the boundaries of what he can do physically and being a bit more rough-and-tumble with him and letting him try things physically a bit more. So you know when he started to be able to get up on to the sofa, I'm probably a bit more just letting him get on with you know getting off and getting back down in his own way! You know just because I sort of, you know that he needs to learn how to tumble and what he can't do and what he can do ... I think I'm definitely more likely to let him get on with that and just let him explore what he can and can't do .... I think that's probably a more you know stereotypical man thing ... and having more rough and tumble play with him, and I definitely do more you know getting down on the floor and physically you know interacting with him and throwing him onto the sofa and these sorts of things than [partner] does. But I think aside from that, I think we're pretty similar overall. (Anthony, equal care sharer)

Notwithstanding the broader interchangeability in their parenting, such accounts may reflect the endurance of certain gendered differences of parenting 'style', the like of which prompt Ranson's concept of 'parenting like a man' (2010, 2015). However, an emphasis on such approaches was not consistent across the sample and, in many other cases, fathers struggled to identify any significant differences between themselves and their partners, or stereotypes appeared to have been turned on their head. Some, for example, said they were more likely to stay indoors with their children than their partners (see Chapter 6) and others emphasised that it was they rather than their partners who tended to place greater emphasis on structure and consistency. Michael outlined how he felt that his children's mother, who was his family's full-time breadwinner at the time, had adopted what he regarded as the typical approach of a breadwinning father, eschewing the structures and consistent approaches he had worked to put in place through leniency and the offer of treats:

> Maybe, because I'm looking after them all the time, I'm probably a little bit stricter with them and will say, no, we're not doing that, whereas ... it's almost ... it is the sort of stereotypical thing where people go, oh you go to dad and you get what you want and it's ... Because dad comes home and he wants you to be happy all the time that you're home because he doesn't see you very much, you get what you want .... Whereas you know [partner] will come in and [child] gets treats and things like that and you know just little things that are ... And then I'll go, [partner], look, I've been trying to work on not getting him to pee in the garden! And she'll go, yeah, just go pee in the corner! Can we not do that?! (Michael, primary caregiver)

Most importantly, perhaps, although some fathers had mentioned an orientation to more typically masculine styles of care, there was little evidence they were avoiding or feeling uncomfortable discharging more traditionally feminine aspects of care such as those relating to emotional comfort. Some even emphasised the achievement of an equivalence between themselves and their partners in this respect, as here:

> If my [older] daughter fell over and hurt herself and needed to run to someone for comfort, I think she is as likely to come to me as my wife, so there's no ... there's no one of

us who provides comfort and solace in that way more than
the other I don't think. (Chris, parental leaver)

While we shall later see that not all the families were quite so equal
in this respect, many talked positively about developing gentler, more
intimate and nurturing aspects of their parenting and the closeness of
the emotional bonds they felt this had led to. In the following extract,
Patrick describes the importance of everyday intimate moments of
interaction with each of his children and the strong affective bonds
he feels these have led to:

> I do value that, and it is, like I say the little things, like that
> five minutes each morning when the boys are off playing
> on their own and I'm doing [daughter]'s hair and we kind
> of talk and get on with it ... when it was just [elder son]
> before number three was born, the kind of, the moments
> when [daughter] was at school, then he was developing
> and the little things that have made him different from
> [daughter], like he was always interested in washing up, so
> we'd come home from after the school run and he'd have
> his chair next to me and he would happily stand there the
> entire duration of me washing up ... and he'd have the clean
> things, have his own little bowl of water and then he'd put
> it in the draining rack. And it was just a little thing that him
> and I did ... And then there's, obviously [younger son]'s
> only one and a bit ... but there's things that are definitely,
> his personality is different enough, there's things that I'm
> enjoying with him, and especially now that I've got the
> two days a week when it's just him and I ... things that
> are just between the two of us are developing a lot more.
> (Patrick, primary carer)

Notwithstanding the differences in parental style identified by
some, the development in the fathers of myriad gentle moments
of intimacy such as these provides an indication that, as a result of
their responsibilities and everyday practice, they had, like the fathers
in previous studies by Brandth and Kvande (2018b) and Ranson
(2015), often begun to embrace the 'affective, relational, emotional,
and inter-dependent qualities of care' regarded by Karla Elliott as the
foundation of 'caring masculinities' (2016: 252). While differences
of style and emphasis were sometimes apparent and while these may
have meant distinctions between motherly and fatherly identities and

practices were not always entirely undone, the range of approaches being developed and recognition of the emotional relationships in many of the accounts remained, we argue, a substantial departure from established parental roles, including those of many of the men's peers. It also suggests that, subsequent to their decision to take on care-sharing, the shift of direction this represented and the challenges of the initial transition, the fathers' competences, self-understandings and horizons had developed – albeit at different rates – towards a sense of parental equivalence between themselves and their partners.

Persistent areas of gender difference

For all the distance that many of the fathers had travelled – and in spite of the striking challenge to established notions of fatherhood that their embrace of interchangeability represented – we often found that one or more of three particular facets of care had continued to be dominated in some way by mothers: emotional comfort, care co-ordination and parent networking. Their fairly regular appearance in our data as areas of enduring gender disparity, we suggest, indicates the capacity of some familiar and deep-rooted motherly roles and burdens to endure, even where arrangements and understandings are comparatively gender-neutral in other respects. While it would be problematic for these to eclipse the extent of the symbolic and functional interchangeability that had been embraced by most of the fathers, they go significantly beyond differences of style and into the realms of responsibility for parenthood and ongoing emotional labour (Miller, 2017). As such, they prompt consideration of the apparent resilience of certain maternal pressures and of the barriers that sometimes can prevent even the most committed of caregiving fathers from reaching a position of full parental equivalence.

Comfort, and affective preferences

As outlined earlier, we identified few indications from the fathers that they were reticent to discharge emotional or affective care, while positive accounts of the development of the more intimate sides of their caregiving were plentiful. Nevertheless, although some felt they had become fully interchangeable with their partners in this respect, in other cases children had retained some sort of a preference for their mother when they were upset or needed affective comfort. Ed, referred to in the previous chapter in relation to his children missing their mother when he first took over as primary caregiver, explained that, although things were gradually improving and his general emotional bond with his girls felt strong, they still tended to prefer their mother when they were upset and this sometimes included days when he was caring for them alone. This had clearly affected his confidence:

> Although I would like to think that I have a very, very strong connection with the girls and a good solid bond, mummy is still ultimately the go to … my ability to kind of comfort the girls is not as great as [partner's] … And [child shouting in background] she may be shouting daddy but she may also be shouting mummy … It's quite gutting, but … I do have to deal with that reality that I will never [laughs] … be mummy! (Ed, primary caregiver)

Similarly, John had found himself anxious and struggling for explanations for his son's preference for his mother when it came to emotional comfort and cuddles in spite of them parenting equally in most respects. Like some others, he had highlighted the period of exclusive maternity leave his partner had taken prior to their decision to share care equally as a potential factor, but also had retained in his mind the possibility of a more natural – and gendered – bond between mother and baby:

> There are … things that you know the baby just wants mum sometimes and that, we can't work out why, why he wants her, not me, when we do spend the same amount of time you know caring for him, maybe it's that nine months' maternity leave, maybe it's just an unspoken mother-child bond. But sometimes you know my wife will get a cuddle, I won't … But then when she's not there, he's fine for that person to be me, so … I've got a little bit upset a couple of times about it, ehm because a couple of times it's happened in public … And as I say, on a Monday, when she's not there … or if she's out at the weekend, he's perfectly happy that she's not there, he really doesn't mind if she's not there because I'm there and that's absolutely fine. And he doesn't push me away. (John, equal care sharer)

Although John was experiencing no problems when his partner was not present, for both him and Ed, their children's ongoing preference for their mother's emotional comfort had led to one or two doubts about their *capacity* as men to achieve full equivalence with their partners in this respect, and had encouraged the retention in their minds of broader gendered understandings of maternal emotional bonds, even amidst their own clear effectiveness and enthusiasm as caregiving fathers. In Ed's case, particularly, the extent of the children's apparent preference for their mother's comfort had helped to precipitate a broader sense that, despite his competence at discharging the wide range of activities associated with full-time caregiving (about which he spoke at length), his children's mother might still have been the more ideal full-time caregiver, had circumstances been different: 'at the moment I just feel as though I do ... as well as I possibly can to sort of make up for not having a mum around almost' (Ed, primary caregiver).

The general sense of inferiority to his partner that Ed was feeling was unusual, however, and most fathers who had experienced such disparities came across as more optimistic at the gradual signs of improvement they were seeing as they spent more time with their children. Jason's confidence and his intimate relationship with his daughter were benefiting from a sense that she gradually was becoming happier turning to him for comfort when he was caring alone, even if she preferred her mum when she was present:

> Mum's still her favourite, if she's feeling a bit down and under the weather ... But now, if mum's not there, she'll happily come to me, and it is nice, whereas before she'd be a bit hesitant ... it's really nice that now I know that I get the benefit of having more time with her. (Jason, primary caregiver)

The achievement of parity with their partners with respect to emotional care, then, was more often regarded as a work in progress than a lost cause in the cases where it was raised – and was also offset somewhat by the aforementioned comfort with which most fathers described their own discharging of emotional and intimate forms of care. Nevertheless, the disparity had the potential in some cases to become a barrier to fathers' ability to act and understand themselves as the full parental equivalent of their partners and, crucially, it also could exert disproportionate emotional pressure on mothers who remained the primary focal point for emotional response. Scott, for example, described how his partner's days with the children sometimes could be more challenging than his because of the extent of their son's affective attachment to her:

> I can put our son down with a toy and sort of go to another room and he'll just keep himself entertained and I can come

back. She can put him down but he whimpers and he wants to be held ... recently, she's basically pretty much holding him on and off the whole day ... Or like sitting with him, she has to be in his vicinity. (Scott, equal care sharer)

Care co-ordination

As noted in Chapter 2, the location of organisational responsibility for caregiving with working mothers is a consistent feature of existing literature on care (Christopher, 2012; Parke, 2013; Irwin and Winterton, 2014; Miller, 2017). Importantly, our findings suggest that this may sometimes endure even when, in other respects, parental roles have become more gender neutral. Pleck and Stueve (2001) have usefully distinguished between 'infrastructural' aspects of maternal co-ordination, concerning management of everyday activities and people in children's lives, and 'executive' components that relate to overall direction. We found this distinction useful in making sense of our own findings in this respect.

In relation to the 'infrastructural' co-ordination, while some fathers were taking on an equal or greater share of everyday planning and organisation, our impression (though it was not always easy to tell) was that mothers were often taking a little greater responsibility than their partners for things like setting up appointments, liaising with childcare providers and organising activities. While common among equal care sharers, this sometimes could even apply to families in which fathers were doing the majority of day-to-day care. In Michael's case, although he regarded himself as a stay-at-home father and was covering the range of daily caregiving and domestic tasks throughout the week, he outlined how his partner had continued to co-ordinate parts of his routines and activities as well as their household budgeting:

She's the sort of organiser of our unit ... she will either organise and book it, or she will say to me, here's the information, this is what you need to do and then I'll phone up and book ... I think it's sort of probably slightly changed now because obviously I need to book it in around all the different things that we'd be doing ... and you know money-wise I actually have no real clue as to what's going on because [partner] does all that, I know what budget I need to keep to for the shop on a Tuesday and do that! (Michael, primary caregiver)

There was a sense, then, that the doing of everyday caring had not always translated for the fathers into full organisational responsibilities.

We also observed apparent disparities in some families when it came to 'executive responsibility', which we take to refer to broader co-ordination – together with associated pressures and liabilities – of children's development, including in relation to medium and long-term decisions about care, activities and orientation (Ranson, 2013). Here, it is important to note that, where this was discussed, fathers typically said that decisions tended to be taken jointly, while some primary caregivers felt they were now taking the lead role in this respect. And sometimes, the men explicitly talked about how the experience of everyday care had developed their understanding, literacy and confidence to an extent that they now felt able to play a substantial part in conversations about their children's development, as here:

> Having more time regularly with the children gives me a much better view of where they are at developmentally and what their needs are in particular areas. So it means I can have a much more productive and collaborative conversation with [partner] about how we want to parent and what things we want to change ... it means that I feel we have a greater degree of kind of common knowledge about them when we're having those discussions compared to when I was working full-time. (Eric, equal care sharer)

There remained, though, an unspoken sense in Eric's account that, although far more able to engage meaningfully and substantively, he still may not normally have been the lead participant in such conversations. Consistent with this, it was sometimes explicitly noted by other fathers that, in spite of most decisions being taken jointly, mothers seemed more often to be the ones to raise issues for discussion or to take the initiative to research issues in order to inform such deliberations. John accepted that, although he contributed extensively to conversations about approaches to parenting, his wife tended to lead these, often in relation to ideas or approaches she had read about:

> My wife is a lot more willing to spend time reading material, which is good for me because she reads it and then ... she'll say what do you think about that? ... and I'll, you know, I'll say, well what, what do you think and what have you read? And we'll tend to agree, what she reads and then

> take from that I tend to agree with, it makes sense, certain
> ways of parenting, so my wife very much leads that. (John,
> equal care sharer)

Notwithstanding the seriousness and sense of responsibility with which the men had taken to their role of caregivers, the indication that partners had sometimes retained a leading role in regard to broader decision-making and planning suggests these mothers may still have often been feeling a greater sense of responsibility with respect to the overall direction of children's upbringing. Even in unusually egalitarian households, then, there were examples of mothers apparently taking on more of the '24/7 thinking responsibility' (Miller, 2017), and the ongoing mental and emotional labour associated with this, than were fathers (Ungerson, 2006; Doucet, 2009).

As with the question of emotional preference, mothers' retention of significant responsibilities for infrastructural and executive aspects of care co-ordination sometimes was connected by fathers – plausibly we think – with their prior responsibility for caregiving during maternity leave in the first months of children's lives. As well as establishing from the outset a strong sense of overall responsibility, this early period seems sometimes to have cemented roles and routines related to liaison with professionals or others where, once connections had been established, their continuation by mothers was understood to reflect convenience or force of habit. Scott explained his partner's continuing primary responsibility for liaising with health professionals and others in these terms:

> Yeah, I'd say it's primarily my partner, mainly because,
> because she had the first six months, that's when you know
> the first, those first sort of checks were done … So, but yeah,
> so with sort of health professionals, etc, it just happened
> just because she took the first sort of six months … it just
> happened that she sort of, she ended up sorting out that.
> (Scott, equal care sharer)

Importantly, however, others mentioned external barriers to their own taking on of such roles, barriers that related to how they were positioned by others outside their immediate family. Several alluded to awkwardness when dealing with midwives, health visitors, doctors and others, or the tendency of professionals to communicate with their partner only – something that, in Chris' case, had prompted responsibility for liaising with them to default to his partner:

> I think my wife tends to take the lead with those [health/support professionals] and I think that is partly because that's the expectation on the part of the people offering those services ... I remember situations where I had been trying to arrange a health visit or something along those lines, but they wanted to speak to my wife, not me ... so it's just easier for her to lead those conversations. (Chris, parental leaver)

Even though many were partially or solely responsible for taking their children to and/or from day care, some of the fathers had found that nurseries also tended to contact their partners rather than them. Brian explained that, even though he had been the one to set up the child's place at nursery because it was linked to his workplace, staff tended to phone his partner rather than him if their child had hurt herself or was unwell.

> I mean it hasn't happened too often thankfully, but I think generally speaking [partner] gets the phone call. Whether that was by design or whether that's just by assumption from the nursery end, I'm not entirely sure. I think they've got both our contact details and I don't, I was the one they dealt with for the actual setting up of the place ... so again, complete guess work on my part, but it could be an assumption, a perfectly benign assumption that ... it's mum who would react first or want to know first. It doesn't particularly trouble me but ... that's the way round that it tends to be. And then immediately I get the phone call from [partner] and get the sort of verbatim what's going on. (Brian, equal care sharer)

As we elaborate in the discussion towards the end of this chapter, factors such as these had the potential to form significant barriers to fully interchangeable parenthood for the fathers and they can be seen as part of a broader gendered environment or habitus (Doucet, 2009) that encourages mothers, fathers and those that surround them to regard women as ultimately responsible for children's wellbeing and development.

Parent networking

While the roles described in the previous two sections remained inconsistent across the sample (and, occasionally, ambiguous within individual accounts) with respect to the presence and extent of disparities between the fathers and their partners, the most striking and consistent area of difference we identified related to activities that involved informal contact or liaison with other parents. The aspect of infrastructural co-ordination most regularly attributed by fathers to their partners rather than themselves, for example, was the organisation of social events with other children and their parents, including parties, playdates and meet-ups. Not surprisingly, this was often put down by the fathers to the predominance of mothers rather than fathers within local parenting networks and the perceived greater ease with which women could liaise with one another. William explained that, while he would typically be the one to make daytime social arrangements with long-standing friends of theirs, the strongly gendered nature of the networks of parents they had met since having a baby made it easier for his partner to take the lead with communicating with them:

> So we've got ... three groups of friends, who were pre-existing friends to the kids arriving, who now all have kids ... And it's, you know, I'm more likely to arrange that, especially if it's say on a Friday ... we might go to the park, sit in the park, so my mum's there and our friends are there and the kids are playing together. At the weekend, it's just whoever's chatted to our friends most recently ... it might be just because [partner]'s a little bit more sociable than I am, but in terms of where it's been someone from nursery, and it might just be because most of the other people who drop off and pick up are ... are female. And it's, there's only really [partner], my wife whose kind of arranged with people we don't know that well. (William, equal care sharer)

In a similar manner to other areas of disparity, fathers also sometimes emphasised how they felt their partners' initial forging of relationships with others during their first few months on maternity leave had meant they were much more embedded in such networks from the beginning and that this made it easier for them to be the ones to engage in communications going forward:

> That's [organising playdates, parties] generally my wife ... And that's because ... a lot of the parents with younger children from the NCT group [group of parents who did a pre-natal course together and stayed in touch], the baby groups that my wife's on her year's maternity ... And that's

still the friendship group at the moment, so she's in contact with them all. (Kevin, primary caregiver)

The strong tendency for arrangements with other parents to be the responsibility of the men's partners connects to what Doucet (2006a, 2009) refers to as 'community responsibility' aspects of parenting which involve key aspects of caregiving that take place outside of individual domestic spheres and among local networks of other parents and children. Because of the importance of these social aspects of care, fathers' marginality to them constitutes a significant limit to their practical interchangeability with their partners as parents, as well as a symbolic reminder of their strongly gendered status as men undertaking roles that are taken on in most families by mothers. Crucially, fathers' lack of involvement in liaising or organising with other parents was invariably connected to broader sets of issues with respect to their comfort within daytime spaces and among groups of mothers – issues that left many of them isolated on the days when they were caring for their children. Because of its importance in our data, this issue is explored in greater depth in Chapter 6. Suffice to say here that it provides a strong example of the way that, outside the safety of the domestic sphere, caregiving fathers can find that the significance of their gender – and the hegemonic expectations associated with it – can come once again to the fore, raising challenges to their developing caregiving roles, identities and horizons (Ranson, 2015; Locke and Yarwood, 2017).

Default maternal responsibility

It is important not to underplay the distance so many of the fathers had travelled towards interchangeable understandings and practices, or the significance of this as a challenge to traditional mother/father distinctions in their households. Neither were the areas of disparity identified in the previous section uniform across the sample: occasionally we did not see clear evidence of any of them and, even where one or more of them did apply, the extent of the difference between mother and father was varied. Yet repeated instances of women retaining a primary position with respect to key aspects of caregiving often highlighted within broader literatures, even in the midst of otherwise interchangeable identities and practices, warrants consideration. This is because it indicates how persistent some aspects of the doing and feeling of gender by parents can be. In part, we would suggest, the explanation lies with the particular rootedness of maternal pressures, expectations and practices, particularly with respect to co-ordination, community responsibility and associated mental work. Yet it is also important to identify barriers that may be making it difficult even for unusually involved fathers to reach equivalence with their partners in these areas.

Maternal pressures

It is likely mothers' retention of centrality with respect to care co-ordination sometimes reflected well-established pressures on working mothers to continue to understand themselves primarily in relation to their maternal role and to feel morally responsible for children's upbringing that are outlined in Chapter 2 (Hochschild, 1989; Doucet, 2009; Ranson, 2013; Miller, 2017). As Doucet points out, mothers often feel guilty returning to work because their gendered habitus has engendered internalised sets of embodied understandings that prompt them to feel 'pulled towards care' and the retention of primary caregiving responsibilities (also see Christopher, 2012). In particular, it is argued, mothers may continue to feel and discharge responsibility for mental and emotional aspects of caregiving – aligning with Ungerson's notion of 'caring about', Miller's '24/7 thinking' and Christopher's coining of the term 'extensive mothering' to describe retention of overall maternal control and emotional labour even where daily care-delivery is carried out by others (Ungerson, 2006; Christopher, 2012; Miller, 2017). And, as we also have outlined earlier in the book, such maternal pressures have escalated with the rise of intensive mothering, whose demand for hyper-involved caregiving is argued to have impacted more acutely on women than their partners (Hays, 1998; Shirani et al., 2012).

What our study indicates is that such pressures and feelings are sufficiently rooted that they can endure even in the unusual circumstance of fathers assuming care roles that are, in many respects, interchangeable with their partners. We have already seen in Chapter 4 that many of the fathers spoke of their partners' feelings of guilt, anxiety and regret when they relinquished their role and status as primary caregiver and it is equally clear – not least from the fathers' emphasis on interchangeability rather than role-reversal – that most mothers had remained substantially involved in caregiving in general as well as sometimes retaining primary burdens with respect to comfort, co-ordination and parental networks. It is unlikely to be coincidence, we would suggest, that aspects of care that connect to ongoing feelings of emotional and moral responsibility for mothering (Doucet 2006a) have come to the fore here. While there was ample evidence of how seriously the fathers were taking their responsibilities, of the pressures they felt and of the care, dedication and thought they put into their days at home, mothers in some examples were still doing a good deal of the ongoing thinking, worrying, planning and co-ordinating of parenthood, sometimes even when their partner was taking on the majority of practical care.

While pressures on women to retain an emphasis on their maternal selves and mother intensively can be attributed partly to the broader gendered habitus that surrounds pregnancy and early years care (Doucet, 2009), our study suggests they were also reinforced by the period of exclusive maternity leave that most of our participants' partners took on prior to the taking on of care-sharing by fathers. It is well-established that maternal dominance in the first period of babies' lives helps set in train enduring hegemonic parental roles (Doucet, 2009; Miller, 2011, 2017; Rehel, 2015). Our findings suggest it also was contributing to the endurance of specific areas of disparity within families that had subsequently adopted more equitable approaches. Several fathers spoke about how, by the time they had taken on equal or primary responsibilities, routines, emotional bonds and relationships with professionals and other parents (see also Chapter 6) had been firmly established, along with an overall sense of responsibility for care that lay with the baby's mother. The retention of particularly strong emotional bonds and responsibility for organising and co-ordinating in and outside of the home by mothers was thereby sometimes experienced by both partners as a somewhat inevitable continuation, in spite of the shift to more interchangeable or paternal-centred care delivery. As well as helping to avoid difficult transitions between maternity leave and shared caring arrangements (see Chapter 4), more equal involvement from caregiving fathers right from the beginning of babies' lives may make it easier for them to become interchangeable with respect to all rather than most responsibilities (Doucet, 2009; Maggararia, 2012; Ranson, 2013, 2015; Rehel, 2015).

Paternal barriers

As well as showing how particular maternal pressures, anxieties and burdens can endure, our evidence highlights barriers that appear to be discouraging some otherwise interchangeable fathers from reaching a sense of equivalence with their partners, particularly with respect to organisational and social aspects of parenting. The first of these emanates directly from the retention of such roles by their partners and the aforementioned pressures this reflects. Some of the fathers explicitly discussed how the rootedness of their partners' maternal identities had made it difficult for them to relinquish organisational tasks. Anthony, for example, described how his partner had continued, in spite of his protests, to organise aspects of his days at home caring when they became equal care sharers and how some aspects of this had endured:

> I think it took a while for [partner] to get used to the fact that she didn't have to do some things for me or for him, so for a while on my days for dropping him off at the nursery she would still lay out his clothes for the day and things like that, and I was saying, well you know you don't ... I'll do that, you know, that's part of my routine and I was quite sort of got into doing that ... there's still that residual, I think she still has that residual thought that there's some of those things that she should be doing because she's the mum, I think that's still her gut reaction or maybe her sort of heart's reaction rather than the logic of, well actually we both, you know, we both can select clothes for him and fix his lunch and put it in his wee rucksack and all that sort of stuff. (Anthony, equal care sharer)

The self-reinforcing impact of mothers' control of care responsibilities on fathers' level of involvement sometimes is understood through the notion of maternal gatekeeping (Fagan and Barnett, 2003; Puhlman and Pasley, 2013; see Chapter 2). This concept, though, implies a one-way controlling of access by mothers, rendering the role of fathers a largely passive one. In our research, the situation was often more complex. First, in these situations women clearly *had* relinquished much care time, responsibility and control to their partners, even if they sometimes had retained aspects of organisational and social control. Second, while maternal role retention may have dissuaded fathers from encroaching into particular areas, this seemed often to involve a two-way process whereby mothers retained control but where, in contrast to Anthony's protestations, fathers often seemed to willingly cede it (Miller, 2017).

Sometimes such ceding of control reflected the force of routine or habit, while on other occasions fathers justified deferring to their partners due to their perceived greater competence in the area in question. A further factor, though, was that the men often perceived anxieties and regrets on the part of their partners about having relinquished everyday care and this had made them keen to avoid monopolising responsibility themselves in order to ensure their partners had space to remain involved. Having not spoken directly to the fathers' partners, it is difficult to be certain as to the accuracy of these perceptions, though we have no particular reason to doubt them. What is clear, we would suggest, is that fathers' anxieties about this sometimes contributed to a concern to ensure that what they saw as their partner's needs, as regards caregiving, were not being undermined by the extent of their own involvement. As well as reducing the likelihood of some fathers challenging their partner's continued control of care co-ordination, this narrative of deferral to their partner's wishes sometimes positioned their partner in the role of *default* caregiver in a broader sense. Unlike some others, David's partner had had few doubts or regrets about him taking on the role of primary carer in their household when the possibility arose, but we were struck by how he outlined that, had she wanted greater involvement, her wishes on this would have taken precedence over his:

> It's a difficult thing for a lot of women to give up as well ...
> it's kind of interesting ... because it's [being primary carer]
> something I actually I wanted to do, [partner] wanted to
> go to work [but] we were like, well what if [partner] didn't
> want to go back to work and she wanted to do it, and
> I was like well 'you take precedence'. She was like 'why?'
> ... And it was interesting ... why would I take that kind
> of position, that kind of default position that if you want
> to do it, as a mother you should have first choice? (David,
> primary caregiver)

Although in this particular case there was little evidence of pressure on David to cede responsibilities to his partner, the extract illustrates how fathers can be prone to give precedence to the perceived wishes of mothers when it comes to caregiving. Rather than mothers 'blocking' fathers' access to care, then, we would suggest that mothers and fathers can mutually reinforce assumptions and practices with respect to what we might term 'default maternal responsibility', and this can be complex and dynamic. Of course, such assumptions also can be strengthened further by apparent evidence of greater motherly competence, or of a child's apparent preference for maternal comfort. At a broader level, they reflect not only the internalised pressures on women to retain caregiving responsibilities and identities (Doucet, 2009), but also the likely absence of such a pre-existing sense of default care responsibility in the gendered habitus of fathers. Rather than maternal gatekeeping, we would suggest it preferable to understand what was sometimes taking place as a collaborative reinforcement of default maternal-centrism, contributed to by both mother and father.

Such maternal-centrism – or 'matrifocality', as Catelain-Menunier (2002) calls it – also is reinforced externally, however, and sometimes in quite direct ways. Fathers' secondary position with respect to some organisational and social aspects of care related not only to the internal dynamics of their partnerships but also to barriers created by the ways people and institutions outside their families positioned and responded to them, foregrounding their gender and holding back aspects of their developing sense of themselves as interchangeable, gender-neutral parents (Ranson, 2015). Most notably, fathers sometimes felt bypassed or ignored in favour of their partners by a variety of early years professionals, from midwives, to doctors, to childcare professionals, and this sometimes influenced whether care responsibilities involving such professionals were embraced. Others commented on the absence of changing facilities in men's toilets, or the gendered presentation of parenting websites or parent and toddler events (see Chapter 6). Such instances might be regarded – alongside a range of other examples – as contributing to an institutionalisation of default maternal responsibility, whereby paternal access to certain organisations and spaces is rendered more difficult and maternal access easier through their gendered orientation. Fathers' particular reticence to engage with female-dominated parenting spaces, however, also reflected broader feelings of being out of place within 'public spaces not often well set up for fathers and babies' (Ranson, 2015: 176) and this particular set of barriers connects also to informal dynamics of gender and public space that we explore in Chapter 6.

Conclusion

In this chapter we have explored how the division of roles between the fathers and their partners had developed in their households since they took on their care-sharing arrangements and the ways they had come to see themselves as parents. We have outlined how the fathers had often become comfortable with an understanding of themselves as broadly interchangeable with and equivalent to their partners, emphasising how this contrasts with some existing studies of primary carer fathers that stress the endurance of more distinctly masculine parental identities. We also highlighted the range of caregiving roles the fathers were taking on, dwelling on the expedient and largely gender-neutral basis on which they understood and played out such roles. Contrasting with its more hegemonic use in discourses that justify traditional care roles, deployment of the notion of practical expediency in the context of the fathers' unusual circumstances formed a key facet of their understandings of themselves as interchangeable and a central driver of their approach to role-sharing. In centring our discussion on the notion of interchangeability, we draw upon Ranson's valuable earlier use of the concept to make sense of domestic situations in which roles are practically shared in a manner that challenges traditional notions of mother and father. However, unlike Ranson's emphasis on 'functional interchangeability', our use of the notion is concerned as much with how the fathers had come to see, feel and present themselves as with the playing out of roles in practice.

That fathers typically expressed such overall comfort with practicalities and identities they saw as interchangeable indicates, we suggest, that they were moving towards the development of 'caring masculinities' that replace traditional emphases on protection or provision with an orientation to interdependence, relationality and positive affectivity (Elliott, 2016). As such, in spite of sometimes having a different style of parenting from their partners, the men were 'undoing', through their unusual caregiving practices, significant facets of normal gendered parental performance in their households and were developing identities and care horizons centred on the notion of broad parental equivalence. Having often adopted their care-sharing arrangements only after a significant period of exclusive maternity leave, the turning point represented by their take-up of such roles had set the fathers on a journey in which their understandings of themselves as parents and their care horizons had, in many cases, been substantially transformed.

We have also identified certain substantive areas of enduring disparity between a number of the fathers and their partners with respect to emotional and organisational aspects of caregiving. While findings were inconsistent across the sample, the centrality of many mothers in one or more of the areas identified indicated the endurance of deep-rooted maternal pressures to be and feel ultimately responsible for care and the specific potential for such pressures to be concentrated by initial periods of exclusive maternity leave. We suggested, however, that a focus on barriers that prevent fathers from embracing full responsibility may be equally important. This includes the ways that mothers and fathers can, between them, collaboratively reinforce continued maternal dominance of some aspects of caregiving, but also how caregiving fathers are positioned by external organisations, professionals and others – institutionalising and reinforcing notions of default maternal responsibility. Also identified in existing work (Doucet, 2006a; Ranson,

2015), our study suggests that a distinction between the domestic and more public/social aspects of parenthood may help understand the challenges caregiving fathers can face and the ways interchangeability and, with it, fathers' developing care horizons, can be constrained, at least in some respects.

Notwithstanding such limitations, there remain grounds for cautious optimism in the interchangeable practices and identities outlined here, the ways they challenged established notions of mother and father and the apparent contentment of most of the fathers with the roles they described. Importantly, most of our sample did not begin their fatherhoods with largely interchangeable understandings of themselves as parents, making it justifiable, we think, to assign at least some of their embrace of such a notion to the impact of their engagement in the everyday practices of caring for children alone, including the skills they were developing, the memories they were creating and the increasingly strong affective bonds they were feeling (Ranson, 2015). Though gender had not been fully undone in their parenting and though sometimes maternal-centrism continued to loom in the background, distinct forms of caregiving masculinities, parenthoods and horizons were emerging.

6

Daytime Social Isolation
from Other Parents

Introduction

Interactions with other parents have long comprised a core part of the daily routine of many mothers who are primary caregivers for young children (Doucet, 2006a). Attendance at organised parent and infant events, children's activities and a range of more informal gatherings in parks, shopping centres, cafes and in one another's houses forms a key element of what Doucet (2006a) refers to as 'community responsibility' for the upbringing of children, while also offering crucial sources of company and support, not least in the first year of babies' lives (Mulcahy et al., 2010). Indeed, such activities and connections, argues Doucet, can form a key facet of contemporary mothering (Doucet, 2006a). As we have outlined in Chapter 2, however, research has suggested that fathers who care for children alone on weekdays may engage less with such spaces and networks and that, when they do, reactions to them can be less than positive (Doucet, 2006a; Merla, 2008; Snitker, 2018) – with potential implications for the extent of the parental responsibilities they are taking on, their own wellbeing and comfort within their role, and the prospects of longer-term commitment to it.

In the previous chapter, we argued that networking with other parents was one area in which differences between mothers and fathers continued to be played out among our sample of men who, in many other respects, had embraced interchangeable approaches to parenting. In this final empirical chapter, we examine the challenges fathers faced in these respects in greater detail, outlining how they often felt out of place within daytime spaces, their difficulties interacting with other parents, and the apparent isolation many were subject to on the days they cared for their children alone. Comparing our findings with existing literature (for example Doucet, 2006a; Ranson, 2010; Solomon, 2017), we explore the reasons why caregiving fathers tend to stay at home alone with their children and the implications for their own wellbeing and for the prospects of broader take-up by men of shared care arrangements. While fathers themselves commonly individualised the issue by putting their isolation down to their own introverted nature, our analysis suggests more collective and structural factors were at play. Although these partly related to intensive mothering pressures on women to take children to a variety of public events, they also involved specific barriers to fathers' participation in such spaces. We explore some of the anxieties and difficulties experienced by fathers within feminised daytime spaces, from shopping centres to playgrounds, and also organised group events such as playgroups and other parent and baby events. Fathers typically knew they would likely be the only man at such events and many recounted awkward experiences that had made them reticent about attending again. Experience of fathers' groups, meanwhile, tended to be little better, since such groups invariably were oriented to breadwinner fathers and held in the evenings or at weekends. Caught between feminised daytime spaces and traditionally masculine fathers' groups, the fathers frequently found themselves feeling out of place.

We examine the implications of these findings for some of the themes raised in previous chapters of the book, including their impact on the establishment of 'interchangeable' parental identities and the development of the men's fatherly care horizons – suggesting that, for many although not all of our fathers, while experiences within the home were largely positive, parenting outside the home and in daytime public spaces presented a particular challenge. We also touch on some practical steps that could be taken to lessen the social isolation experienced by many of our respondents.

'Just the two of us': Fathers' lack of contact with other parents

Not all the fathers in the sample were isolated from networks of other parents on the days they cared for their children. Robert and Stephen both described having attended playgroups and other activities targeted at parents and children, and appeared to have derived some benefit from such interactions. Robert, in describing his typical day, explained that 'We will often then go out somewhere, at around about kind of 9.30, 10 o'clock-ish, we'll head off to a stay-and-play [parent and baby group] or visit a relative or something' (Robert, equal care sharer). Similarly, Stephen had frequently attended a similar type of group with his daughter:

> You know morning coffee groups and stuff like that … you get a coffee and a biscuit, the kid gets a biscuit and they get to play with all these toys … So I do a few, I used to do a few of those, I'll be doing one on Friday because I've got my daughter and it's in the local church, not that we're religious, but my daughter enjoys it and has made friends there. (Stephen, equal care sharer)

Within the sample as a whole, however, Stephen and Robert's regular contact with other parents was unusual and most of the fathers, in contrast, noted that they made much less use of playgroups and other structured group activities than did their partner when she was in sole charge of the children. Jason, for example, commented, 'My partner was very good at it [taking part in organised activities such as playgroups], I'm not so much' (Jason, primary caregiver). Similarly, a large majority of the fathers reported that they had fewer social interactions in general with other parents than did their partner or other mothers. Thomas' comment was typical:

> My wife, my partner, she's often going to see other mothers like to, in town, to have a walk or have a coffee or … But myself, yeah, it's more, it's …. Yeah, no I don't, I don't meet people on those Fridays, it's just my son and I. (Thomas, equal care sharer)

Such fathers also indicated that, as well as attending fewer meet-ups with groups of other parents, they tended to have fewer individual interactions with other adults than their partners did or had done when they were on maternity leave. Although there were a few notable exceptions (such as Ed who described how he had one friend who was a stay-at-home dad and how it was very helpful to know at least one person who was going through the same experience), in general the fathers described relatively isolated days when they had little contact with other mothers or fathers. In the following quotation, for example, Michael describes how his partner had been able to meet up with various female friends who had children, because they had also been at home during the day, whereas his male friends who had children were typically at work and he had relatively few female friends to see:

> When she [partner] was off, she did it, she met up for play
> dates a lot more than me. I think it's, for me because ...
> I meet some of my [female] friends that have children, but
> on the whole it's [partner's] friends who are off, caring for
> their children, whereas my male friends are all at work,
> I haven't got any other male friends who are looking after
> their children. So it tends to be a little less [compared with]
> what [partner] used to do. (Michael, primary caregiver)

Scott also drew a clear distinction between the parental socialising
undertaken by his partner and him:

Scott: She [partner] also has sort of a group of friends
              that she sometimes meets up with and so I think
              for example today she's meeting up with them,
              whereas I don't have that kind of, that network ...
              I meet, so my sister works near me, so I sometimes
              meet her and some of my friends sometimes,
              because they're freelance some of them, I can just
              meet them for a tea or a coffee but they haven't
              got kids.

Interviewer: So you don't generally sort of go to things where
              other people have got kids and ...?

Scott: No, apart from like to the park or to the swings...,
              I might have a conversation with, usually a mother.
              (Scott, equal care sharer)

Although, unlike some, Scott did have some adult contact on the days
he was caring alone for their son, it was typically family members or
friends without children who were making time to see him during
their working day, rather than other parents – and contact with the
latter was limited to occasional pleasantries with others in the park.
The implication here is that his partner's network was, in contrast to his
own, comprised of other parents – thus providing a forum in which to
regularly discuss child-related issues and allow children to play together.

Indeed, it was striking that many of our interviewees (nearly three-
quarters) indicated they were spending the majority of the days when
they were in sole charge of their children either at home by themselves
or visiting local cafes or parks – again by themselves. John's description
of his day is typical: 'Mostly on my own together, on our own together,
yeah, the two of us' (John, equal care sharer). Here, our findings tend to
support other studies of fathers, conducted over the past decade and a

half and referred to in Chapter 2. Existing research in Canada by Doucet (2006b) and Ranson (2010), in Belgium by Merla (2008) and the US by Solomon (2017) indicates that many such fathers have less contact with other parents than do mothers and that, as a consequence, they sometimes can lead rather solitary week-day lives with little adult contact (also see Medved, 2016). Recent UK research on fathers on parental leave and grandfathers in parenting spaces has indicated a similarly isolating experience (Tarrant, 2016; O'Brien and Twamley, 2017).

Of course, relative social isolation during the day is experienced by some mothers, too. Miller (2005) notes that this is particularly the case for some very new mothers, who limit their presence in public space because of feelings of insecurity in their maternal identity. Moreover, Das (2019) has shown how mothers may avoid public spaces if they experience difficulties in the early weeks and months of their child's life, while other scholars have argued that mothers from some traditionally marginalised groups also find it more difficult to join baby groups and other forms of parent network (for example Wenham, 2016). Nevertheless, our data suggest that there is also an important and consistent gender dimension to the experiences of the fathers in our sample, evident in both the comparisons they drew between themselves and their partners, and some of the specific experiences they described. We explore this in more detail in the following section, as we consider some of the reasons for the fathers' lack of social interaction, beginning with the explanations proffered by the fathers themselves.

Explaining the relative absence of parental social interaction

Self-ascribed introversion

In their own explanations of their lack of contact with other parents, the fathers often focussed in their initial responses on their own personal characteristics or preferences. Indeed, a marked feature of the fathers' narratives was the frequency with which the words 'introvert' and/or 'unsociable' were used. Over half the sample used this kind of language in relation to discussions about their lack of contact with other parents; the following quotations are typical:

> I suppose partly I am, I'm something of an introvert, so I'm perfectly [happy on] ... my own, at my own time, you know this is seven weeks where there's relatively few people talking at me, which is nice. (Chris, parental leaver)

I'm not the most social person so ... especially if it was a group of people I don't know, I would be very out of place and uncomfortable with it, so I didn't really want to [go out]. (James, equal care sharer)

I felt, I did feel awkward [in the baby group] but it's hard for me to judge whether that is a normal feeling to have or not because I am quite a socially anxious person anyway. (John, equal care sharer)

It is, of course, possible that introverted individuals may have been over-represented in our sample. Alternatively, this language could also be taken to support some older sociological studies of gender and friendship, which maintained that men are less likely than women to form intimate relationships outside the family or to desire confiding and emotionally supportive friendships (Spencer and Pahl, 2006). Doucet (2006a) relates the lack of integration into parent networks evident in her sample of Canadian fathers to gender differences in the ways in which friendships are played out. Traditional notions of masculinity, she argues, discourage men from both discussing personal issues with one another and forming close friendships with members of the opposite sex. (We return to these points later in the chapter.)

While it seems plausible that such inhibitions may have played a role in some of the fathers' experiences, further analysis of our data suggests other factors may have been of greater importance. Beneath the veneer of comments about introversion and unsociability were others that indicated that many fathers would have valued social contact with other parents and/or had made attempts to initiate such contact. Indeed, some fathers spoke about the social isolation they sometimes felt when at home with their child, thus suggesting that this situation was not necessarily one that they would have chosen for themselves. Chris, for example, who had explained his lack of social interaction on the grounds that he was 'something of an introvert' and happy on his own, later went on to acknowledge that he did not always view his circumstances so positively:

The significant majority of the other parents who are arranging play dates for children of a similar age to my daughter are women. So ... I have experienced, I don't mean deliberate but I've experienced a certain amount of isolation. (Chris, parental leaver)

In other cases, this tension was expressed less directly. Timothy explained that he did not mix with other adults on the days when he cares for his son because of his dislike of socialising and his preference for what he viewed as more structured activities:

> Because I definitely do less group socialising than the stay-at-home mums that we know certainly in this area. [...] A lot of them use the group socialising as part of their day to day structure, so they always meet up with a group of their friends and kids on a day to day basis, whereas I don't … I think the socialising side of things … I think it's more to do with my personality and my coping mechanisms than it is to do with the fact that I'm a dad not a mum. … Because I work on such a structured day, the baby groups and socialising, by its nature isn't … Which I don't cope with as well! (Timothy, primary caregiver)

In other parts of the interview, however, he emphasised his enjoyment of socialising at the weekend, when he and his partner spent time with friends she had made while on maternity leave. He also described how he had felt able to attend a small playgroup in a village hall in the past, but that at some events he had tended to feel awkward as a result of difficulties integrating or feeling accepted by the mothers there because of his gender:

> I was going along, before nursery, I was going along every Tuesday to the one in the local village hall, and that wasn't too bad because it was quite a small group … The bigger groups, they do a soft play at the [name of centre] on Thursday, which we tend to go along to every now and again …
>
> You don't really get accepted into the mothers' circle in the corner, I always tend to find that I end up playing with my son and other people's kids in the soft play…. rather than sitting round in the circle with the mothers drinking tea … When I do sit down with them, you get funny looks and people are sort of a bit wary as to why you're there and … it … it doesn't really sort of work! (Timothy, primary caregiver)

This quotation suggests that while Timothy's introversion may have contributed in some way to his preference for caring alone for his son, this was not the whole story. He had clearly made attempts to attend events and converse with other parents but, with some exceptions, these had not worked out and this seemed to contribute to his becoming disillusioned. We develop some of the themes touched upon in Timothy's narrative in further detail later – namely the sense of feeling 'out of place' that many of the fathers experienced in groups dominated by mothers.

We can see a similar tension in Scott's account of his day-to-day activities. As with Timothy, he initially attributed his lack of engagement with organised groups to his unsociability, but then went on to talk about the envy he felt at the dense networks of mothers he had observed. He also described the considerable effort he went to on his days in sole charge of his children to find some sort of company – driving significant distances across the city in which he lived in order to meet family members:

> I think, I'm not, I'm not a very like … I don't often go up to strangers or go up to people and talk to them, I'm not very socially … well I'm not a very socially social person as it were, I'm quite insular, I always have been, I like my own space and those sorts of things.
>
> And you know, I did, I did make more of an effort as well to see like my mum or my gran, I'd sort of take him to … because they wanted to see him anyway, but I'd make more of an effort to go up sort of to [location across city] to see them, almost to have that kind of interaction as well. And I was sometimes a bit jealous when I saw like groups of mothers with their prams, all chatting to each other, and I was sort of solo with him and I did kind of think, maybe I should be a bit more sociable, maybe. (Scott, equal care sharer)

These apparent inconsistencies in the fathers' narratives suggest their practices are unlikely to be explained entirely by a positive decision to spend time alone with their child or general pre-existing inhibitions about social contact with others. In the sections that follow, we argue that a range of other social factors are also likely to have affected their practices. These include the potential absence of some of the pressures mothers may feel to socialise with other parents, but particularly relate, we suggest, to some specific gender-related barriers.

Differing needs and pressures

It is likely that at least some of the reported differences between the fathers and their female partners can be explained by, first, the particular needs of women on maternity leave and, second, the pressures to engage in 'intensive parenting' (Hays, 1998). In the first few weeks and months after a baby's birth, interaction with other parents going through similar experiences can be a very important source of support (Mulcahy et al., 2010). As we explained in Chapter 4, in our sample, it was primarily the mothers who had assumed the role of primary caregiver in this early phase of the child's life. This may have contributed to the bonds they formed with other parents (typically mothers who were also on maternity leave) being closer and stronger than those forged subsequently by their partners. They may have had a greater need of support at this particular point – because of the challenges of taking on a new role as parent – than in later stages of parenthood. As described in previous chapters, most of the fathers had not taken extended parental leave; the majority had assumed their role as primary or equal care sharer only after their partner had completed a significant period of maternity leave. In spite of the challenges of their transitions into their care roles (see Chapter 4), they were already accustomed to parenthood in a broader sense and, in most cases, had taken on part-time rather than full-time care roles and were working for part of the week. As a result, it is possible that they may have had a less urgent drive to find daytime support and company than their partners had done immediately after their child's birth.

In addition, women may experience pressure to become involved in organised baby- or toddler-related groups or activities because they feel a strong expectation that this is a socially prescribed aspect of 'good mothering'. Brian alludes to this, in relation to his partner's experience of maternity leave:

> You could also equally say there is perhaps a sense of obligation that comes with that time off [maternity leave], a sense in which, well … what's the point in me being off if I'm not putting things in place … and structures and networks in place for the benefit of my child … And sometimes that's a sort of probably an unnecessary pressure … but I think it is there and probably unavoidable. So I think … there is an awful lot of well-intentioned emphasis during pregnancy on the need to find other mums with, who you know have children of a similar age. (Brian, equal care sharer)

This 'obligation', articulated with respect to his partner, to embed their child in stimulating social networks and activities, relates to the prescriptions of intensive mothering. As well as emphasising the time and commitment that should be devoted to bringing up one's child, it is also often understood to include a pressure to attend various activities and organised groups – to develop specific skills and interests, as well as boosting intelligence through stimulating new experiences (Thomson et al., 2011). Although some of our data suggest that fathers, too, can experience the pressures related to intensive parenting (see discussion in Chapter 4), comments such as Brian's earlier offer support for the notion that there remain differences in how susceptible mothers and fathers are to such pressures. Here, then, there may be some comparability with the fathers in Shirani et al.'s (2012) research, who typically felt more able than their partners to resist pressures to follow expert advice and avoid at least some of the prescriptions of intensive parenting. While it is difficult to be certain, we think, following on from our discussions in Chapter 5 about maternal pressures and moral responsibility, that it is possible some of the fathers may have experienced less acute obligations than their partners to seek out and attend organised activities.

Nevertheless, what came through even more strongly in our data was that most of the men we spoke to had experienced particular gender-related barriers that had dissuaded them from participating in daytime parental spaces. Specifically, our evidence suggests that, whether or not their needs or pressures to participate were as great as those of their partners, many of the fathers would have liked to spend more time in daytime spaces and activities with other parents had they had access to environments in which they felt comfortable as men caring for young children. We discuss the barriers that seemed to prevent this in the subsequent section.

Barriers experienced by fathers

Feeling 'out of place' in parenting-related daytime spaces

There is a large literature on the ways in which, historically, women have been excluded from public space. Indeed, women who have conspicuously occupied streets or other public arenas have often been seen as unnatural or unsexed (McDowell and Sharp, 1997), and continue to experience harassment and other forms of abuse in such places (Bastomski and Smith, 2017). Nevertheless, despite the significant evidence of the enduring masculine nature of much public space, many of the fathers in our sample articulated clear feelings of being 'out of place' that they experienced within some daytime public spaces. While this sometimes could connect to certain negative reactions or judgements from others (as we explore in the next section), it also related to broader aspects of the environments in which they found themselves and the way these could make them feel. Specifically, this related to: the sense of visible difference they felt (often being the only man in a particular space); a perception that they were intruding on women-only spaces and conversations; and the naming and presentation of some particular parental groups and activities.

Feeling 'out of place' was articulated particularly clearly with respect to organised activities such as baby groups. Although we noted earlier that Stephen was one of the few fathers in the sample who had attended parent and baby groups on a regular basis, even he had not always enjoyed these experiences. Indeed, he described being the only father at child-focussed activities and groups as 'demoralising', and specifically recounted the difficulty of joining in conversations with the mothers who were there:

> I know most of them [mothers in the group] but it is very much a three line conversation ... you don't go much beyond that, whereas they can talk about ... [problems] they had with their birth or you know all that; they're not going to have that conversation with me. (Stephen, equal care sharer)

There was no criticism of these mothers in Stephen's account, just a sense that he had relatively few points of connection with them, and that the conversations they wanted to have with each other often related to their identity as *mothers* specifically, rather than parents in general. To some extent this feeling of being out of place was exacerbated by the long-standing nature of many such groups. As noted earlier, many groups are founded when women are on maternity leave. Entering such well-established groups at a later point can be difficult for men, as Patrick and Kevin explained:

> And I do, you know, the mums tend to know each other a little bit more from all the ... antenatal groups, so they all continue moving through together and all stuff like that and ... whereas I'm sort of maybe a bit more of an outsider. (Patrick, primary caregiver)

> In the first three or four months I tried quite hard to meet a few other people through baby groups and bits and pieces.

But …. a lot of mums tend to be in groups already. (Kevin, primary caregiver)

This sense of being 'out of place' was also reinforced by the names of some of the organised groups, which were taken by some to suggest they were not for fathers at all. Jeremy, for example, explained that he felt unable to go to groups with 'mummy' or 'mother' in the title, noting that while 'quite often those things will have, "Oh but everybody's welcome" … it's like, well you've called it something that's … not inclusive of me' (Jeremy, equal care sharer). Here, there are clear commonalities with the experiences documented in Ranson's (2010) study of caregiving fathers: a significant minority of her respondents did make use of baby groups – something revealingly described by one as 'breaking cover' – but they typically commented on the 'gender barrier' within such environments and awkwardness of being the only man. Similarly, although there was diversity among her primary caregiver fathers, Doucet (2006a) argues that 'community engagement' overall was considerably lower than for mothers, and frequently characterised by gendered awkwardness:

> [E]very stay-at-home father described an uncomfortable or downright painful experience in playgroups or, more generally, in the parenting community. Some fathers glanced into the windows of the culture and quickly made the decision to avoid mother-dominated settings; they cited lack of time, fears that their child would catch a cold or flu, or the kids' schedules. Sometimes these reasons seemed justified. Other times it was clear that they are just avoiding one of the most female-dominated areas of early parenthood. (139)

As noted earlier, as well as feeling uncomfortable within organised groups or events, fathers in our research sometimes also discussed feeling out of place with respect to daytime public spaces more generally. Again, this was often related to what they believed to be the visible difference between them as men with small children and the vast majority of other people they saw during their day-to-day encounters. Brian and Michael, for example, both spoke of how being the only father within environments dominated by women and children had prompted intense feelings of self-consciousness when out and about with their child. Robert, referred to earlier in relation to his (unusual) regular attendance of playgroups, indicated how such feelings sometimes could be unwittingly exacerbated by event organisers:

I don't know if I'd call it a difficulty but there is an annoying tendency for people to assume that everyone in the room is a woman, and so they'll say things like, and now all the mums do X … I have found that sometimes, if they're going around dropping off a leaflet, talking about the next, you know a future event, they'll hand it to the woman sat next to me, on the assumption that she must be my wife. And I have to go, yeah, can I have one of those too? (Robert, equal care sharer)

As alluded to earlier, it is important to recognise that the fathers in our sample may not be alone in feeling marginalised within daytime parenting spaces. Studies suggest that mothers too sometimes can feel awkward or ostracised within such spaces (Thomson et al., 2011), particularly those from working class or minority groups (Mulcahy et al., 2010). Nevertheless, the narratives of these fathers indicate their difficulties related specifically to their gendered status as men 'out of place'. As such, our research suggests that some public daytime spaces can be experienced as gendered and that men can sometimes feel, as Doucet puts it, like 'a threat to *estrogen-filled worlds*' (2006b: 74, italics in original). On weekdays, places such as shopping centres, schools, parks, swimming pools and playgroups are often highly female-dominated, while the topics of conversation favoured by mothers of small children may not necessarily be ones fathers feel comfortable with (Merla, 2008; Medved, 2016). Moreover, images used in health and social care spaces can also focus primarily on mothers (see Wolf, 2007; Jupp, 2013). Given that friendship is typically understood as a relationship based on perceptions of similarity (Spencer and Pahl, 2006), it may be unsurprising that – given the way in which many fathers felt so out of place within these spaces – relationships with other parents were hard to establish.

Fear of being judged

The potentially isolating impact of this sense of being 'out of place' was exacerbated, in some cases, by specific feelings of being judged, which were sometimes based on awkward previous experiences. Some fathers spoke about gendered judgements about their not being in full-time employment; their level of competence at caring for their children; and/or their motivations for wanting to be a primary or equal care sharer. These were made both in relation to some of the groups the fathers had attended (or which they had at least thought about attending) and daytime public spaces more generally. The following quotations are illustrative:

> People react differently because you're a dad doing things. Even things as simple as you're in a shop, you know, you're doing the shopping … And the amount of weird looks you get you know if you're, because you're the dad doing this thing … it's like "Why is there a dad doing things on a Fri … not in work on a Friday?"-type things. (Andrew, equal care sharer)

> The very minority of men have done some horrible stuff and I think people are worried that it's going to happen to their child, and if they see a man with a child, I think, or a man in a setting where there are a lot of children, I think sometimes you feel a bit … sometimes I feel that on me. (Michael, primary caregiver)

Brian was explicit about how his perception of such judgements encouraged him to avoid public spaces for much of the time and stay at home with his daughter:

> Society, no matter how much things change, still has a kind of in-built assumption that … a mother has a natural instinct for [childcare] and a dad doesn't … I don't think it's necessarily that I think people would be harshly judging, just that they would be observing, possibly even pitying in some respects … that's almost worse if somebody … 'The poor sod, he can't, you know, oh look mum's left him with the kid for the day and he doesn't know how to push the buggy round, you know, the wheels keep locking up.' And I don't want that almost as much as being harshly judged, I'd rather just not be judged at all, I'd rather it goes back to the, if I'm in my home environment … I really don't give a damn because it's my world. (Brian, equal care sharer)

All of the judgements or perceived judgements described by the fathers – in the extracts we have provided in this chapter and other interview data – centre on the notion of their deviation from traditional understandings of masculinity, particularly with respect to employment and childcare. Indeed, there is evidence here to support Shirani et al.'s (2012) contention that there continues to be a strong, if often implicit, gendered morality around parenting. Extending existing work (Doucet and Merla, 2007; Merla, 2008; Medved, 2016), our study highlights the nature and strength of fathers' feelings of being judged and gazed at with suspicion within public spaces, and the impact of such feelings on their fathering practices. It is striking that, while in many respects these fathers had become comfortable with their non-traditional role as primary or equal carers within their family and home environment, they felt markedly different with respect to how they were seen by others in public space. This is significant for development of the men's fatherly care horizons, as we explore later. The discussion in this chapter has also built on some of the points we made in Chapter 5 to suggest that it is not just the judgements and interactions of early years professionals that can serve to limit parental interchangeability but, in some cases, those of other parents and the broader cross-section of people encountered in daytime public settings.

Difficulty of meeting other caregiving fathers

Difficulties engaging with groups of mothers and daytime spaces sometimes had prompted some fathers to seek out other dads with whom they could spend time on their days at home but success, in this respect, had been minimal. A small number of our respondents had been able to connect with other fathers through the use of online support groups on social media platforms. Jason was particularly positive about the benefits of engaging with other fathers through internet fora, including a sense that conversations sometimes could be less 'awkward' online than traditional male social environments:

> [It] is a really good resource actually, just because you can turn around and get it from other dads. You don't need to know them or anything, and the whole point of it is that you seek advice and you can just turn around and put up a post and then you get it, I mean you don't have to go seek this out down the pub or with your mates or anything because sometimes that can be a bit awkward, it's just really good to be able to do that with dads. (Jason, equal care sharer)

The positive nature of such experiences suggests that increasing awareness of such online sources of company and support could be of significant value to caregiving fathers (see Das and Hodkinson, 2019a). Such spaces have the potential to enable them to connect with other men in similar situations, share experiences and discuss difficulties in a supportive environment. Nevertheless, unless they are connected to offline groups or events, they are liable to offer a different form of connection from face-to-face encounters, with the latter providing a chance for dads to spend time in one another's company while caring for their children and enable children themselves to have the chance to play with one another too.

Consistent with this, many of our respondents implied that they would be interested in meeting up with other caregiving fathers to socialise with during the day, but few had succeeded in doing so. 'Dads' groups' were rarely considered to be an effective solution to respondents' difficulties with female-dominated spaces because, in their understanding, such groups tended to be oriented towards breadwinner fathers, and also − some of our respondents claimed − helped to reinforce the notion that broader 'parents' groups' were primarily for mothers. In contrast to some previous studies that emphasise the need for traditionally masculine company as a form of gender compensation for involved fathers (Doucet 2004, 2006a), several of our respondents felt reluctant to attend dads' groups precisely because of the traditional male paternal identities they were believed to represent. Robert, for example, was deterred from going along to his local dads' group because of his belief that the conversation would focus only on traditional male pursuits, and that his 'unconventional' masculinity, centred on bringing up his children as an equal care sharer, would feel out of place. Timothy, meanwhile, described two dads' groups in his local area that he felt may have provided a valuable point of contact for 'breadwinner dads' but did little to bring together dads who sought contact during weekdays while caring for their children:

> I contacted the local childcare centre to find out if there were any dads' groups for contact with other fathers as it were, and unfortunately they only have two ... dads' meetings a week, one of which was a Tuesday, and that's in the local pub at half past five in the evening .... which is for the dads ... when they've got home from work and they've had half an hour with their kids and they want to get out the house, they can go to the dads' group ... The other dads' meeting was on a Saturday afternoon ... and it's a chance for dads to take their kids along to give the mothers a break. (Timothy, primary caregiver)

A similar point was made by David, who was interested in attending a dads' group, but on weekdays when he was in sole charge of his son, not at the weekend, and was critical of the message he felt that the weekend-only nature of fathers groups sent out about normative father behaviour:

> [At the local library] they do [have a dads' group], it's called Dads' Boogie or something. But it's on a Saturday morning. ... It's like I'm not bringing him on a Saturday morning, that's the time when [partner] is about! So there's kind of an implicit message there that, you know, Dads' Boogie's on Saturday because dad's at work during the week. (David, primary caregiver)

The perceived hegemonic orientation of some fathers' groups – in terms of their timing and perceived orientation – had made them seem unsuitable for the particular needs of some caregiving fathers, then. Like the Belgian stay-at-home dads examined by Merla (2008) over a decade ago, fathers in our study sometimes had found themselves caught between female-dominated daytime parenting spaces on the one hand and masculine or breadwinner-oriented dads' groups on the other. For different reasons, neither were ideally suited to their needs and both had the potential to make them feel out of place.

Implications for fathers and wider society

Although, as we have noted, the relative social isolation of caregiving fathers has been discussed in previous studies, such research has tended to be broadly positive about prospects for change. Indeed, as well as identifying a substantial minority of men in her study who had successfully integrated into parent networks (something also true of Ranson's (2010) study), Doucet (2006a) signals an optimistic note about the future, suggesting that men are becoming more accepted in parents' groups and finding it easier to establish friendships with mothers. Moreover, recent research on US stay-at-home fathers by Solomon (2017) identifies a mixture of positive and more marginalising experiences in daytime parenting spaces. Nevertheless, the extent of the lack of engagement with parent networks across our sample of British caregiving fathers suggests that, some years after its exploration in earlier work, it remains a significant issue. Whereas, in Doucet's research (2006a), over a quarter of fathers had been successful in establishing parent networks, in ours, difficulties with parent networks or daytime public spaces, though not universal, were consistently cited across most of the sample. Doucet's main examples of successfully networked fathers, meanwhile, were fathers of older children – who had become involved in school associations or sports activities. This may underline early years parenting as an especially isolating period for fathers caring alone during the week. It is also noteworthy that the experiences of our fathers seemed similar irrespective of whether they were primary or equal care sharers, even if the overall impact has the potential to be greater for the former due to their greater concentration of time at home caring. In this part of the chapter, we draw on the evidence we have presented earlier to explore the implications of fathers' relative isolation from parent networks and other forms of daytime sociability for: their wellbeing; our understandings of sociality and friendship; the gendering of public space and the development of fatherly care horizons; and conceptualisations of the 'ideal worker'.

Fathers' wellbeing

As well as affecting the extent to which they were taking on parental 'community responsibility' (Doucet, 2006a) in the way mothers often do, the apparent social isolation of the fathers in our study from parent networks during the days they had sole charge of their children raises questions about their wellbeing. Recent scholarship has highlighted the potential for fathers, as well as mothers, to suffer from depression, anxiety and other forms of mental ill-health in the post-natal period – but also the difficulty, for many fathers, of acknowledging such problems during a period when they feel they should be providing support to their partner (Das and Hodkinson, 2019a). While most of the fathers in our sample reported being broadly content with their caregiving arrangements, some recognised possible negative consequences of spending so much time alone with their child. For example, Jason commented 'I wish I didn't do as much of it on my own, so I do try and make myself go out' (Jason, primary caregiver) – largely for the benefit of his daughter, while Kevin (also a primary caregiver) explained that he was keen for his daughter to attend some sessions at the local nursery so that she had the opportunity to interact with other children.

However, while most of these concerns were framed in relation to *children's* wellbeing, it is likely that fathers themselves may also have suffered as result of their prolonged periods of social isolation, particularly in the case of those spending substantial proportions of the week in sole charge of their children. Such isolation was discussed explicitly by some of our respondents, including Chris whom we cited earlier in the chapter. In addition, Scott was aware that on his days caring alone he had been desperate for adult conversation such that when his partner came home 'I'd be like chat, chat, chat, chat. ... She'd be like, I'm tired, what are you talking about?' (Chris, equal care sharer). He also spoke of the regret he felt at not making friends through attending a parents' group like his partner had done when she was on maternity leave. John also saw disadvantages in not being more engaged within parent networks, and hoped that this would become easier as his son grew older:

> So I would like to be able to do more things and it will get easier as he becomes older, not only because he'll be at school but also there are things that, you know I've got a friend of mine takes his daughter to, I think it's called Diddy Kicks, so it's like you know toddlers playing football. (John, equal care sharer)

In this extract, the two parent networks John mentions – that associated with the school and a football group – can be seen as less stereotypically 'feminine' in their orientation than many he had encountered by the time of the interview. There were also various other fathers in our sample who indicated that they had had periods when they were anxious or struggling with the pressures of caring for their child. Ed, for example, noted that while, overall, he had enjoyed caring for his child, '[it] isn't to say that it hasn't been tough because it's been really, it has been really, really tough but ... and mentally you know I've found it really challenging' (Ed, primary caregiver). While Ed did not explicitly link this type of experience to his relative lack of integration in parental networks, it is likely that company and sharing concerns with others in similar situations may help to ameliorate them (Das and Hodkinson, 2019b). Indeed, Stephen – one of the few fathers in the sample who appeared to have established connections with other parents during his caregiving days – emphasised the practical support such relationships could offer and, sometimes, the associated reduction in stress levels:

> On Monday we went and I looked after, my daughter was playing with this other lady's daughter, so she took her son and I took my son and they were playing, so we just swapped it between us while they were playing, made life easier because the other one wasn't running off .... Yeah, there's a lot of teaming goes on. (Stephen, equal care sharer)

Meanwhile, the importance of just getting out of the house was also highlighted by James:

> We can't just sit at home all the time, it would not be good for either of us .... It does make the day go quicker as well, to be honest, if we're stuck at home on a really bad weather day for instance, if we're literally stuck inside, it drags. (James, equal care sharer)

While, on the face of it, such a task can seem straightforward, it is clear from the evidence presented in this chapter that it is one that can clearly be made significantly more difficult if you feel out of place or are afraid of being judged outside the house as a result of gender differences.

While some previous research has noted that fathers parenting alone can feel isolated and lonely (Brandth and Kvande, 2018), other studies have emphasised, instead, associations between the primary care of an infant and subjective happiness (O'Brien et al., 2017). Without disputing this, our research is significant in reiterating that – alongside many positive benefits to fathers and their families – primary or equal paternal care still has the potential to be associated with particular forms of isolation.

Sociability and friendship

As we have discussed earlier, the reasons for the fathers' comparative lack of engagement with parent networks were complex. It remains possible that, collectively, fathers' desire for parental company may be less acute than, for example, that of mothers in the initial post-partum period. They may also sometimes feel less pressure than mothers when it comes to intensive parenting and associated drives to facilitate their children's participation in public activities. Nevertheless, we outlined how our respondents tended initially to explain that they were unsociable and/or introverted but that such explanations appeared not to tell the full story. This initial recourse to individualistic explanations, we argue, can be seen as an example of what Furlong and Cartmel (2007) have called the 'epistemological fallacy': the impact of social structures, such as class and gender becomes 'increasingly obscure as collectivist traditions weaken and individualist values intensify' (2–3). People, then, come to understand the world as negotiable primarily on individualised terms. Such explanations may also in some cases be understood as 'face-saving' strategies, however. Playing down one's desire for social connection may be preferable to a discourse centred on social endeavours that might be construed as unsuccessful.

The narratives of our fathers also speak to wider debates about friendship in contemporary society. Indeed, as we alluded to previously, one of the explanations offered in the literature, to explain fathers' relative social isolation, focuses on the way in which friendship practices more generally are differentiated by gender. Doucet (2006a), for example, while recognising, empirically, the ostracism fathers sometimes face in spaces dominated by mothers (see also Doucet, 2006b), relates the bulk of her conceptual argument in this area to masculine inhibitions regarding gender and friendships. She writes:

> The majority of fathers in my study comment that the friendship and connection necessitated by the daily work of care are often beyond what they have known from their own experiences, having grown up as boys, engaging in traditional male friendships or believing that men and women simply form friendships differently. (2006a: 151)

Moreover, she argues that the enduring dominance of hegemonic masculinity makes it difficult for stay-at-home dads to make friends with one another – because of the assumption that talking about child-rearing is not an appropriate topic of conversation – or with mothers – because of concerns that such friendships will be viewed with suspicion by spouses and others.

In our study, there were some examples of fathers articulating what they believed to be gender differences in the ways in which friendship is practised and/or the focus of friend interactions. Timothy, for example, thought that a lot of parent and baby groups were 'based around sharing to cope'. He went on to say that he was not sure whether his own reluctance to participate was 'because I'm not much of a sharer' or 'because men [in general] aren't sharers' (Timothy, primary caregiver). Andrew also drew distinctions between how male and female friendships were practised, when explaining why few men attended parent groups:

> I think it might be male conversation as well, because male conversation isn't about … bottom wiping and feeding, you know, it isn't about the job stuff, it's just one … one of the things I have noticed is you don't get men together talking about issues with nappies, issues with this sort of stuff, issues with toilet training, that sort of thing, you get

men talking together about politics or football or those sort of things. (Andrew, equal care sharer)

Nevertheless, much of the data we have presented in earlier parts of this chapter indicates that the difficulties experienced by the fathers in our sample were attributable less to gender differences in approaches to friend-making per se, and more to the particular ways they had felt out of place and subject to the judgement of others within parent networks or daytime spaces through established gendered structures and circumstances.

Notwithstanding masculine approaches to friendships, then, our discussion has focussed primarily on these other factors. Fathers' awareness of how their caregiving activities jarred with hegemonic masculinity and how this could lead to awkwardness or marginalisation pervaded this discussion. While this appeared to be unproblematic in the home and even with work colleagues (with one or two exceptions), it was brought into sharp relief in public settings. Indeed, many respondents avoided baby groups and other organised activities – and, sometimes, engaging in public space more generally – because of feeling out of place within feminised daytime spaces and a specific fear of being judged on the basis of their transgressions of traditional notions of masculinity and fatherhood. Moreover, the reluctance of some to participate in what they regarded as traditional, breadwinner-oriented dads' groups also reflected concerns about their positioning vis-à-vis hegemonic masculinity. In contrast to Doucet's (2006a) research, there was little indication that the majority of our respondents avoided such groups because of a fear of establishing an emotional connection with other men or an awkwardness discussing their role as parents with other fathers. On the contrary, many would have welcomed male contact that centred on their non-traditional role as equal or primary caregivers for their children (connecting perhaps with the positive experiences of men who attended the 'dads-only' parenting programme reported by Dolan (2014) and community groups for young fathers (Hanna, 2018)). In addition to all this, however, we have suggested the way in which parental leave is structured may have had a significant impact. Maternity leave (and also ante- and post-natal groups attended by women) had, in many cases, facilitated the construction of close networks of mothers, which were hard for fathers to engage with at the later point at which they 'took over' some or most daily caregiving from their partner (typically when she returned to work after maternity leave). Most of our fathers had taken on a primary or equal caring role several months after their child had been born, once social networks among mothers of similar-aged children were already well-established.

As noted previously, sociological studies have traditionally recognised differences between the friendships of men and those of women, and explained these in terms of the different social spaces they occupy (Allan, 1996). For example, writing over 30 years ago, Gillespie et al. (1985) argued that men typically had a larger number of friends than women, because of the greater opportunities for friend-making through work, whereas women's interactions were more limited, because they were tied to the home. More recent studies, however, have suggested that these gender differences have become less marked as men and women's lives have become more similar. In particular, it is argued that women's increasing involvement in the labour market has brought about significant positive change to their networks in this sphere (Pahl, 2000; Spencer and Pahl, 2006). Our research indicates, however, that the movement of men into the traditionally female spaces of care (albeit on a much smaller scale) has not wrought similar change with respect to social networks connected to parenting. Indeed, the evidence we have outlined throughout this chapter has suggested that it has, in contrast, been associated with the maintenance of strikingly gender-distinct patterns of social interaction.

Gender, public space and circumscribed care horizons

The dads' narratives discussed in this chapter also articulate with broader debates about the intersections of gender and public space and their impact on fatherly identities and care horizons. As noted earlier, there is a substantial literature that documents how women have been excluded from public space by, for example, the ways in which towns and cities have been planned, the association between public space and employment, and fear of sexual harassment and other types of uncivil behaviour (for example Bastomski and Smith, 2017). Nevertheless, our data demonstrate that the relationship between gender and public space is complex, and that, in some circumstances, men can experience spatial exclusion. Many of the fathers whom we interviewed spoke of their unease at being 'out and about' when caring for their child or children in spaces they experienced as female-dominated. The fathers' descriptions of these spaces reflect what Boterman and Bridge (2014) observed in their comparative study of parenting spaces in London and Amsterdam (discussed in Chapter 2). In relation to the former, they note that 'certain neighbourhood spaces are strongly feminised and associated with young motherhood in highly visible ways' (257).

Similarly, Doucet maintains that involved fathers in her study were wary of 'worlds populated mainly by mothers and mothering networks which sometimes cast suspicious scrutiny on male participants' (2006b: 704).

Moreover, the narratives of the fathers in our research suggest a temporal dimension to such processes of exclusion: it was typically during the working day that they felt 'out of place' in certain public spaces – particularly those associated with leisure and parenting. McDowell (1999) has argued that a specific space may, over the course of a particular period of time (potentially as short as a day), 'be occupied by a series of social groups whose practices imbue the same spaces with different meanings at different times' (168). On the basis of our data, we do not, of course, claim that fathers are excluded as a matter of course from daytime public space; rather, that within particular parenting-centred spaces during the working day men caring alone for young children can sometimes feel out of place.

The reasons provided by the fathers for feeling this way were based, as we have documented earlier, on their sense of difference from the women who frequented many of the baby groups and leisure spaces they had visited, but also the comments made by others about their 'out-of-place' position, and their own fears (even if never realised) that they would be seen in this way. Here, in the unusual context of a sample of fathers caring for young children during the day, we can see an example of the operation of gender in particular spaces and times that seems to complicate the traditional binary association of masculinity with public space and femininity with private space. In this respect, we build on existing work that highlights nuances and changes in the gendering of space (Spain, 2014). Thus, while in many spaces and times it remains difficult for women to occupy public space with the same ease as men, the case of fathers who have taken on the traditionally feminine role of caregiver provides an example where such patterns had been reversed – albeit in specific spaces (such as parents' groups, shops, parks and swimming pools) and at specific times (during the working day).

Presence and visibility within such spaces is important, not just for the social integration and wellbeing of fathers themselves, but also for *bringing about* social change. As Evans (2016) has argued, public 'exposure' of non-traditional patterns is important in affecting change to dominant practices. Evans contends, for example, that flexibility in the gender division of labour has tended to foster, rather than follow, changes in gender ideologies. In our research, the relative invisibility of our respondents within parenting networks and spaces may suggest that the significant challenges their practices were making to traditional divisions of labour may have had less effect in changing the attitudes and practices of others than if they felt more comfortable in public spaces and integrated in parent networks. For the same reason, their invisibility may have reinforced the isolation of other fathers in a similar position. Clearly, however, there are important interdependencies here; a key reason why the fathers tended to avoid such 'exposure' was, at least in part, precisely because of what they perceived to be the traditional and judgemental attitudes of others.

Relatedly, the fathers' feelings of being 'out of place' in such spaces highlight some of the limits to the development of fatherly care horizons centred on interchangeability or equivalence with their partners. Although nearly all of our sample had successfully taken on new ways of thinking about paternal roles and embraced the opportunity to spend more time caring for their young children (see Chapter 5), the evidence presented in this chapter shows that they were not equally comfortable with their role in all social situations. While nearly all enthused about the positive implications for their family and them personally, this was often held in tension with a more ambivalent view about their positioning outside the home and family unit. Moreover, while as we demonstrated in Chapter 5, most fathers saw themselves as, in many respects, interchangeable with their partner, many were conscious of the stark differences evident with respect to their social interactions with other parents and, for some, their movement through public space. Although rarely expressed by our respondents in these terms, it seems likely that this disjuncture – between their comfort at taking on non-traditional roles in the home and their greater discomfort at performing the same role in daytime public settings – has a bearing on the nature of the fathers' developing care horizons and perhaps also their identity as primary or equal caregivers. The fathers' narratives, which emphasised their awareness of difference from their partner in this respect, and a belief that their caregiving role was not always fully accepted by others, suggests that, despite the broader sense of parental equivalence they alluded to in their domestic life, they were aware of the limits to their 'interchangeability' and the impediments to developing longer-term identities and horizons consistent with care-sharing. In their public encounters, gender came strongly back into play, often reinforcing stereotypes and seemingly making it difficult for fathers to carry out their caregiving in an unselfconscious manner. While the non-traditional role taken on by the fathers was largely validated within their home and, in most cases, by wider family and colleagues, the lack of affirmation evident in public space may have left them in a form of 'no-man's land' outside the home – in which the new identities they had taken on often did not feel fully recognised or accepted. This seems significant and potentially damaging for fathers taking on sole care for even only one day a week, as well as their peers who are caregiving alone for considerably longer periods of time.

'Ideal workers' and hegemonic masculinity

The experiences of the fathers outlined in the data we have presented so far clearly relate to enduring norms about gender roles and, in particular, expectations – and *perceived* expectations – that men will typically be at work during the day, rather than present in leisure-related public spaces. Here, there are strong links to the concept of the 'ideal worker' discussed in some detail in Chapter 3, and alluded to more generally in Chapter 2. Ideal workers are assumed to prioritise commitments to the workplace over those to the home, and be happy to devote long hours to their employment, when necessary. Moreover, an equivalence is often assumed between masculinity and ideal worker norms. As the narratives of the fathers in our study indicate, apparent rejection of the 'ideal worker' frame can be interpreted by others as also a rejection of masculinity. Nevertheless, evidence from other countries suggests that where such expectations about ideal workers are brought into question – for example, through policies that incentivise the uptake of paternal leave and/or encourage more egalitarian parenting practices – men's experiences within public space are rather different. Indeed, Boterman and Bridge (2014) have argued that in Amsterdam, where it is almost as common to see children being looked after on weekdays by their fathers as their mothers, highly feminised social spaces such as cafes are much less common than in London. Similarly, in her study of parenting practices in Helsinki, Lilius (2017) reports that 'latte dads' (that is fathers who spend time in coffee shops, when looking after their children) are as common a phenomenon as 'latte mums', and that there is no great difference in the spatiality of mothering and fathering. (It should be noted, however, that her sample was comprised entirely of highly educated men and women.) In both cases, parental leave policies have been held at least partially responsible for these changes in fathers' behaviour and wider societal attitudes (see discussion of such policies in Chapter 3).

Conclusion

Building on the discussion in Chapter 5 about how differences in parental networking can be seen as an important limitation to the concept of parental interchangeability, this chapter has focussed in more detail on the social interactions of our interviewees with other parents and their experiences of daytime public spaces. We have shown how, in spite of usually feeling positive overall about their experiences, many of the men in the sample had relatively little contact with other parents during the time they were caring for their child/children alone and some felt uncomfortable outside their homes when caring on weekdays. Although many explained their preference for spending time alone with their child in terms of their own 'introverted' or 'unsociable' nature, we have suggested such individualised initial narratives underplay the ways in which systemic barriers related to their gender were constraining their interactions. We have argued that such barriers connect to a sense of feeling 'out of place' and a fear of being judged in relation to their gender within feminised public spaces – alongside the difficulty of meeting other fathers with responsibility for day-to-day care. Such barriers, we contend, suggest that, even in cases where fathers take on caregiving roles that challenge traditional roles, substantial gender barriers continue to persist with respect to their integration within parenting communities and public spaces.

As well as illustrating the enduring gender segregation of men's and women's friendships in this sphere, this could have implications for fathers' wellbeing, the scope of their fatherly care horizons, their identity as caregiving fathers, and the extent and longevity of their roles as caregiving fathers. The fathers' social isolation and lack of engagement in playgroups and the like also underlines this as a particularly clear limit to the otherwise relatively pervasive sense of mother and father as interchangeable in the families, which was discussed in detail in Chapter 5. Furthermore, through rendering their care-sharing as relatively 'invisible', their limited engagement with public parenting spaces may lessen the effectiveness of their progressive activities in contributing to the broader undoing of gender ideologies than if fathers were fully integrated into parenting networks.

While the challenges referred to in the chapter reflect broader and deep-rooted sets of assumptions, judgements and anxieties relating to gender and masculinity that are difficult to change, there remain some aspects to such experiences that highlight policy and practical changes that could make things easier. Developed in further detail in the next chapter, these relate most directly to how organised events for parents and young children are presented and oriented, and to the availability of suitable groups and events for fathers on weekdays. Fathers' experiences in parent networks and public spaces, though, also connect to broader practical questions returned to at various points in this book, not least the impact for the fathers of taking up significant caregiving responsibilities after the establishment of routines and relationships by their partner while she was on maternity leave. Attention, then, to paternity leave entitlements may have positive implications for caregiving fathers' connections with other parents, as well as for other aspects of their experience. Likewise, the broader reconfiguring of expectations with respect to fathers, breadwinning and notions of the 'ideal worker' (see Chapter 3), including through policy change, may help reduce some of the judgements to which fathers felt subject. We explore such questions in greater detail in Chapter 7, as part of the development of broader conclusions and reflections with respect to the various dimensions of fathers' experiences of their care-sharing roles.

7

Care-sharing Futures

Introduction

Our premise for much of this book is that, when fathers share care for young children, this has the potential to be beneficial for them, their partners and families and, on a broader scale, for the alleviation of longstanding gender inequalities. Yet, in spite of gradual transformations in popular understandings of fathers as caregivers, the time mothers typically spend on periods of leave and juggling full- or part-time work with primary care responsibilities continues to generate disproportionate burdens on them and hamper the development of their working selves. While external forms of childcare can partially alleviate this, greater maternal participation in the workforce without reciprocal movement of men towards caregiving moves us towards a 'universal breadwinner' approach (Fraser, 1996) that embraces traditionally masculine understandings of career intensity and the 'ideal worker', while devaluing caregiving and, ultimately, leaving much of the burden for it with women anyway (Hochschild, 1989). In contrast, movement towards a 'universal carer model' (Fraser, 1996) characterised by greater sharing of both care and paid work by men and women has the potential to alleviate this maternal care burden while also addressing difficulties with high intensity work cultures and opening up possibilities for men to move beyond the shackles of dominant masculinities (Elliott, 2016).

It is against such a context that this book has engaged with the journeys of heterosexual fathers who already have broken with established practice to take on an equal or greater share of early years caregiving for young children. Having carried out a detailed examination of existing literature on both fathering in general and 'involved' fathers, and explored the impact and significance of different policy approaches to paternal early years involvement, we went on to delve deeply into the experiences of a sample of UK fathers with a range of different approaches and arrangements to the sharing of care. Among other things we explored what prompted them to take on such arrangements; what the process of their transitioning into such roles involved; how roles and responsibilities became distributed; how they came to see themselves as caregivers as compared to their partners; what challenges they faced and what limits there were to the scope of their caregiving; and how their experiences inside the home compared with those in parenting spaces, institutions and networks outside it. Underlying our examination of such questions have been developing conceptual themes relating to the extent to which established gendered practice and hegemonic masculinities were being 'undone' (Deutsch, 2007) by the men's experiences, and the nature and extent of their own journeys, particularly with respect to the development or transformation of what we have termed their fatherly care horizons. Equally important throughout our discussion have been the lessons that might be drawn from the fathers' journeys for policymakers and for practitioners who engage with or support early years parents.

In this final chapter, we draw together key findings about and explanations of the men's experiences and outline conclusions and recommendations. We begin by returning to our interviews with the fathers for a final time in order to address how the men in the study reflected on their experience as a whole and what lay in their horizons with respect to the future for them as parents and carers. We then tie this together with the findings and explanations from previous chapters to discuss some detailed empirical and conceptual conclusions on fathers and early years care-sharing involvement. These conclusions then feed into practical recommendations for policymakers and practitioners that centre on easing some of the challenges caregiving fathers can face and creating practical and ideological environments conducive to greater numbers of fathers taking on such roles in the future.

Care-sharing futures and the negotiation of crossroads

Throughout our exploration of the experiences of fathers in the Sharing Care project, we have returned on a few occasions to our notion of fatherly care horizons. Through this term we have sought to explore the men's shifting sense of what they see as feasible, likely or appropriate for them as fathers and carers, starting with the initial decision to take up their unusual caring roles and then in relation to how their initial and ongoing experiences became intertwined with a

174

developing sense of their parental roles, responsibilities and identities. We have outlined the turning point that becoming care-sharing fathers often represented and the ways that, through their caregiving practices, fathers had often begun to develop a sense of themselves as somewhat interchangeable with their partners in respect of much of their care. We have also, however, identified specific limits to the scope of some of their otherwise extensive caregiving, areas that continued to fall primarily to their children's mother, and barriers that sometimes stood in the way of the fathers reaching a sense of full parental equivalence. But what of the fathers' overall reflections on their care-sharing journeys so far – and, perhaps more importantly still – their visions of how their caregiving arrangements and identities may develop in the future?

When we asked fathers to reflect on their experience as a whole, most responded in positive terms, focusing on perceived benefits of their arrangements to themselves, their partners and their children. Many highlighted the contribution they felt they were making to enabling their young children to be cared for at home for some or all of the week, the satisfaction they took from supporting their partners' careers and wellbeing, and their own ability to have some respite from paid work and/or a better sense of balance to their weekly lives. For Jeremy, who shared responsibilities equally with his partner in a flexible way that changed from week to week, the primary benefit related to the achievement of balance and equality for both himself and his partner with respect to life in and out of the home. In some ways his response encapsulates the vision behind Fraser's aforementioned universal care model (1996): 'we feel like we get the best of both worlds, and we both get to have quite a lot of time with the kids, we both get to go out and do things in the world and ... feel we're part of ... society' (Jeremy, equal care sharer).

Meanwhile, although he was doing a greater share of care than his partner, Jason felt their shared care arrangement – which he described as a 'risk' to begin with – had benefited both of them, not only in terms of life balance but the enthusiasm and commitment they were now both able to bring to parenting itself. His partner, as he saw it, was enjoying parenting more because it no longer was her primary activity, while for him the ample time spent with his daughter during his days caring eased previous anxieties about not doing enough to bond with her in the evenings after work:

> She [partner], she wants to play with her daughter more,
> she wants to take her out more, she wants to get involved

move with her, she ... she's much better, much better. And I wasn't when I came home, I ... needed time to chill out and stuff and decompress ... So all my days off, I do more with her, I'll take her out, I'll play with her, I'll relax with her and I'll just spend time with her. So it's worked a lot better, and I think both of us are a lot happier for it but we needed to take the risk that it was going to be worse to do it in the first place, and it has worked out better, we're both a lot happier with the way it is. (Jason, primary caregiver)

Most importantly, perhaps, in spite of undoubted struggles along the way, most of the fathers referred to the fulfilment they got from spending significant time alone with their children and the enhanced care competencies, emotional bonds and attachments they felt they had developed. Andrew reflected on the affective closeness he had developed with his daughter through caring for her alone one day a week and the intimate knowledge he had developed of her 'world' through myriad shared experiences:

My daughter's now getting to the stage where she's learning to hug properly, you know, and she will come over and she will be [mimes hug]. And it's not a, it's not daddy's this dark, distant figure that's used for discipline and things like that ... you're part of it, you're part of their world, you're very much part of this world, you know, you have experiences that they've never had with mum, you know being able to chase the new baby elephant at the zoo, you know with the toddler, it's just brilliant! (Andrew, equal care sharer)

Some of the fathers connected this enhanced emotional connection and familiarity with the specific benefits – in the present and future – of parental interchangeability. That children had become comfortable with different aspects of care being discharged by either parent was deemed to have generated relationships with both that would endure, while enabling roles to switch with minimum fuss, something contrasted by John with some other families he knew:

We've seen friends who have got slightly older children who ... if mum wants a night out, dad has a really difficult time putting the baby to sleep ... Or you know when they become toddlers I think it becomes harder because dad's never done it, it's always mum, and I don't want that ...

he's just as happy with having stories and bedtime with me as he is with my wife. (John, equal care sharer)

In this way, fathers' reflections on their experience clearly connected to the future they envisaged for the caregiving relationships in which they had invested so much. Having often begun their fatherhoods with their partner as full-time and primary carer, most talked about how the skills, capacities and self-belief they had developed as carers would enable them to continue to take on a wide range of childrearing tasks and responsibilities in the future (something supported by existing literature, for example Ranson, 2010). For Anthony, the bonds being developed through his role as an equal parent, including caring for his son one day a week, had acquired great significance as part of his vision for the future of a relationship he hoped would remain as close as possible:

> That's quite an important thing to me to think about ... what we're doing now is really setting up, hopefully ... a stronger relationship throughout his life, it's not just about him as a baby or a toddler or you know, it's not just about right now ... you're sort of building something that will last a lifetime hopefully, I suppose that's what we think we're doing is that you know hopefully we'll have that solid relationship later on in life, that he will hopefully feel that he can come to me as easily as he could go to his mum when he's pissed off when he's 15 about something or other. (Anthony, equal care sharer)

John set out a similar vision of future relationships, while also placing emphasis on the extent to which being a parent and caregiver had become a core part of his own identity:

> Well obviously longer term benefits I can't be sure of, but hopefully longer term [child] will always feel close to me or nearly as close to me as he does to his mum and ... yeah and I look forward to hopefully him growing up feeling ... feeling that I'm as important as she is. In the more, now, the current benefits, I like, I really enjoy being as involved in his upbringing. So if we're having conversations with friends about children and sometimes the dads might be a bit quiet, I'm not, I'm just as involved and that, and maybe that's just me being ... I like to know about things, I like to

> be involved and I like to know about things … I enjoy being
> as much a parent as my wife is. (John, equal care sharer)

The fathers' longer-term care horizons, then, were clearly encompassing notions of extensive caregiving involvement and enduring close relationships as part of what they saw as feasible and appropriate for them in the future. Importantly, though, this did not always mean the continuation of their primary or equal care roles was fully assured. While some expressed clear determination to maintain their responsibilities for the foreseeable future and some even speculated about expanding their roles, for others, the possibility of reverting to an involved and committed, yet more secondary care role remained, whether in the near or more distant future. In one unusual case, a stark reversion was already planned. Unlike many of the other families, following a period during which he had been primary carer for his first child, Chris' career and salary had recently become the ones on which his household most depended and this meant he had been limited to two relatively short (two weeks, then seven weeks) periods of parental leave for his second. While emphasising the significance of the bonds he felt had been developed while at home, he described with a sense of inevitability the prospect of returning to his demanding full-time role and long commute:

Chris:	I don't think I'm necessarily looking forward to going back to work but then I'm not, it's not something I'm dreading, it's just a transition … I'm strongly of the opinion that I have a closer relationship to my son than I would have done otherwise and that's, that's been a good investment … that relationship has … noticeably strengthened during the seven weeks … So I think this has been very valuable for that … I don't think that's something that will fade.
Interviewer:	What will the arrangement be in terms of how much time you spend with him? Will you be, as you described, sort of pretty much out at work all day, every day?
Chris:	Yeah, there's unfortunately no real way around that. What with commuting to [city] and so on. So we'll just have to see how it goes, but that's something that you know is not ideal but it's what pays the mortgage. (Chris, shared parental leave)

While it was an isolated case (and contrasted with other examples in the study where fathers had set up more permanent shared care arrangements after paternity leave), this example illustrates how the inherent temporariness of parental leave as a work/care arrangement means it may not always lead to longer-term shared care arrangements unless other circumstances mitigate in favour of this (see Brandth and Kvande, 2018b). The coming to an end of such a period, we would suggest, represents a 'caregiving crossroads', with the potential either to set in train new care-sharing arrangements, or – as here – a reversion to more established roles.

Although the arrangements of fathers working flexibly to care on one or more days a week did not have this in-built temporariness, their futures as caregivers also were subject to predictable or unpredictable events that had the potential to become a caregiving crossroads for them. Some were unsure whether their children starting school would prompt a return to a more usual full-time routine or a different approach to flexible working, for example. Patrick described the likelihood of scaling down his current care responsibilities once his children were in school but indicated an intention to explore self-employed working arrangements with his partner that would continue to allow caring to be shared between them:

> We're already talking about different things, a year from now [oldest child] will be just about to start full-time school, [youngest child] will be ... a couple of months away start, getting his fifteen hours [subsidised weekly day care], so there's automatically two days in a week when I then can start committing to a full-time job, and obviously a year after that, they'll all be in school full-time and what we do exactly, we don't know yet ... once they're all kind of school age, a bit more independent, maybe we'll find either a franchise of the [pub chain] or a private place or managers for some other pub company ... we could more than easily arrange the rotas so we're there for the school pick-up and things. (Patrick, primary caregiver)

Another notable crossroads event for the fathers' caregiving was the arrival of a second (or third and so on) baby. Interestingly, in spite of their broader embrace of shared parenting, in most of the cases where this was mentioned in the interviews the fathers seemed to view it as unlikely they would take significant parental leave and that, therefore, primary care responsibilities would return to their partner, at least temporarily. In Kevin's understanding, his current role as primary carer would cease when they had a second child, with his partner taking a year of maternity leave and him renewing his career focus for a time. He indicated a hope that, after she returned to work, he might be able to take up a similar care-sharing role through working part-time, but once again this was uncertain:

Interviewer: And how long did you plan to continue with this arrangement or ...?

Kevin: Erm ... if I'm entirely honest, until my wife gets pregnant again! I think we, we always talked about it being at least 12 months, I had it more in my mind that it would probably be about 18 months ... And by that time I'll be ready to look for promotion opportunities and my wife will be going on maternity, hopefully at some point.

Interviewer: Right, right. And so if, if you had another child, your wife took some maternity leave and she went back to work after that, would you imagine that you continue working full-time then or is this ...?

Kevin: If I could make it work with the office, I'd like to do it again. And do another 12, 24 months of part-time. Because it would be nice to spend equal amounts of time with the kids. (Kevin, primary caregiver)

In some ways, fathers' willingness to switch in and out of their roles in response to different circumstances, events or crossroads could be taken as further evidence of their expedient, interchangeable approach to parenting (see Chapter 5). Importantly, however, there was a strong sense in Kevin's and some other examples that the way future parental leave was apportioned was a decision that rested primarily with the mother's wishes and that these should take precedence: 'she really enjoys being back at work full-time actually, but saying that, if we have another one, she wants to take another twelve months off, to get that full length of time with the baby' (Kevin, primary caregiver). Such examples speak to the way that, as we also explored in Chapter 5, a discourse of default maternal responsibility – especially in the first year after having a baby – still sometimes seemed to endure, even among families that had embraced notions of care-sharing and, in some cases, paternal primary care.

It was clear, then, that most of the fathers felt their arrangements had been positive for them and their families and that the bonds and skills they had developed had great significance for their future caregiving roles and relationships. There remained uncertainties, though, with respect to exactly what care and work arrangements would ensue as their children's lives developed, and the possibility of reverting to a role more centred on a secondary carer status (whether temporarily or permanently) seemed often to be present. Whether this represented a largely non-gendered facet of flexible approaches to parenting and breadwinning that centred on interchangeability (a willingness to switch between care or work orientations as needed) in response to developing circumstances or, rather, an enduring sense that, in spite of everything, the children's mother somehow had retained the position of default caregiver, was not always easy to determine. From the indications available to us we would suggest that, in different degrees, elements of both may often have been present. Equally, however, we rarely saw evidence that fathers were keen to relinquish their substantial caring roles and plenty that they felt keen to continue should circumstances favour this. The underlying point, then, is not that the fathers' commitments were short-term, but that uncertainties with respect to the future underline the importance of devoting attention to how we might make it easier for fatherly involvement to continue through the various crossroads families encounter, rather than merely hoping that early involvement will automatically ensure this.

Sharing care: Shifting horizons and developing fatherhoods

In placing this discussion of the fathers' overall reflections and outlooks together with the detailed examination of their motivations, experiences and perspectives in the previous chapters, we now turn to the overall findings and conclusions from the Sharing Care project, and their implications for understandings of fatherhoods, families and gender.

Becoming a care-sharing father

The question of what factors prompt fathers take on an equal or greater share of care for young children has been the subject of existing research in different national contexts, including in studies of primary carer fathers and fathers on parental leave. In addressing this question for the fathers in our study, we sought to expand the discussion to equal care sharer fathers as well as primary carers and parental leavers, and also to centre our exploration particularly on the role of pre-existing orientations and shifting circumstances as part of the decision-making process. We drew, in this respect, on a distinction outlined in some previous research between decisions rooted in choices and ideals, and those prompted more by necessity, expediency and circumstance (Merla, 2008; Chelsey, 2011; Solomon, 2014). By thinking about decision-making through the frame of fatherly care horizons, we were able to broaden such a distinction into an overall examination of whether care-sharing already lay within fathers' visions for themselves as parents – rooted in existing identities, habitus and relationships – or whether something had prompted a shift, or turning point, in what they could see as an appropriate, viable or realistic path for them. What this helped us to show is that, while many of the fathers were middle class and broadly liberal minded, with an initial comfort with broader notions of gender equality and fatherly involvement, only some of them had envisaged taking on an equal or greater share of early years care as a result of clear pre-existing ideals, ambitions or orientations. For the others, the development of relatively unusual sets of circumstances had been a key factor in transforming – sometimes gradually and sometimes more suddenly – their fatherly outlooks, and precipitating a significant practical, affective and symbolic change of direction for their families. Even in the case of those fathers who had already envisaged taking on an equal or primary share of caregiving, the actual assumption of such responsibilities often still represented a fairly dramatic practical turning point, because of the overwhelming centrality of their partner to the first part of their babies' lives.

Making sense of such continuities and transformations in fathers' journeys toward the taking on of primary or equal care-sharing roles is essential to understanding their experiences. It enables us to see how existing aspects of social position, relationships and ideals may hold great importance, but rarely enable care roles that go 'against the grain' (Ranson, 2010) in the absence of circumstances that render such roles practically expedient. There are, after all, many middle class, liberal-minded fathers with aspirations for care involvement and 'being there', most of whom do not envisage taking on an equal or greater share of caregiving (Dermott, 2008; Miller, 2017). Our horizons, and the spaces they help open or close for us, then, reflect a multitude of long-, medium- and short-term factors, from broad social positionings to more idiosyncratic features, events, interactions or circumstances (Hodkinson and Sparkes, 1997). What our research shows is that, while transformations in longer-term attitudes may be important, the development of care horizons and practices that go against established trends may be achieved best by helping to generate practical circumstances conducive to the sharing of care by fathers.

A further core observation from our exploration of how the fathers came to take on their care-sharing roles is the extent of maternal domination of the first period of babies' lives, even in the case of such unusually egalitarian families. Our findings support Doucet's highlighting of the first year of parenting in particular as one in which motherly and fatherly roles, rooted in broader gendered habitus, become sharply differentiated, with belief in a unique mother–infant bond at this time seemingly near-universal (Doucet, 2009; also see Miller, 2017). 'This early phase of parenting' argues Doucet, 'is one where the biological and social differences between women and men are magnified so that they can take on enormous dimensions' (Doucet, 2009: 93). That so few of the fathers in our study had taken parental leave – and that even those who had done so took on the bulk of their responsibilities only after several months dominated by their partners – provides a powerful indication of the extent of the barriers to care-sharing during this period. Our conclusions are a little more complex, however, when it comes to Doucet's emphasis on how far this early phase can 'entrench women and men into long-standing gender differences in their parenting and employment opportunities' (Doucet, 2009). After all, another of our key findings is that dramatic transformations of horizons, roles and responsibilities remain possible during or after this first period, suggesting that greater attention might be devoted to supporting/encouraging families to engage in such caregiving transformations 12 months or so into babies' lives. Yet, conversely, aspects of our investigation also have highlighted how useful greater paternal involvement during the first year might have been to the fathers and their families, not just in reducing what sometimes were stressful transitions but also enabling the eventual relieving of maternal primary care burdens to be as comprehensive as possible.

Embracing caregiving and shifting paternal masculinities

Following the initial transformations involved in their taking on of primary or equal caregiver responsibilities, our research suggests the fathers' care horizons and parental identities had continued to travel towards a deeper and longer-standing embrace of the notion of care-sharing as they became more comfortable in their roles. Drawing on theories that emphasise the connections between the everyday doing of care and the development of caregiving identities, we suggest the men often were challenging or undoing traditional understandings of fatherhood (Deutsch, 2001, 2007) and, in doing so, taking significant steps towards an embrace of caregiving masculinities (Elliott, 2016). Though the fathers indicated a range of experiences with respect to how, exactly, caregiving roles were allocated and discharged, they often spoke of themselves as having become broadly equivalent to their partners with respect to their capacity, willingness and overall approach to everyday caregiving. Whether they were primary or equal carers, few seemed particularly keen to differentiate themselves as fathers as opposed to mothers, preferring a discourse that centred on an embrace of more neutral notions of parenthood and on the idea of their interchangeability with their partners. This does not mean gender was absent from their identities or practice, or that there were no limits to their embrace of traditionally maternal burdens, but most were keen to highlight the expedient way tasks were allocated and the wide range of roles with which they had become comfortable, including those focused on emotional comfort and affectivity. While some did discuss a propensity for masculine 'rough and tumble' styles of play, most struggled to identify clear substantive differences between themselves and their partners with respect to their caregiving approach while, in contrast to other studies (Doucet, 2004; Merla, 2008; Chelsey, 2011), emphasis on 'compensatory' breadwinning activities, DIY activities or other masculine pursuits in their accounts was minimal.

The extent of the men's journeys toward the normalisation of such practices in their lives and the embrace of interchangeable caregiving identities should be understood, we suggest, in the context of the traditionally gendered way in which most of their fatherhoods had begun – as breadwinner fathers with their partner on maternity leave. For many, the decision to take on such roles had been a change of direction and for most, the process of taking on some or most daily caregiving practices from their partner had entailed significant challenges. Yet, so far as it was possible for us to tell, they had, through the extent and regularity of their caregiving since then, and the competences, confidence and bonds developed, come to embrace the notion of themselves as care-sharing, nurturing parents, able and willing to discharge tasks or roles according to need. And, as we have shown at the beginning of this chapter, it is equally clear that this had long-term future significance to the fathers, most of whom envisaged extensive ongoing care involvement and enduring bonds, comparable to those between their children and their partner, throughout their children's upbringing and beyond.

Crucial here, we would suggest, are the sets of experiences and competences fathers acquired while caring alone, without their partner present (Brandth and Kvande, 2018b) – and the connections between such practice, their parental identities and their care horizons. It is not just that there seemed to be a degree of functional interchangeability to their roles, as Ranson (2010) would have it, but that this was linked to transformations in how fathers envisaged themselves as such. The emphasis placed in Ranson's (2015) later work on affectivity and embodiment in early years caregiving practice helps us understand how fathers' fast-developing bonds with their children had enabled them to begin to understand themselves as interchangeable with their child's mother. As with the group of parental leave fathers studied by Brandth and Kvande (2018b: 87), the fathers often seemed to be 'thriving on being loved, and appreciated', as well as on 'feelings of joy and pride in being needed and wanted'. If it was the combination of circumstances, broader habitus and orientation that first enabled sharing care to enter their horizons and become a probability, it was the repeated, affective nature of their everyday care practice, together with growing bonds, confidence and sense of responsibility, that enabled fathers' caregiving journeys to develop towards the embrace of nurturing masculine identities and the possibility of longer-term care-sharing and close, enduring bonds.

The persistence of default maternal responsibility

While the distance many of the fathers had travelled since deciding to take on their caregiving roles was striking, we also have explored challenges, limits and barriers to their embrace of traditionally maternal responsibilities and to the transformation of their fatherly identities. For many, the initial period after care roles were transferred between their partner and themselves was challenging. Becoming accustomed to the practicalities of care and the weight of responsibility that can accompany caring alone sometimes led to considerable anxiety, while the difficulties the men's partners sometimes seemed to have had with handing over caregiving responsibilities could engender feelings of guilt for both parties and, sometimes, a reluctance by mothers to fully relinquish control and by fathers to claim it. Once new routines and practices had become established, everyday care practice became easier, but challenges sometimes prevented fathers from achieving full equivalence with their partners in all respects. Though fathers keenly embraced nurturing and emotional sides of parenting, children sometimes had retained a clear preference for their mother's comfort.

Mothers themselves, meanwhile, had often tended to retain greater responsibility for organisational aspects of parenting, and, sometimes, the emotional labour and sense of moral responsibility associated with this. Most strikingly, consistent with the findings of some other studies of primary carer fathers (for example Doucet, 2006a; Solomon, 2017), fathers had often struggled to connect, spend time or communicate with other parents and tended to feel out of place in daytime parenting spaces and communities. The presence of such challenges and disparities, even in the context of care-sharing journeys that had progressed so far, highlights enduring and persistent aspects of maternal-centrism, reinforced sometimes within the fathers' domestic spheres but more starkly still within spaces and networks outside them.

The domestic sphere was, in many respects, where fathers seemed to feel most comfortable in their embrace of caregiving. Nevertheless, challenges to the scope of their roles within this domain often centred on pressures on their partners to retain control or involvement and the interplay of this with fathers' seeming willingness to cede such control. Of importance here is an underlying assumption of default maternal responsibility that seemed to underlie at least some of the accounts. That is, even where the practical administering of care was shared out equally or where fathers were taking on the greater share of such responsibilities, there sometimes remained a sense that mothers were regarded as having 'first preference' on care involvement and co-ordination, with fathers reluctant to encroach too far into territory regarded as rightfully their partner's, unless there were the clearest indications she was comfortable to vacate or share it. In turn, consistent with extensive literature on working mothers elsewhere (for example Christopher, 2012; Miller, 2017), mothers themselves had, according to the fathers, often found it difficult to fully relinquish responsibilities and identities set in train during the first phase of their children's lives and rooted in broader maternal expectations and cultures of intensive mothering (Hays, 1998; Shirani et al., 2012). While some may seek to understand such a domestic dynamic through the concept of maternal gatekeeping (Fagan and Barnett, 2003; Puhlman and Pasley, 2013), the notion of mothers excluding fathers through their monopolisation of responsibilities does not adequately capture the mutual and interactive nature of the process whereby default maternal responsibility can be reinforced. As Miller has argued (see Chapter 2), 'practices of caregiving are complex, contingent and dynamic. Both parents are able to exert … behaviours that 'block' and/or facilitate care' (2017: 140).

Our research also illustrates the particular role of women's domination of care during the first period of babies' lives in cementing particular understandings of the maternal self in a manner that can endure even when fathers take on greater responsibilities thereafter. The considerable extra time the fathers' partners had spent with their children during this time, together with the extensive primary responsibilities they had taken on, meant that routines, bonds, skills, relationships and ownerships already had been established by the time fathers became involved, as had fathers' status as secondary in respect of most of these. Miller describes the significance of mothers' primary responsibility for care in the first few months as follows:

> Their expertise develops more quickly during this time, and so they come to share and orchestrate baby care information with the father. This can involve lists and verbal 'briefings', and fathers' practices are likely to be overseen, as they more slowly ... become accomplished at aspects of caring. (2017: 137)

Now, as we have noted, subsequent take-up of unusual care roles by the fathers in the study, and the extent of their affective and symbolic journeys towards interchangeable notions of parenting, suggest that significant aspects of this early establishment of roles can, in fact, be undone at a later point. Yet we also showed how all that is established during maternity leave could exacerbate some of the challenges of sharing care later. First, it ensured that the take-up by fathers of parental leave or equal/primary care roles entailed a sharp transformation of responsibilities that could be both practically and emotionally challenging. Second, it contributed to ongoing maternal pressures and to the establishment of an undercurrent of default maternal responsibility, even in families highly committed to egalitarian or reversed roles. Specifically, the early establishment of bonds, we think, is likely to have made it more difficult for some fathers to reach parity with their partners when it came to their children's emotional preferences, made it more likely that mothers would retain responsibility for aspects of co-ordination and parental direction, and established mothers in relationships with practitioners and parent networks in such a way that it felt easier for them to take responsibility for their continuation thereafter.

Such internal pressures relating to the interplay between fathers and their partners with respect to the taking on or receding of responsibilities worked alongside some more overt boundaries that many of them faced outside the home. Such boundaries could make it more challenging for fathers to engage in aspects of parenting centred on the networks of other people and institutions that early years parents typically encounter. The tendency for some mothers to still take the lead in liaising with health visitors, doctors, childcare providers and others, then, was likely encouraged not only by internal domestic dynamics but by the deeply gendered maternal orientation of some such professionals and institutions. Of course, the tendency for health visitors, doctors and childcare professionals routinely to seek contact with mothers rather than fathers does not in itself prevent the latter from taking on responsibility for such roles, any more than a relative paucity of father-accessible baby change facilities might prevent a father from taking their child out in the day. It does, however, make such roles a little more complicated for them to discharge than for their partner, as well as signalling a broader reminder of how far fathers' gender sets them apart in a world of early years support centred on default maternal responsibility.

It was within and among networks of other parents, however, that fathers most consistently and strongly experienced feeling out of place. Consistent with existing studies of fathers on parental leave or stay-at-home dads (Doucet, 2006b; Merla, 2008; Ranson, 2015; Solomon, 2017), this had been the most difficult and anxiety-inducing aspects of parenting for most of the fathers on their days caring alone. For many, their experience contrasted sharply with the comfort and friendships their partner seemed to have experienced in daytime parenting spaces. Unlike Doucet (2006b) and Solomon (2017), we saw few indications that men are becoming more integrated in parenting communities – on the contrary, the similarity between our findings and those of studies from a decade or more ago is striking. As a result, few of the fathers regularly spent time with other parents and children and, for those that did, this was more likely to be existing friends or relatives than other parents in their communities. For some, even spending time alone with their child in parks and other spaces could feel stressful because of their fear of being judged by others. While partly attributable to lower pressures to participate in public activities associated with intensive parenting, or a broader reluctance on the part of the fathers to spend time with others, our primary explanation for the fathers' predicament relates to their feeling out of place in spaces that were oriented to and/or dominated by women and where they were often the only caregiving man (Doucet, 2009; Boterman and Bridge, 2014). Although the fathers sometimes played it down, such barriers had consequences. Most obviously, it was more difficult for fathers to fully embrace what Doucet (2006a) calls 'community responsibility' aspects of parenting – including liaising, organising and spending time caring for children with other parents – and hence this became the most significant barrier to achieving full practical interchangeability with their partners. It also had potential implications for their wellbeing, with some admitting they sometimes felt lonely on their caregiving days. Although we did not encounter direct indications of mental health difficulties, and most seemed to be enjoying their caregiving overall, broader evidence of the struggles new fathers can experience in the months and years after having a baby is mounting (O'Brien et al., 2017; Das and Hodkinson, 2019b) and, against this context, such evidence of isolation ought to be a concern. More fundamentally, fathers' anxieties about spending time in daytime parenting spaces, alongside the direct negative experiences of some, had served to bring their status as men to the forefront of their parental selves once more and thereby to hold back in some respects their embrace of gender-neutral notions of parenting, their undoing of dominant masculinities and the development of their care horizons. That mothers sometimes seemed to retain the status of default caregiver, even if their current role was secondary may, perhaps, be unsurprising against such a context.

While it would be remiss to underestimate the significance of such barriers, the distinctions between caring inside and outside the domestic sphere and the limits to the scope or ease of father's caregiving journeys, it remains the case that most of the fathers reflected on their overall experiences as care-sharing fathers in positive terms. Our exploration of the challenges they faced and the limits of their roles has much potential to inform discussions on how these might be alleviated (as we explore in the next section). Yet what remains most notable about our findings is, we would argue, the extent of the distance many of the fathers had travelled, from involved but often breadwinner-focused dads with a partner on maternity leave, to care-immersed men who had come to see themselves as – broadly speaking – interchangeable with and equivalent to their children's mothers.

Making care-sharing easier: Recommendations for policy and practice

In addition to the broader lessons it offers to our understandings of journeys of caregiving fatherhood, the findings of the Sharing Care project also enable us to identify some observations and lessons for policymakers and practitioners, in light of the international and UK policy contexts we outlined in Chapter 3. These lessons relate both to how we can make it more feasible for fathers to envisage and take on equal or primary care roles for young children, and how we can ease, enhance and extend the experience of those who do take on such roles and that of their families. For, as we have argued earlier in the book, creating circumstances conducive to effective care-sharing from early in children's lives has the potential to make a significant contribution towards longer-term equalisation in men and women's caregiving and career opportunities and, in doing so, realising a society centred on universalisation of caregiving along the lines envisaged by Fraser (1996).

Facilitating long-term care-sharing

The first lesson to be drawn is that there are a wide range of different ways in which fathers can play an equal or greater role in early years caregiving. While some were on parental leave and others occupied the role of unemployed stay-at-home dad, most of the fathers in our sample were combining either a primary or equal care role with different approaches to full- or part-time work, leaving either their partner or outside forms of care integral to the arrangement also. As we have shown in Chapter 3, policy efforts to increase fathers' early years involvement, both in the UK and elsewhere, have been overwhelmingly centred on parental leave. While our research does nothing to suggest that such efforts are misplaced (quite the contrary, as we outline in due course), we have shown how possible it is for fathers to shift their direction and take on equal or greater proportions of caregiving for children at a later point through working flexibly. This, we think, indicates the importance of broadening our understandings of the range of ways care-sharing might work, when such sharing might begin, and how we might support and ease its take-up, whether during or beyond the first year of children's lives.

That significant care-sharing during the first 6–12 months of care after birth had often not been considered by care-sharing families in the study illustrates the extent to which understandings of this first period remain centred on the most deep-seated notions of mother-centred nurturing. As we showed in Chapter 3, the rootedness of such maternal understandings of this period of time may be such that they continue to ensure mothers shoulder much of the caregiving burden during it, even in countries such as Sweden, where paternal leave policy is at its most progressive (Wells and Sakardi, 2012). We also have suggested that, while it may well make such an outcome much more likely (Haas and Hwang, 2019b), parental leave does not, in itself, ensure that shared care arrangements continue in the longer term, the inbuilt ephemerality of leave ensuring it likely ends at a caregiving crossroads, rather than a simple, one-way path to enduring equality. While this does not suggest progressive parental leave policies are misplaced, it does indicate that policymakers must attend to other ways they could support the sharing of care and, in particular, how to make it easier for fathers to set up and sustain longer-term sharing arrangements.

This may encompass different aspects of policy, not least support for affordable and easily accessible childcare that, as we have shown, often forms a central part of care-sharing arrangements. However, support for flexible working and, specifically, creating conditions conducive to flexible working for men and fathers, is arguably the most significant area for policy attention. As we have shown, for example, current UK law offers employees only the right to *request* flexible working and does not impose any obligation on employers to accede to such requests or advertise jobs as open to flexibility, and the consideration of policy options with respect to such limitations would be valuable (House of Commons Women and Equalities Committee, 2018). Studies also suggest that UK fathers are currently far less likely to request to work flexibly than are mothers (Radcliffe and Cassell, 2015). Even in countries with the most facilitative environments, fathers seeking work arrangements that would enable them to take on a fair share of caregiving can come up against significant difficulties with employers, in cultures centred on the notion of the ideal worker and, sometimes, on traditional understandings of men as primary breadwinners (Haas and Hwang, 2019a). It was notable in the Sharing Care study that, while some complained of minor difficulties with colleagues, most of the men suggested that their employers had been supportive of their arrangements. While this was, on the face of it, a positive finding, it is worth remembering that these fathers were highly unusual in their arrangements and that the policies and cultures in their workplaces may also have been atypical. The fathers also were unusual in often feeling less career-oriented than their partners, which may have made it easier for them to accept the risk of damaging their employment prospects. If the kinds of care-sharing in which these unusual fathers were engaged are to become more widespread, it will be necessary to enable more career-minded fathers to work flexibly, without seriously curtailing their future careers. Creating policy and work cultures that enable fathers – and mothers – to work flexibly without fear of damaging their future prospects, then, is an area of great importance that is not always afforded the attention it warrants in debates about early years fatherly involvement.

Supporting parental leave

While drawing attention to the importance of supporting semi-permanent work arrangements that may enable care-sharing throughout and potentially beyond children's early years, our findings also illustrate the potential value of enabling and encouraging fathers to take significant time off work during the first 6–12 months of their babies' lives. Complete equality of care between women and men during this period may be unrealistic in the short term, but the potential value of extensive fatherly involvement during this time, including significant periods caring alone for their baby, as a means to ease and enhance paternal caregiving thereafter, is difficult to dispute (Karu and Tremblay, 2018). After all, taking on primary or equal care responsibilities *without* having shared parental leave beforehand often involved a sharp turning point for the fathers in our study, and a challenging and anxiety-laden initial transition. And, notwithstanding the successes and competences many fathers had established in their embrace of interchangeable parenting, their clear-cut secondary position during the immediate post-natal period in most cases surely contributed to enduring areas of disparity between themselves and their partners as carers, and sometimes to the broader sense of default maternal responsibility that could linger beneath their care arrangements.

While it could play a significant role in reinforcing maternal-centrism and setting up responsibilities and assumptions that endured, the resilience of exclusive maternity leave itself also, of course, reflected deeply-rooted *existing* assumptions about the particular importance of mothers during the first year of babies' lives (Doucet, 2009; Miller, 2017). Against the context of such understandings – and alongside a plethora of practical factors – it is not difficult to see why *transferable* leave policies (where leave entitlement can be taken by either partner: see Chapter 3) such as the UK's Shared Parental Leave scheme, are unlikely to prompt significant change. Such an approach, we would suggest, provides a near-perfect example of a policy couched in 'gender-neutral' language that in practice reinforces maternal responsibility (see Kilkey, 2006). Indeed, the UK's Shared Parental Leave scheme is specifically wedded to ideologies of maternal responsibility as *default* because, in practice, the leave is initially assigned to the mother and has to be transferred to the father in order for it to be shared (see Twamley and Schober, 2018). Through highlighting the challenges fathers and their partners can face when taking on counter-hegemonic roles without having shared parental leave, then, our project offers support for the introduction of longer periods of non-transferable leave for fathers (the so-called 'daddy quota') as well as for its greater compensation.

Addressing and catering for caregiving fathers

While some of the challenges faced by fathers connect to the primary role of their partners in the first period of babies' lives, or to broader assumptions and pressures reinforced through internal dynamics within their households, our findings also highlight the difficulties the men could have engaging with institutions, professionals, other parents and parenting spaces outside the home when caring alone. Such findings point to the ways cultures of default maternal responsibility can be institutionalised in early years support networks and highlight how practitioners and others might provide greater support for caregiving fathers, enabling them to expand the scope of their parenting and enhance their experience.

First, while some post-natal services may for good reason need to be oriented specifically to mothers, perinatal and early years institutions might review whether they are inadvertently or unnecessarily excluding fathers, or making it more difficult for them to undertake particular dimensions of care. A wide range of practices might be looked at here, from addressing mothers and not fathers in the name, orientation or advertising of events or parent groups that have no need to be women-only, to the ways information is presented on support websites, to the automatic contacting of mothers rather than fathers by health visitors, doctors, childcare providers and others. While they may be understandable from a practical point of view, we have shown how such practices can regularly remind caregiving fathers of their outsider status within feminised worlds of caregiving, and can work together with other factors to discourage their involvement in organisational and social dimensions of care outside the home. Such organisations also should consider, if they are not already, positive and proactive ways in which they might encourage fathers to engage with them.

Second, there is a pressing need to increase the number, range and visibility of early years fathers' groups. Alongside their broader challenges in daytime spaces, fathers in the Sharing Care project often outlined how difficult it was to make meaningful connections with other fathers, while some emphasised that those events or groups they were aware of seemed to be oriented – through their timing, location or cultural character – to breadwinner fathers, rather than to those who were caring for children alone during the day. The setting up – by government-funded early years providers or charitable organisations – of groups specifically oriented to fathers caring for babies and toddlers alone during weekdays, then, has the potential to provide a substantial boost to such fathers' ability and enthusiasm to spend time with their children among communities of other parents and to enhance their comfort in public spaces. And if such measures were to form part of broader attempts to connect new fathers with one another – both off- and online – such an initiative may have the potential to make a significant contribution to efforts to improve paternal wellbeing more generally, amidst evidence of the role isolation can play in post-natal mental health struggles (Das and Hodkinson, 2019b).

Understandings or practicalities?

A theme that has pervaded our discussions throughout the book of what might prompt fathers to take on unusual care roles and what might ease their journeys into such roles is the relationship between understandings and practicalities. At face value, a good deal of what we have established suggests that, consistent with prevailing policy viewpoints on the subject (for example Bünning and Pollmann-Schult, 2016), it is the establishment of practical circumstances that render care-sharing viable and expedient that is likely to make the most difference. Many of the fathers we spoke to were not ideologically driven towards gender-neutral care-sharing, for example, and such unusual arrangements often did not lie within their original horizons of fatherhood. More often than not, it was finances, career practicalities or other such factors that had been the most important prompt for shifts in their care horizons, with a more fulsome embrace of notions of parental interchangeability in their identities and values often seeming to develop from this as part of their practical and affective journeys of caregiving. In policy terms, such evidence may suggest, then, that campaigns by government or others to persuade families to share parental leave, or proliferating images of caregiving fathers carrying babies on websites, may have less impact overall than policies that make it practically more advantageous for fathers to share leave, or to share care in the longer term by working flexibly (see Chapter 3). Similarly, practicalities could be of most importance in resolving some of the challenges caregiving fathers can face. Undertaking greater everyday care involvement during the early months of babies' lives may be what would most help address the issue of children's enduring tendency to prefer mothers' comfort, for example. Fathers' comfort within daytime parenting spaces and institutions may be enhanced most by the practical scenario of professionals, other parents and institutions routinely treating them as equal or first port of call for their children and, ultimately, of dads being able to see more other dads, as well as mums, when they spend time within such spaces.

Yet, the interaction between practicalities and ideals and between short- and longer-term factors is not one-directional or simple, as our earlier development of the concept of fatherly care horizons shows. We have already outlined, for example, how – even in those countries where practical circumstances are most conducive to sharing – significant early years discrepancies between men and women remain. Conversely, in our study of fathers who did share care, while many did not seem to have been driven primarily by gender-neutral early years ideals, such factors were of importance to some and, for the rest, their broader existing orientations must surely have made it easier for them to turn towards an embrace of primary or equal care roles when the possibility presented itself. So, while practicalities may remain key, continued emphasis by government, employers and early years providers on discourse and imagery that helps render early years care-sharing visible and normal may still have the potential to make receptiveness to the possibility of care-sharing more widespread or, better still, enable more fathers to see care-sharing at the centre of their horizons from the outset. To take a simple example, fathers too often constitute little more than a footnote on ante- and post-natal parenting advice websites and literature that are implicitly (and sometimes explicitly) addressed to women, with the emphasis in content that *is* addressed to men tending to position them principally as supporters of their partners before, during and after birth (Das and Hodkinson, 2019b). While the importance of such support is undoubted, a drive to address fathers as fully involved and potentially equal or primary caregivers may contribute – alongside other measures – to a shift in fathers' initial horizons in this respect. In a broader sense, attention to the reconfiguring of assumptions about what constitutes an 'ideal worker' among employers and throughout society may help greater numbers of fathers to envisage making adjustments to their work in order to share care, whether through parental leave, flexible working or both. Such shifts in cultural understanding are something that policymakers and employers can help to change through the language they use, the actions they take and the policies they put in place. More generally, policy needs to convey more effectively that men's contribution is not tied exclusively to their participation in the labour market and that adjusting work to care for children contributes to both individual and social good.

Concluding thoughts

As we have noted previously, in 2019 the UK government launched a consultation on proposals designed to promote fatherly involvement in UK care, accompanied by a newspaper article written by the outgoing prime minister outlining a desire to challenge assumptions that 'it is the lot of the mother to be primary carer' and acknowledging the impact of this on disparities in pay and career opportunities for men and women (May, 2019). Encouragingly, as well as entailing proposals for extended non-transferable paternity leave, the consultation included possible extended requirements on employers with respect to flexible working. While the destination of such proposals under a new, more right-wing government remains unclear, their launch by a Conservative prime minister represents, we would suggest, evidence of the growing consensus on the importance of enabling fathers to play a greater role in early years care and the potential impact of this on broader gender equality and relations. It appears to underline a shift in UK policy discourse (if not policy, as yet) away from the dualism of 'care parity' approaches (centred on supporting/recognising women's care work) and 'universal breadwinner' models (that seek to facilitate mother's employment opportunities without encouraging greater care responsibilities from men) (Fraser, 1996). While a great deal remains to be settled, perhaps the time is right for the taking of decisive steps towards Fraser's 'universal caregiver' model, based on the sharing of both paid work and caregiving by parents.

There are of course, some limits to our own contribution to such debates – and some obvious suggestions we can make for future research. We focused – deliberately – on the perspectives of fathers in care-sharing families in order to highlight and detail such experience but greater emphasis on the journeys of mothers within such families, and of the interplay between the perspectives of mothers and fathers, clearly would be of value in future work. Similarly, while it enabled a valuable examination of the gendered dynamic between mothers and fathers, our heterosexual sample did not include the experience of same-sex parents of either gender in the way that some previous studies have (for example Ranson, 2010). While we would not accept that our sample *size* is any sort of a weakness for this qualitative, detail-focused study, its white and middle class orientation, like the samples of some previous studies of fathers, clearly entails limitations to the range of experience that we were able to explore. This, too, is a point worthy of attention in future work. Finally, our focus on the trajectories, horizons and journeys of the fathers means that, had resources have allowed it, we would dearly have loved to return to their lives a few years later in order to examine how far their care-sharing identities had progressed, or regressed, and how myriad crossroads had been negotiated as their children became older. The possibility remains for us to do so, of course, but this will have to be for another project.

Notwithstanding such future avenues, the Sharing Care project has provided findings, insight and understanding that are, we believe, timely and relevant to broader debates on the topic both in and beyond the UK. Most importantly, we would emphasise that for all the challenges and limits discussed, the overall experiences of the fathers offer a strong endorsement of the potential for men to share early years care and of the significance of such a role in potentially transforming fathers' identities, masculinities and care horizons. Even as stark outliers within thoroughly maternal-centric cultures, the fathers' caregiving journeys demonstrated how everyday involvement in the myriad practicalities of care can enable the development of interchangeable understandings of parenthood considerably more gender-neutral than those that prevail in the worlds that surround them. Nevertheless, their experience powerfully highlights how deep-rooted assumptions of what we termed default maternal responsibility can be and the ways such assumptions and their consequences can hold back the scope of fathers' care roles, or leave their longevity uncertain. For this reason, as well as legislating to make it easier for fathers to take on care-sharing roles, policymakers and practitioners should prioritise the promotion of measures that address the challenges caregiving fathers and their families are liable to face, particularly those that relate to their interactions with the outside world. For, as well as helping enable their caregiving responsibilities to be as comprehensive and fulfilling as possible, such measures may help such responsibilities to endure through the many crossroads that fathers, their partners and their families encounter.

Appendix: Table of Participants

Pseudonym	Age	Occupation	Care status
Aaron	39	IT analyst	equal care sharer
Andrew	49	pensions administrator	equal care sharer
Anthony	39	researcher	equal care sharer
Brian	35	administrator	equal care sharer
Chris	47	client services manager	parental leaver
David	43	unemployed	primary caregiver
Ed	38	unemployed	primary caregiver
Eric	33	clinical psychologist	equal care sharer
James	37	research technician	equal care sharer
Jason	26	transport organiser	primary caregiver
Jeremy	43	theatre director	equal care sharer
John	38	administrator	equal care sharer
Joseph	43	industrial chemist	parental leaver
Keith	40	IT specialist	primary caregiver
Kevin	33	civil servant	primary caregiver
Michael	35	unemployed	primary caregiver
Patrick	33	restaurant supervisor	primary caregiver
Robert	37	civil servant	equal care sharer
Ryan	41	lecturer	equal care sharer
Scott	31	charity worker	equal care sharer
Stephen	43	financial advisor	equal care sharer
Thomas	30	IT consultant	equal care sharer
Timothy	34	event production	primary caregiver
William	32	lecturer	equal care sharer

All interviews were carried out between June and September 2016.

References

Allan, G. (1996) *Kinship and Friendship in Modern Britain*, Oxford: Oxford University Press.

Almqvist, A. (2008) 'Why most Swedish fathers and few French fathers use paid parental leave', *Fathering*, 6(2): 192–200.

Anderson, E. (2011) *Inclusive Masculinity: The Changing Nature of Masculinities*, London: Routledge.

Andreasson, J. and Johansson, T. (2016) 'Global narratives of fatherhood. Fathering and masculinity on the internet', *International Review of Sociology*, 26(3): 483–96.

Baird, M. and O'Brien, M. (2015) 'Dynamics of parental leave in Anglophone countries: The paradox of state expansion in liberal welfare regimes', *Community, Work and Family*, 18(2): 198–217.

Bass, C. (2015) 'Preparing for parenthood? Gender, aspirations and the reproduction of labor market inequality', *Gender and Society*, 29(3): 362–85.

Bastomski, S. and Smith, P. (2017) 'Gender, fear, and public places: How negative encounters with strangers harm women', *Sex Roles*, 76: 73–88.

Bergqvist, C. and Saxonberg, S. (2017) 'The state as norm-builder? The take-up of parental leave in Norway and Sweden', *Social Policy and Administration*, 51(7): 1470–87.

Birkett, H. and Forbes, S. (2019) 'Where's dad? Exploring the low take-up of inclusive parenting policies in the UK', *Policy Studies* (advance online access).

Bloksgaard, L. and Rostgaard, T. (2015) 'Denmark country note', in P. Moss (ed) *International Review of Leave Policies and Research 2015*. Available online at: www.leavenetwork.org/lp_and_r_reports/

Borve, H. and Bungum, B. (2015) 'Norwegian working fathers in global working life', *Gender, Work and Organization*, 22(4): 309–23.

Boterman, W. and Bridge, G. (2014) 'Gender, class and space in the field of parenthood: Middle-class fractions in Amsterdam and London', *Transactions of the Institute of British Geographers*, 40(2): 49–261.

Bourdieu, P. (1977) *Outline of a Theory of Practice*, Cambridge: Cambridge University Press.

Boyer, K., Dermott, E., James, A. and MacLeavy, J. (2017) 'Regendering care in the aftermath of recession', *Dialogues in Human Geography*, 7(1): 65–73.

Brandth, B. and Kvande, E. (1998) 'Masculinities and child care: The reconstruction of fathering', *The Sociological Review*, 46(2): 293–313.

Brandth, B. and Kvande, E. (2003) 'Father presence in child care', in A. M. Jensen and L. McKee (eds) *Children and the Changing Family: Between Transformation and Negotiation*, London: Routledge Falmer, pp. 61–75.

Brandth, B. and Kvande, E. (2018a) 'Fathers' sense of entitlement to ear-marked and shared parental leave', *The Sociological Review* (advance online access).

Brandth, B. and Kvande, E. (2018b) 'Masculinity and fathering alone during parental leave', *Men and Masculinities*, 2(1): 72–90.

Brandth, B. and Kvande, E. (2019) 'Workplace support of fathers' parental leave use in Norway', *Community, Work and Family*, 22(1): 43–57.

Bryan, M. and Sevilla, A. (2017) 'Flexible working in the UK and its impact on couples' time coordination', *Review of Economics of the Household*, 15(4): 1415–37.

Bünning, M. and Pollmann-Schult, M. (2016) 'Family policies and fathers' working hours: Cross-national differences in the paternal labour supply', *Work, Employment and Society*, 30(2): 256–74.

Castelain-Menunier, D. (2002) 'The place of fatherhood and the parental role: Tensions, ambivalence and contradictions', *Current Sociology*, 50(2): 185–201.

Castro-García, C. and Pazos-Moran, M. (2016) 'Parental leave policy and gender equality in Europe', *Feminist Economics*, 22(3): 51–73.

Cheal, D. (2002) *Sociology of Family Life*, Basingstoke: Palgrave.

Chelsey, N. (2011) 'Stay at home fathers and breadwinning mothers', *Gender and Society*, 25(5): 642–64.

Christopher, K. (2012) 'Extensive mothering', *Gender and Society* 26: 73–96.

Coles, L., Hewitt, B. and Martin, B. (2017) 'Contemporary fatherhood: Social, demographic and attitudinal factors associated with involved fathering and long work hours', *Journal of Sociology* (advance online access).

Connell, R. (2005) *Masculinities* (2nd edn), Cambridge: Polity Press.

Craig, L. and Mullen, K. (2011) 'How mothers and fathers share childcare: A cross-national time-use comparison', *American Sociological Review*, 76(6): 834–61.

Crompton, R. (1999) 'Discussion and conclusion', in R. Crompton (ed) *Restructuring Gender Relations and Employment: The Decline of the Male Breadwinner*, Oxford: Oxford University Press, pp 201–14.

Daly, M. (2010) 'Shifts in family policy in the UK under New Labour', *Journal of European Social Policy*, 20(5): 433–43.

Das, R. (2019) *Early Motherhood in Digital Societies: The Perinatal Ideal*, London: Routledge.

Das, R. and Hodkinson, P. (2019a) 'Tapestries of intimacy: Networked intimacies and new fathers' emotional self-disclosure of mental health struggles', *Social Media and Society* (advance online access). DOI: https://journals.sagepub.com/doi/full/10.1177/2056305119846488.

Das, R. and Hodkinson, P. (2019b) *Is Dad OK? New Fathers and Mental Health Difficulties*. Available online at: https://ournctstory.nct.org.uk/is-dad-ok-new-fathers-and-mental-health-difficulties/?fbclid=IwAR3EtC4BzgdOMOMAI2xDr34yUyEmoTU26XY1mu9wxSNzTqcWiHLP_ENUkAk.

DBIS (Department for Business, Innovation and Skills) (2014) *New Right for Fathers and Partners to Attend Antenatal Appointments*. Available online at: https://www.gov.uk/government/news/new-right-for-fathers-and-partners-to-attend-antenatal-appointments.

DBIS (Department for Business, Energy and Industrial Strategy) (2017) *Written Submission to the Women and Equalities Committee* (FWP0054). Available online at: http://data.parliament.uk/writtenevidence/committeeevidence.svc/evidencedocument/women-and-equalities-committee/fathers-and-the-workplace/written/48234.pdf.

Deakin, H. and Wakefield, K. (2013) 'Skype interviewing: Reflections of two PhD researchers', *Qualitative Research*, 14(5): 603–16.

Dermott, E. (2008) *Intimate Fatherhood. A Sociological Analysis*, London: Routledge.

Dermott, E. and Miller, T. (2015) 'More than the sum of its parts? Contemporary fatherhood policy, practice and discourse', *Families, Relationships and Societies* 4(2): 183–95.

Deutsch, F. (2001) 'Equally shared parenting', *Current Directions in Psychological Science*, 10(1): 25–8.

Deutsch, F. (2007) 'Undoing gender', *Gender and Society*, 21(1): 106–27.

Dolan, A. (2014) ' "I've learnt what a dad should do": The interaction of masculine and fathering identities among men who attended a "dads only" parenting programme', *Sociology*, 48(4): 812–28.

Doucet, A. (2004) ' "It's almost like I have a job but I don't get paid": Fathers at home reconfiguring work, care and masculinity', *Fathering* 2(3): 277–303.

Doucet, A. (2006a) *Do Men Mother?*, Toronto: University of Toronto Press.

Doucet, A. (2006b) ' "Estrogen-filled worlds": Fathers as primary caregivers and embodiment, *The Sociological Review*, 54(4): 696–716.

Doucet, A. (2009) 'Dad and baby in the first year: Gendered responsibilities and embodiment', *Annals of the American Academy of Political and Social Science*, 624(1): 78–98.

Doucet, A. and Lee, R. (2014) 'Fathering, feminism(s), gender and sexualities: Connections, tensions and new pathways', *Journal of Family Theory and Review*, 6: 355–73.

Doucet, A. and Merla, L. (2007) 'Stay-at-home fathering: A strategy for balancing work and home in Canadian and Belgian families', *Community, Work and Family*, 10(4): 455–73.

Duncan, S. and Edwards, S. (1997) 'Lone mothers and paid work – rational economic man or gendered moral rationalities?', *Feminist Economics*, 3(2): 29–61.

Eek, F. and Axmon, A. (2013) 'Attitude and flexibility are the most important workplace factors for working parents' wellbeing, stress and work engagement', *Scandinavian Journal of Public Health*, 41(7): 692–705.

Eerola, P. and Mykkänen, J. (2013) 'Paternal masculinities in early fatherhood: Dominant and counter narratives by Finnish first-time fathers', *Journal of Family Issues*, 36(12): 1674–701.

Elliott, K. (2016) 'Caring masculinities: Theorizing an emerging concept', *Men and Masculinities*, 19(3): 240–59.

Enderstein, A. and Boonzaier, F. (2015) 'Narratives of young South African fathers: Redefining masculinity through fatherhood', *Journal of Gender Studies*, 24(5): 512–27.

Esping-Anderson, G. (1990) *The Three Worlds of Welfare Capitalism*, Cambridge: Polity Press.

Evans, A. (2016) 'The decline of the male breadwinner and persistence of the female carer', *Annals of the American Association of Geographers*, 106(5): 1135–51.

Fagan, J. and Barnett, M. (2003) 'The relationship between maternal gatekeeping, paternal competence, mothers' attitudes about the father role, and father involvement', *Journal of Family Issues*, 24(8): 1020–41.

Faircloth, C. (2013) *Militant Lactivism? Attachment Parenting and Intensive Motherhood in the UK and France*, Oxford and New York: Berghahn Books.

Farstad, G. and Stefansen, K. (2015) 'Involved fatherhood in the Nordic context: Dominant narratives, divergent approaches', *NORMA: International Journal for Masculinity Studies*, 10(1): 55–70.

Fatherhood Institute (2016) *2016 Fairness in Families Index*, London: The Fatherhood Institute.

Featherstone, B. (2009) *Contemporary Fathering. Theory, Policy and Practice*, Bristol: Policy Press.

Fortin, N., Bell, B. and Böhm, M. (2017) 'Top earnings inequality and the gender pay gap: Canada, Sweden, and the United Kingdom', *Labour Economics*, 47: 107–23.

Fox, E., Pascall, G. and Warren, T. (2009) 'Work–family policies, participation and practices: Fathers and childcare in Europe, *Community, Work and Family*, 12(3): 313–26.

Fraser, N. (1996) *Justice Interruptus. Critical Reflections on the 'Post-socialist' Condition*, New York: Routledge.

Furlong, A. and Cartmel, F. (2007) *Young People and Social Change*, Maidenhead: Open University Press.

Gatrell, C. (2007) 'Whose child is it anyway? The negotiation of paternal entitlements within marriage', *The Sociological Review*, 55(2): 352–72.

Gatrell, C. and Cooper, C. (2016) 'A sense of entitlement? Fathers, mothers and organizational support for family and career', *Community, Work and Family*, 19(2): 134–47.

Gatrell, C. and Dermott, E. (2019) 'Introduction', in E. Dermott and C. Gatrell (eds) *Fathers, Families and Relationships: Researching Everyday Lives*, Bristol: Policy Press: 1–10.

Giddens, A. (1984) *The Constitution of Society: Outline of the Theory of Structuration*, Cambridge: Polity Press.

Giddens, A. (1991) *Modernity and Self-identity: Self and Society in the Late Modern Age*, Cambridge: Polity Press.

Gillespie, D., Krannich, R. and Leffler, A. (1985) 'The missing cell: Amiability, hostility and gender differentiation in rural community networks', *The Social Science Journal*, 22, 17–30.

Goffman, E. (1976) *Gender Advertisements*, London: Macmillan.

Gornick, J. and Meyers, M. (2004) 'Supporting a dual-earner / dual-carer society: Policy lessons from abroad', in J. Heymann and C. Beem (eds) *A Democracy that Works: The Public Dimensions of the Work and Family Debate*, New York: The New Press.

Gottzen, L. (2011) 'Involved fatherhood? Exploring the educational work of middle class men', *Gender and Education*, 23(5): 619–34.

Gregory, A. and Milner, S. (2011) 'Fathers and work–life balance in France and the UK: Policy and practice', *International Journal of Sociology and Social Policy*, 31(1–2): 34–52.

Haas, L. and Hwang, P. (2019a) 'Policy is not enough – the influence of the gendered workplace on fathers' use of parental leave in Sweden', *Community, Work and Family*, 22(1): 58–76.

Haas, L. and Hwang, P. (2019b) 'Workplace support and European fathers' use of state policies promoting shared childcare', *Community, Work and Family*, 22(1): 1–22.

Haas, L. and Rostgaard, T. (2011) 'Fathers' rights to paid parental leave in the Nordic countries: Consequences for the gendered division of leave', *Community, Work and Family*, 14(2): 177–95.

Hanna, E. (2018) *Supporting Young Men as Fathers. Gendered Understandings of Group-Based Community Provisions*, London: Palgrave.

Hays, S. (1998) *The Cultural Contradictions of Motherhood*, New Haven, CT: Yale University Press.

Henwood, K., Shirani, F and Coltart, C. (2015) 'Investing in involvement: Men moving through fatherhood', in J. Holland and R. Edwards (eds) *Understanding Families Over Time*, London: Palgrave: 88–105.

Hochschild, A. (1989) *The Second Shift*, New York: Avon Books.

Hodkinson, P. and Brooks, R. (2018) 'Interchangeable parents? The roles and identities of primary and equal carer fathers of young children', *Current Sociology* (advance online access). DOI: https://doi.org/10.1177/0011392118807530.

Hodkinson, P. and Sparkes, A. (1997) 'Careership: A sociological theory of career decision-making', *British Journal of Sociology of Education*, 18(1): 29–44.

House of Commons Women and Equalities Committee (2018) *Fathers and the Workplace. First Report of Session 2017–18* London, House of Commons. Available online at: https://publications.parliament.uk/pa/cm201719/cmselect/cmwomeq/358/358.pdf.

Humberd, B., Ladge, J. and Harrington, B. (2015) 'The 'new' dad: Navigating fathering identities within organizational contexts', *Journal of Business Psychology*, 30: 249–66.

Irwin, S. and Winterton, M. (2014) 'Gender and work-family conflict: A secondary analysis of timescapes data', in J. Hollands and R. Edwards (eds) *Understanding Families Over Time*, London: Palgrave: 142–60.

Ives, J. (2014) 'Men, maternity and moral residue: Negotiating the moral demands of the transition to first-time fatherhood', *Sociology of Health and Illness*, 36(7): 1003–19.

Ives, J. (2019) 'Framing fatherhood: The ethics and philosophy of researching fatherhoods' in E. Dermott and C. Gatrell (eds) *Fathers, Families and Relationships: Researching Everyday Lives*, Bristol: Policy Press: 11–30.

Jensen, T. (2018) *Parenting the Crisis. The Cultural Politics of Parental Blame*, Bristol: Policy Press.

Johansson, T. and Andreasson, J. (2017) *Fatherhood in Transition. Masculinity, Identity and Everyday Life*, Basingstoke: Palgrave.

Jupp, E. (2013) 'Enacting parenting policy? The hybrid spaces of Sure Start children's centres', *Children's Geographies*, 11(2): 173–87.

Karu, M. (2012) 'Parental leave in Estonia: Does familization of fathers lead to defamilization of mothers?' *NORA – Nordic Journal of Feminist and Gender Research*, 20(2): 94–108.

Karu, M. and Tremblay, D.-G. (2018) 'Fathers on parental leave: An analysis of rights and take-up in 29 countries', *Community, Work and Family*, 21(3): 344–63.

Kaufman, G. (2013) *Superdads. How Fathers Balance Work and Family in the 21st Century*, New York: New York University Press.

Kaufman, G. (2018) 'Barriers to equality: Why British fathers do not use parental leave', *Community, Work and Family*, 21(3): 310–25.

Kilkey, M. (2006) 'New Labour and reconciling work and family life: Making it fathers' business?', *Social Policy and Society*, 5(2): 167–75.

Kitterød, R. and Rønsen, M. (2017) 'Does involved fathering produce a larger total workload for fathers than for mothers? Evidence from Norway', *Family Relations*, 66: 468–83.

Koslowski, A. and Kadar-Satat, G. (2019) 'Fathers at work: Explaining the gaps between entitlement to leave policies and uptake', *Community, Work and Family*, 22(2): 129–45.

Kremer, M. (2007) *How Welfare States Care. Culture, Gender and Parenting in Europe*, Amsterdam: Amsterdam University Press.

Lappegård, T. (2012) 'Couples' parental leave practices: The role of the workplace situation', *Journal of Family and Economic Issues*, 33: 298–305.

Latshaw, B. (2015) 'From mopping to mowing: Masculinity and housework in stay-at-home father households', *Journal of Men's Studies*, 23(3): 252–70.

Latshaw, B. and Hale, S. (2016) ' "The domestic handoff": Stay-at-home fathers' time-use in female breadwinner households', *Journal of Family Studies*, 22(2): 97–120.

Lee, J.Y. and Lee, S.J. (2018) 'Caring is masculine: Stay-at-home fathers and masculine identity', *Psychology of Men and Masculinity*, 19(1): 47–58.

Lewis, C. (2013) 'Fatherhood and fathering research in the UK: Cultural change and diversity', in D. Shwalb, B. Shwalb and M. Lamb (eds) *Fathers in Cultural Context*, London: Routledge, pp 332–57.

Lewis, J. and Campbell, M. (2007) 'UK work/family balance policies and gender equality, 1997–2005', *Social Politics*, 14(1): 4–30.

Lewis, J. and Campbell, M. (2008) 'What's in a name? "Work and family" or "work and life" balance policies in the UK since 1997 and the implications for the pursuit of gender equality', *Social Policy and Administration*, 42(5): 524–41.

Lilius, J. (2016) 'Domestication of urban space? Mothering and fathering while on family leave in the inner city of Helsinki', *Gender, Place and Culture*, 23(12): 1763–73.

Lilius, J. (2017) 'Urban space in the everyday lives of mothers and fathers on family leave in Helsinki', *European Urban and Regional Studies*, 24(1):104–18.

Liong, M. (2017) 'Sacrifice for the family: Representation and practice of stay-at-home fathers in the intersection of masculinity and class in Hong Kong', *Journal of Gender Studies*, 26(4): 402–17.

Lo Iacono, V., Symonds, P. and Brown, D. (2016). 'Skype as a tool for qualitative research interviews', *Sociological Research Online* 21, 2.

Locke, A. (2016) 'Masculinity, subjectivities and caregiving in the British press: The case of the stay-at-home father', in E. Podnieks (ed) *Pops in Pop Culture. Fatherhood, Masculinity and the New Man*, Basingstoke: Palgrave, pp 195–212.

Locke, A. and Yarwood, G. (2017) 'Exploring the depths of gender, parenting and "work": Critical discourse psychology and the "missing voices" of involved fatherhood', *Community, Work and Family*, 20(1): 4–18.

Maggararia, S. (2012) 'Tensions between fatherhood and the social construction of masculinity in Italy', *Current Sociology*, 61(1): 76–92.

May, T. (2019) 'For the whole family' sake, fathers need more paternity leave', *The Guardian*, 19 July 2019. Available online at: https://www.theguardian.com/commentisfree/2019/jul/18/family-fathers-paternity-leave-theresa-may.

Mayer, M. and Le Bourdais, C. (2018) 'Sharing parental leave among dual-earner couples in Canada: Does reserved paternity leave make a difference?', *Population Research and Policy Review* (advance online access).

McDowell, L. (1999) *Gender, Identity and Place*, Cambridge: Polity Press.

McDowell, L. and Sharp, J. (eds) (1997) *Space, Gender, Knowledge. Feminist Readings*, London: Arnold.

Meah, A. and Jackson, P. (2016) 'The complex landscape of contemporary fathering in the UK', *Social and Cultural Geography*, 17(4): 491–510.

Medved, C. (2016) 'Stay-at-home fathering as a feminist opportunity: Perpetuating, resisting and transforming gender relations of caring and earning', *Journal of Family Communication*, 16(1): 16–31.

Merla, L. (2008) 'Determinants, costs and meanings of Belgian stay-at-home fathers: An international comparison', *Fathering*, 6(2): 113–32.

Miller, T. (2005) *Making Sense of Motherhood: A Narrative Approach*, Cambridge: Cambridge University Press.

Miller, T. (2011) *Making Sense of Fatherhood. Gender, Caring and Work*, Cambridge: Cambridge University Press.

Miller, T. (2017) *Making Sense of Parenthood. Caring, Gender and Family Lives*, Cambridge: Cambridge University Press.

Miller, T. (2019) 'Qualitative longitudinal research: Researching fatherhood and fathers' experiences', in E. Dermott and C. Gatrell (eds) *Fathers, Families and Relationships: Researching Everyday Lives*, Bristol: Policy Press.

Miller, T. and Nash, M. (2016) ' "I just think something like the 'Bubs and Pubs' class is what men should be having": Paternal subjectivities and preparing for first-time fatherhood in Australia and the United Kingdom', *Journal of Sociology*, 53(3): 541–56.

Milner, S. (2010) ' "Choice" and "flexibility" in reconciling work and family: Towards a convergence in policy discourse on work and family in France and the UK?', *Policy and Politics*, 38(1): 3–21.

Mulcahy, C., Parry, D. and Glover, T. (2010) 'Play-group politics: A critical social capital exploration of exclusion and conformity in mothers' groups', *Leisure Studies*, 29(1): 3–27.

Närvi, J. and Salmi, M. (2019) 'Quite an encumbrance? Work-related obstacles to Finnish fathers' take-up of parental leave', *Community, Work and Family*, 22: 123–42.

Neale, B. (2016) 'Young fatherhood: Lived experiences and policy challenges', *Social Policy and Society*, 15(1): 75–83.

Neale, B. and Davies, L. (2015) 'Young Breadwinner Fathers? Journeys through Education, Employment and Training', Briefing Paper. Available online at: https://followingfathers.leeds.ac.uk/wp-content/uploads/sites/79/2015/10/Brieifing-Paper-4-V6.pdf.

Neale, B., Patrick, R. and Lau Clayton, C (2015) 'Becoming a young father: Transitions into early parenthood', Briefing Paper. Available online at: https://followingfathers.leeds.ac.uk/wp-content/uploads/sites/79/2015/10/Brieifing-Paper-1-web.pdf.

Newsome, L. (2017) 'Female leadership and welfare state reform: The development of Australia's first national paid parental leave scheme', *Australian Journal of Political Science*, 52(4): 537–49.

Nordberg, T. (2019) 'Managers' views on employees' parental leave: Problems and solutions within different institutional logics', *Acta Sociologica*, 62(1): 81–95.

Norman, H., Elliot, M. and Fagan, C. (2014) 'Which fathers are the most involved in taking care of their toddlers in the UK? An investigation of the predictors of paternal involvement', *Community, Work and Family*, 17(2): 163–80.

Norman, H., Elliot, M. and Fagan, C. (2018) 'Does fathers' involvement in childcare and housework affect couples' relationships stability?', *Social Science Quarterly*, 99(5): 1599–613.

Norman, H. and Fagan, C. (2017) 'Shared parental leave: Is it working? Lessons from other countries', *Working Families Blog*. Available online at: https://www.workingfamilies.org.uk/workflex-blog/shared-parental-leave-in-the-uk-is-it-working-lessons-from-other-countries/.

O'Brien, M. (2013) 'Fitting fathers into work–family policies: International challenges in turbulent times', *International Journal of Sociology and Social Policy*, 33(9/10): 542–64.

O'Brien, M., Connolly, S., Speight, S., Aldrich, M. and Poole, E. (2016) 'The United Kingdom', in M. Adler and K. Lenz (eds) *Father Involvement in the Early Years. An International Comparison of Policy and Practice*, Bristol: Policy Press, pp 157–91.

O'Brien, A., McNeil, K., Fletcher, R., Conrad, A., Wilson, A., Jones, D. and Chan, S. (2017) 'New fathers' perinatal depression and anxiety – treatment options: An integrative review', *American Journal of Men's Health*, 11(4): 863–76.

O'Brien M. and Twamley K. (2017) 'Fathers taking leave alone in the UK – A gift exchange between mother and father?', in M. O'Brien and K. Wall (eds) *Comparative Perspectives on Work–Life Balance and Gender Equality*, Cham: Springer.

Ohmae, K. (1995) *The Death of the Nation-State*, London: HarperCollins

ONS (Office for National Statistics) (2018a) 'Understanding the Gender Pay Gap in the UK', *ONS Report*. Available online at: https://www.ons.gov.uk/employmentandlabourmarket/peopleinwork/earningsandworkinghours/articles/understandingthegenderpaygapintheuk/2018-01-17#a-breakdown-of-the-gender-pay-gap.

ONS (Office for National Statistics) (2018b) 'Gender Pay Gap in the UK', *ONS Report*. Available online at: https://www.ons.gov.uk/employmentandlabourmarket/peopleinwork/earningsandworkinghours/bulletins/genderpaygapintheuk/2018.

Orgad, S. (2015) 'Incongruous encounters: Media representations and lived experiences of stay-at-home mothers', *Feminist Media Studies*, 16(3): 478–94.

Orgad, S. (2019) *Heading Home. Motherhood, Work and the Failed Promise of Equality*, New York: Columbia University Press.

O'Reilly, J., Smith, M., Deakin, S. and Burchell, B. (2015) 'Equal pay as a moving target: International perspectives on forty-years of addressing the gender pay gap', *Cambridge Journal of Economics*, 39(2): 299–317.

Pahl, R. (2000) *On Friendship*, Cambridge: Polity Press.

Park, J. (2018) 'Public fathering, private mothering: Gendered transnational parenting and class reproduction among elite Korean students', *Gender and Society*, 32(4): 563–86.

Parke, R. (2013) Future Families: Diverse Forms, *Rich Possibilities*, London: Wiley Blackwell.

Petts, R., Shafer, K. and Essig, L. (2018) 'Does adherence to masculine norms shape fathering behaviour?' *Journal of Marriage and Family*, 80: 704–20.

Pew Research Centre (2015) 'Raising kids and running a household: How working parents share the load', *Social and Demographic Trends Report*. Available online at: https://www.pewsocialtrends.org/2015/11/04/raising-kids-and-running-a-household-how-working-parents-share-the-load/.

Pleck, J and Stueve, J. (2001) 'Time and paternal involvement by US residential fathers', in K. Daly (ed) *Minding the Time in Family Experience*, Oxford: JAI Elsevier Science, pp 205–26.

Puhlman, D. and Pasley, K. (2013) 'Rethinking maternal gatekeeping', *Journal of Family Theory and Review*, 5: 176–93.

Radcliffe, L. and Cassell, C. (2015) 'Flexible working, work–family conflict and maternal gatekeeping: The daily experience of dual-earner couples', *Journal of Occupational and Organizational Psychology*, 88(4): 835–55.

Ranson, G. (2010) *Against the Grain. Couples, Gender and the Reframing of Parenting*, Toronto: University of Toronto Press.

Ranson, G. (2013) 'Who's really in charge? Mothers and executive responsibility in 'non-traditional' families', *Families, Relationships and Societies*, 2(1): 79–95.

Ranson, G. (2015) *Fathering, Masculinity and the Embodiment of Care*, Basingstoke: Palgrave.

Ray, R., Gornick, J. and Schmitt, J. (2010) 'Who cares? Assessing generosity and gender equality in parental leave policy designs in 21 countries', *Journal of European Social Policy*, 20(3): 196–216.

Rehel, E. (2015) 'When dad stays home too: Paternity leave, gender and parenting', *Gender and Society*, 28(1): 110–32.

Risman, B. and Johnson-Sumerford, D. (1998) 'Doing it fairly: A study of post-gender marriages', *Journal of Marriage and the Family*, 60: 23–40.

Riva, E., Lucchini, M., den Dulk, L. and Ollier-Malaterre, A. (2018) 'The skill profile of the employees and the provision of flexible working hours in the workplace: A multilevel analysis across European countries', *Industrial Relations Journal*, 49(2): 128–52.

Robila, M. (2012) 'Family policies in Eastern Europe: A focus on parental leave', *Journal of Child and Family Studies*, 21: 32–41.

Salway, S., Chowbey, P. and Clarke, L. (2009) *Understanding the Experiences of Asian Fathers in Britain*, York: Joseph Rowntree Foundation.

Scourfield, J. and Drakeford, M. (2002) 'New Labour and the "problem of men"', *Critical Social Policy*, 22(4): 619–40.

Shirani, F. and Henwood, K. (2011) 'Continuity and change in a qualitative, longitudinal study of fatherhood: Relevance without responsibility', *International Journal of Social Research Methodology*, 14(1): 17–29.

Shirani, F., Henwood, K. and Coltart, C. (2012) 'Meeting the challenge of intensive parenting culture: Gender, risk management and the moral parent', *Sociology*, 46(1): 25–40.

Shirani, F., Parkhill, K., Butler, C., Groves, C., Pidgeon, N. and Henwood, K. (2016) 'Asking about the future: Methodological insights from energy biographies', *International Journal of Social Research Methodology*, 19(4): 429–44.

Sigurdardottir, H. and Garðarsdóttir, O. (2018) 'Backlash in gender equality? Fathers' parental leave during a time of economic crisis', *Journal of European Social Policy*, 28(4): 342–56.

Snitker, A. (2018) 'Not Mr. Mom: Navigating discourses for stay-at-home fathers', *Journal of Men's Studies*, 26(2): 203–21.

Solomon, C. (2014) ' "I feel like a rock star": Fatherhood for stay-at-home fathers, *Fathering*, 12(1): 52–70.

Solomon, C. (2017) *The Lives of Stay-At-Home Fathers*, Bingley: Emerald.

Spain, D. (2014) 'Gender and urban space', *Annual Review of Sociology*, 40: 581–98.

Spencer, L. and Pahl, R. (2006) *Rethinking Friendship*, Princeton, NJ: Princeton University Press.

Stevens, E. (2015) 'Understanding discursive barriers to involved fatherhood: The case of American stay-at-home fathers', *Journal of Family Studies*, 21(1): 22–37.

Strauss, A. (1962) 'Transformations of identity', in A. Rose (ed) *Human behaviour and Social Processes: An Interactionist Approach*, London: Routledge and Kegan Paul.

Stropnik, N., Humer, Z., Mrčela, A. and Štebe, J. (2019) 'The problem is in practice: Policy support and employer support for fathers' participation in childcare in Slovenia', *Community, Work and Family*, 22(1): 77–95.

Suwada, K. (2017) *Men, Fathering and the Gender Trap: Sweden and Poland Compared*, Basingstoke: Palgrave.

Tarrant, A. (2016) 'The spatial and gendered politics of displaying family: Exploring material cultures in grandfathers' homes', *Gender, Place and Culture*, 23(7): 966–82.

Tarrant, A. (2017) 'The myth of the fatherless society', *The Conversation*. Available online at: https://theconversation.com/the-myth-of-the-fatherless-society-73166.

Tarrant, A. (2018) 'Care in an age of austerity: Men's care responsibilities in low income families', *Ethics and Social Welfare*, 12(1): 34–48.

Thomas, G., Lupton, D. and Pederson, S. (2017) '"The appy for a happy pappy": Expectant fatherhood and pregnancy apps, *Journal of Gender Studies* (advance online access).

Thomson, R., Bell, R., Holland, J., Henderson, S., McGrellis, S. and Sharpe, S. (2002) 'Critical moments: Choice, chance and opportunity in young people's narratives of transition', *Sociology*, 36(2): 335–54.

Thomson, R. and Holland, J. (2002) 'Imagined adulthood: Resources, plans and contradictions', *Gender and Education*, 14(4): 337–50.

Thomson, R., Kehily, M.J., Hadfield, L. and Sharpe, S. (2011) *Making Modern Mothers*, Bristol: Policy Press.

Tipping, S., Chanfraeu, J., Perry, J. and Tait, C. (2012) *The Fourth Work-Life Balance Employee Survey, Employment Relations Series, No. 122*, London: Department for Business, Innovation and Skills.

Twamley, K. and Schober, P. (2018) 'Shared Parental Leave: Exploring variations in attitudes, eligibility, knowledge and take-up intentions of expectant mothers in London', *Journal of Social Policy* (advance online access).

Ungerson, C. (2006) 'Gender, care, and the welfare state', in K. Davis, M. Evans and J. Lorber (eds) *Handbook of Gender and Women's Studies*, London: Sage, pp 272–86.

Vincent, C. (2017) '"The children have only got one education and you have to make sure it's a good one": Parenting and parent–school relations in a neo-liberal age', *Gender and Education* (advance online access).

Walker, O. (2018) 'Shared parental leave suffers auspicious start', *Financial Times*, 8 August 2018.

Wells, M. and Sarkadi, A. (2012) 'Do father-friendly policies promote father-friendly child-rearing practices? A review of swedish parental leave and child health centres', *Journal of Child and Family Studies*, 21(1): 25–31.

Wenham, A. (2016) ' "I know I'm a good mum – no one can tell me different." Young mothers negotiating a stigmatised identity through time', *Families, Relationships and Societies*, 5(1), 127–44.

West, A., Lewis, S., Ram, B., Barnes, J., Leach, P., Sylva, K. and Stein, A. (2009) 'Why do some fathers become primary caregivers for their infants? A qualitative study', *Childcare Health Development*, 25(2): 208–16.

West, C. and Zimmerman, D. (1987) 'Doing gender', *Gender and Society*, 1(2): 125–51.

Windebank, J. (2017) 'Change in work–family reconciliation policy in France and the UK since 2008: The influence of economic crisis and austerity', *Journal of International and Comparative Social Policy*, 33(1): 55–72.

Wolf, J.B. (2007) 'Is breast really best? Risk and total motherhood in the National Breastfeeding Awareness campaign', *Journal of Health Politics, Policy and Law*, 32(4): 595–636.

Index